The Pakistani Economy

The Pakistani Economy

❧

Economic Growth and Structural Reform

Robert E. Looney

Westport, Connecticut
London

Library of Congress Cataloging-in-Publication Data

Looney, Robert E.
   The Pakistani economy : economic growth and structural reform /
Robert E. Looney.
     p. cm.
   Includes bibliographical references and index.
   ISBN 0–275–94737–8 (alk. paper)
   1. Pakistan—Economic policy. 2. Pakistan—Economic conditions.
I. Title.
HC440.5.L66   1997
338.95491—dc21   96–37731

British Library Cataloguing in Publication Data is available.

Library of Congress Catalog Card Number: 96–37731
ISBN: 0–275–94737–8

First published in 1997

Praeger Publishers, 88 Post Road West, Westport, CT 06881
An imprint of Greenwood Publishing Group, Inc.

Printed in the United States of America

The paper used in this book complies with the
Permanent Paper Standard issued by the National
Information Standards Organization (Z39.48–1984).

10 9 8 7 6 5 4 3 2 1

For Christopher

Contents

PART II
SECTORAL ANALYSIS

Tables and Figure

TABLES

FIGURE

Part I

PROGRESS TOWARD LIBERALIZATION AND ECONOMIC REFORM

Introduction

OVERVIEW

Pakistan's economy grew relatively rapidly during the 1980s with strong export performance and modest inflation. Gross Domestic Product (GDP) grew at over 6 percent and the dollar value of exports grew by almost 9 percent per annum, while the annual inflation rate was about 7 percent. Agriculture grew by over 4 percent per annum; industry grew by almost 7 percent.

Despite this healthy performance, the underlying structure of the economy contained certain weaknesses. The savings rate was low, particularly in the public sector. The fiscal budget was heavily dependent on trade taxes for revenues. The domestic tax structure was inelastic. Current expenditures went largely to debt servicing, subsidies on farm and agricultural imports, and defense expenditures. Development expenditures were inadequate to build and maintain the necessary physical infrastructure. Human resource development was the responsibility of the provincial governments, which lacked the resource base to adequately fund social services. The population was growing extremely rapidly at well over 3 percent per annum.

Because of these problems, social indicators lagged behind those of countries at a similar level of development. The financial sector and most heavy industry, as well as rail transport and telecommunications, were state-owned and mired with heavy losses and inefficiency. The private economy remained heavily regulated, with high tariff protection and pervasive foreign exchange controls.

The government's response to these problems has been to initiate several stabilization/reform packages. Initially, these programs were introduced in the late 1970s to deal with serious balance of payments problems stemming from the sharp increases in oil prices and the decline in prices for several of Pakistan's key exports. Later in the 1980s there was a growing emphasis on structural adjustment to strengthen productive capacity. These policies were designed to improve resource allocation, promote domestic investment and savings, and strengthen external competitiveness.

More recently, in early 1991, the government announced a far-reaching package of economic reforms intended to stimulate economic growth through increased private-sector investment and productivity. The main thrust of the new program is to free up markets and reduce the economic role of the government. In terms of implementation, the reforms center around disinvestment of public enterprises, deregulation and denationalization (Rosett 1991).

Despite the difficult domestic economic conditions and the several changes in government since 1991, the Pakistan authorities have shown remarkable continuity in their approach to economic policy. The main thrust of their approach has been an emphasis on liberalization. In this context they have made important gains (IMF 1996, 1) in the area of privatization and deregulation of economic activities; introduced significant reforms in the financial system and in the conduct of monetary policy; gradually steered the taxation system away from international trade taxes and toward greater reliance on domestic taxes; and removed all restrictions on current international payments as well as several restrictions on capital flow.

The second area (IMF 1996) in which the authorities have shown continuity is emphasis on demand management, although implementation has been uneven. Their initiatives in this area enabled the country to receive substantial financial support from the International Monetary Fund.

OBJECTIVES

The purpose of this study is to assess Pakistan's experience with economic reforms. What essential elements are involved in the reforms? What problems arose in implementing past reforms? Are these potential difficulties recognized and adequately addressed today? What are the implications for short run-stability and longer run growth?

The study is divided into three parts. Part I provides a brief overview of the reform process, with an assessment of the gains made to date. The impact of these reforms on the economic freedom of the country's citizens is assessed in light of gains made elsewhere in the developing world. Because many of the reforms are sector-specific in providing incentives for private-sector investment their sectoral dimension is dealt with in Part II. Finally, the related fiscal fiscal/stabilization environment is examined in Part III, where the study concludes with an examination of the country's policy options to the year 2000.

1

Pakistan's Attempts at Economic Reform

OVERVIEW

Pakistan's initial economic reforms and stabilization efforts in the late 1970s were introduced (Aghevli, Kim et al. 1987) to deal with a series of balance of payments problems stemming from the sharp increases in oil prices and the decline in prices for several of its key exports. Later in the 1980s, there was a growing emphasis on structural adjustment to strengthen productive capacity. These policies were designed to improve resource allocation, promote domestic investment and savings, and strengthen external competitiveness.

In contrast, the reforms in the 1990s have focused more on stimulating economic growth through increased private-sector investment and productivity. The main thrust of these programs is to free up markets, thereby reducing the economic role of the government. In terms of implementation, the reforms center on disinvestment of public enterprises, deregulation, and denationalization (Rosett 1991).

Although there are some notable exceptions, ultimately most of the government's current reform efforts are related to problems created by previous public policies in the industrial sector. The industrial sector's difficulties have, in turn, affected the manner in which the public sector has designed and conducted its fiscal policy. In turn, fiscal and budgetary policies have modified the patterns of industrial growth. The new reform efforts are an attempt to break out of this vicious cycle.

EVOLUTION OF INDUSTRIAL POLICY

Prior to 1977, Pakistan's experience with industrialization passed through three distinct phases. During the 1950s, the country followed a policy of import substitution behind high protection. This phase resulted in rapid but somewhat inefficient growth. During the 1960s, the government embarked on an export promotion strategy but maintained protective barriers for its domestic industry.

In 1972, reacting to the high concentration of industrial ownership and some shortcomings of previous policies, the government opted for direct management of industry. It nationalized many agricultural processing units and large industrial firms as well as all domestic banks and life insurance companies. Nationalization was accompanied by a strong campaign to influence public opinion against the private sector. The government also introduced many of the regulations to control the private sector that were still in place in the late 1980s (IBRD 1983, 56).

The manufacturing sector as a whole was among the fastest growing segments of the economy during the 1950s and 1960s resulting in a doubling of its share of gross domestic product (from 8 to 16 percent) within these two decades. In the fifties, the predominant source of growth was the import-substitution segment of industry, whereas in the sixties it was domestic demand which took the lead. In the early 1970s a number of factors were responsible for a considerable slowing down of industrial growth. Among the most influential determinants were (Sarmad 1984a, 20 ff.) the following:

1. Exhaustion of the import substitution potential in consumer industries (which held a share of about 80 percent in the large-scale industries' value added by the end of the sixties)
2. Their excessive protection resulting in inefficient production; over- capitalization and over-capacities due to capital cheapening policy measures as well as major infrastructural and energy bottlenecks (UNIDO 1990, 73)

With the change of government in 1977 came a change in strategy. Under the Fifth Plan, the government sought to reverse previous policies by assigning to the private sector the leading role in industrial development. The Fifth Plan formulated a strategy that was export- as well as import-substitution-oriented and restricted the public-sector investment program in favor of an expanded role for the private sector. To encourage the private sector, the government: denationalized most agricultural processing and a few industrial units, introduced safeguards against nationalization, widened areas open to the private sector, restricted public-sector industrial investment to the completion on ongoing projects, adopted a more liberal trade policy, and introduced a wide range of industrial incentives.

Policy initiatives in pursuit of deregulation and liberalization continued during the 1982/83 to 1987/88 period and included the following:

1. An increase in the investment sanction limit
2. Drastic reductions in the list of specified industries which require government sanction
3. Reduction of tariffs on a number of raw materials, and intermediate and capital goods
4. Introduction of a three-year liberal trade policy
5. An upgrade of the Industrial Incentives Reform Cell (IIRC) to a Tariff Commission in 1989 to make recommendations on fiscal anomalies and effective protection

The new course of deregulation and liberalization had a mixed impact on private-sector investment during the Sixth Five-Year Plan (1983/84 to 1987/88). Private investment in small scale, agro-industries and nonmetallic minerals exceeded the plan target. In textiles, chemicals pharmaceuticals, rubber, and miscellaneous products, private investment was in line with the targets of the plan period. In petrochemicals and fertilizers, however, it fell far short of expectations. Finally, private investment was only 67 percent of the plan target in basic metal and other engineering industries.

The private sector has generally been reluctant to invest in long-generation capital-intensive industries in the absence of long-term commitments for protection and incentives. Low tariffs on imported capital goods have meant strong competitive pressures from foreign producers. This is one major reason for low private investment in engineering industries. Lack of a secure and inexpensive supply of gas inhibited private investment in the fertilizer industry. The high cost of some of the industrial inputs has made export industries less attractive than import-substituting industries.

During the Seventh Plan period (1988/89 to 1992/93) policies and incentives were formulated to encourage investment in key industries such as engineering and high technologies and to stimulate the modernization of agro-processing industries. Emphasis was placed on more efficient export-oriented and sophisticated industries and on fostering the process of industrialization in less-developed areas.

The Seventh Plan anticipated a substantial increase in private investment. Of the projected private investment of Rs 87.6 billion (compared with Rs 9 billion for the public sector), Rs 22 billion was earmarked for the engineering goods industry; Rs 19.6 billion for the agro-based and small-scale industries; Rs 24.9 billion for the textile industry; and Rs 14 billion for the chemical industry. The remaining Rs 7.1 billion was planned for other industries.

It was hoped that the new wave of liberalization and fresh incentives would attract the private sector to important priority sectors where supply shortages persist, that is, electricity generation, telecommunications, and roads. Here the government intended to create a $600 million private-sector fund in order to promote private investment in electricity generation. This investment fund is likely to receive contributions from both bilateral and multilateral agencies.

The Seventh Five-Year Plan (GOP 1988) commenced at a time when the IMF/World Bank-induced conditionality was accepted by the government for a three-year period. It is important to examine the prospects for industrial growth in the light of the influence of the IMF and World Bank recommendations on industrial policy in Pakistan. In fact, despite rapid growth and some reform initiatives introduced during the 1981 to 1988 period, Pakistan's economy still retained a number of key structural weaknesses. The macroeconomic weaknesses included (IBRD 1991, 4):

1. A negative government saving with an excessive budget deficit, a narrow and inelastic revenue base overly dependent on trade taxes, high consumption expenditures and inadequate development expenditures
2. An unsustainable debt service level
3. An inefficient financial sector with mostly public ownership, directed credit, segmented markets and weak commercial banks
4. A highly regulated economy with public ownership, industrial licensing and pervasive price controls
5. A non-competitive and distorting trade regime with import licensing, bans, exemptions, and high tariffs

Before the end of FY88 the deteriorating resource position caused a financial crisis. The budget deficit reached 8.5 percent of gross domestic product (GDP) and the current account deficit doubled to 4.3 percent of gross national product (GNP). Inflation accelerated to over 9 percent. Reserves feel by half from $886 million to $438 million equal to less than three weeks of imports.

THE MACROECONOMIC REFORM PROGRAM

Reacting to the crisis, the Government of Pakistan committed itself to reforms designed to restore the resource balances to sustainable levels by the end of FY91 and to improve the efficiency of the economy. In terms of specifics the objectives of the program were to (IBRD 1991, 4):

1. Reduce the budget deficit to less than 5 percent of GDP and the external current account deficit to 2.5 percent of GNP while raising foreign exchange reserves to seven weeks of imports
2. Sustain real GDP growth above 5 percent per annum reducing the rate of inflation to 6 percent and containing the growth of domestic credit and money supply to the some of real GDP growth and the target rate of inflation

As a result of these reforms, national savings were expected to increase by more than the fall in foreign savings, hence allowing an increase in the investment rate by more than 1 percent of the GDP. The objectives of the adjustment program were to be achieved through policy reforms in the financial trade and industry, agriculture, and energy sectors, as well as in the fiscal area.

Fiscal Reforms. Fiscal measures were to include resource mobilization, efforts to increase the elasticity of the tax system through the introduction of a general sales tax; restructuring of the income tax system; the removal of most exemptions from custom duties on imports; and prices increases for public utilities. Expenditures were to be restrained by curbing the growth of current expenditures (including cuts in defense expenditures and subsides) while ensuring that development expenditures grew more rapidly than GDP, in particular for economic infrastructure and the social sectors. The fiscal adjustment was to be achieved by increasing revenues to over 20 percent of GDP and by reducing expenditures to 25 percent.

Financial Reforms. Policies to strengthen the financial sector included streamlining regulations and managerial reforms and the financial restructuring of commercial banks. To relieve the burden on these institutions of low-cost borrowing by the government and to reduce market segmentation, market-based rates were to be established by auctioning treasury bills; these rates were to become benchmarks for other rates in the economy.

Industrial and Trade Policy. The first phase of industrial and trade policy reform was to replace bans and other nontariff barriers with tariffs and to lower the maximum tariff from 225 percent to 100 percent by July 1990. Further tariff reductions were to follow. The government was committed to continue to manage the exchange rate flexibly and reduce industrial regulations.

Agriculture and Energy. Reforms in agriculture and energy were designed to improve sectoral efficiency and improve resource mobilization. The agricultural reforms addressed adjustments in the prices of key crops and inputs, including water and fertilizer. In energy, the measures aimed at raising prices of electricity, petroleum products, and natural gas to improve efficiency in use, raise resources to finance further investment, and pave the way for more private-sector participation.

The reform program attracted wide external support from multinational and bilateral agencies:

1. In December 1988 the IMF Board approved a three-year structural adjustment facility for a total of SDR 347 million.
2. The World Bank supported the reform program with sectoral adjustment loans for agriculture (approved in August 1988 for $200 million, the financial sector (March 1989 for $150 million) and energy (June 1989 for $250 million).
3. The Asian Development Bank supported industrial and financial reforms with an industrial-sector program loan (December 1988 for $200 million). Several bilateral creditors, including the Arab Emirates States and Japan, provided balance of payments support in the context of sector loans.

Macroeconomic performance in the first two years of the adjustment program were slow and uneven. In FY89 the government implemented the measures envisaged mostly on schedule and achieved improvements in a number of macroeconomic indicators. However, exogenous shocks, in particular floods in August/September 1988, and a deterioration in the country's terms of trade took their toll and required an extending the target date for the completion of the program to FY92, while the timetable for implementing reform measures remained unchanged.

In FY90, serious slippages occurred in implementing reform measures in the financial sector, in containing liquidity growth, and in fiscal policy. As a result, the reform program was substantially off track at the end of the second year, although the government was still able to meet the balance of payments targets.

Adverse external developments and slow implementation of stabilization and adjustment measures have, in general, left Pakistan's economy short of achieving the objectives of the original three-year reform program formulated in 1988:

1. Although GOP growth remained in the vicinity of 5 percent, other key targets such as budgetary revenues, expenditures and the current account deficit of the balance of payments and reserve levels, money, credit and inflation, and saving and investment fell short of their targets
2. Implementation of sectoral adjustment measures in agriculture, energy trade, finance and industry was slow and incomplete
3. Perhaps of greatest consequence for the welfare of Pakistan over the long term, development expenditures were constrained by the slow progress in the stabilization and adjustment program. While expenditures came down as expected, development expenditures bore the brunt of the cuts; defense expenditures continued to grow and to exceed their targeted levels

Because of the stabilization measures (and the way in which overall spending was allocated), public development spending during the reform period was lower than before the reform program started. During FY89–90, development expenditures averaged 6.4 percent of GDP compared to 6.7 for the period FY85 to FY88. This was not the intention of the original Seventh Plan, which envisaged development expenditures rising faster than total expenditures to form a base of almost 7 percent of GDP. Nor was their fall a target of the original reform program, which envisaged maintaining development expenditure at no lower than 6.5 percent of GDP and slowly increasing them as resource mobilization and current expenditure cuts allowed.

Even this initial level of development expenditure was expected to be supplemented by considerably more private-sector investment in infrastructure than in fact took place. Consequently, from a macroeconomic point of view, development expenditures were considerably lower than originally envisaged in the reform program, with negative consequences for Pakistan's social and physical infrastructure as well as for future economic growth.

THE 1990–91 ECONOMIC REFORMS

Shortly after taking office in November 1990 the Sharif administration followed up on its election pledges by appointing six committees for formulating policies aimed at transforming Pakistan into a rapidly industrializing, self-reliant economy through comprehensive liberalization, decontrol, privatization, and investment promotion. These committees were set up in six areas:

1. Exchange and payment reforms
2. Industrial policy and investment
3. Deregulation and disinvestment
4. Tax reform
5. Increasing exports
6. Self-reliance

The first committee to report was that of Exchange and Payment Reforms. Its recommendations were accepted and promptly implemented. Essentially these reforms opened the capital account to much freer foreign exchange transactions, allowing residents to hold foreign exchange in foreign currency accounts in domestic commercial banks and transfer their foreign exchange abroad freely.

The Deregulations and Disinvestment Committee recommended the ease of public entities in the financial and manufacturing sector. The government subsequently formed a Privatization Commission to carry out these sales and initiated the sale of one of the nationalized commercial banks, The Muslim Commercial Bank. Other sales of public entities, both nationalized commercial banks and other public entities, are planned to follow.

Even before these committees were able to complete their reports, the government announced a series of investment incentives and liberalizations that included tax holidays and exemptions and equal treatment of foreign and domestic companies.

In terms of implementation,

1. Financial-sector reforms were reactivated, including the auction of government debt
2. Investment and import licensing were virtually eliminated
3. The Water and Power Development Authority, the Oil and Gas Development Corporation, the National Highway Authority, and Pakistan Telephone and Telegraph Corporation were all given more autonomy to carry out their functions with less government control
4. Meetings of the National Finance Commission and the Council for Common Interests were held to press for agreement on long-standing and major development issues with particular emphasis on revising the share of revenues allocated to individual provinces and achieving a more efficient allocation of water resources

To summarize, the basic changes in the financial area (Banker 1991) included,

Foreign Exchange. Foreign currency accounts can be opened by all Pakistanis and foreigners, and no questions will be asked about the source of the funds. Also, there will be no restriction on bringing in, possessing our taking out foreign currency. Resident Pakistanis can now maintain accounts abroad.

Investment. Nonresident Pakistanis and foreigners can now invest in the shares of Pakistani companies; remittances of principal and dividends are permissible, subject to payment of capital gains tax. Foreign-controlled companies can borrow for their working capital and fixed investment needs from domestic credit institutions without permission from the central bank.

Banking. Foreign currency account holders are eligible for rupee loans against the security of their foreign balances. Foreign banks operating in Pakistan can now underwrite shares, with prescribed limits, as can local banks.

The intent of these measures is to attract back some of the US \$15 to \$20 billion in Pakistani deposits held abroad.

Clearly, the objective of the stabilization and reform policies is not stabilization or privatization per say, but instead the environment they will presumably create enabling the private sector to become a dynamic force in the country's development. A critical concern arises, therefore, regarding the compatibility of these programs with that ultimate objective. In short, these programs and their associated effects must be evaluated in terms of their ability to generate higher levels of sustained growth in efficient output.

One policy variable the government has relied on over the years is its infrastructure programs. How effective have they been in this regard? Have they been curtailed during the recent phases of stabilization/reform? and, if so, why? Have the effects of expanded infrastructure been offset by other government actions, and, if so, in which areas? Specifically, what effect has government deficits and increased levels of debt had on private-sector investment in the various sectors such as manufacturing, agriculture, and the services? These issues are empirically examined in Part II.

General Observations

With the advent of the Sharif administration, the process of liberalization was speeded up. While the Bhutto administration remains fully committed to the progressive expansion of the private sector, it is only at a more calculated pace. There has been a sharp reduction in the number of industries reserved for the public sector, and new avenues are open to the private sector. The government also commits itself not to nationalize any industrial unit in the future.

The government's program of privatization of the economy is consistent with the widely held view in Pakistan that the private-sector investment has had a much greater impact on real output than that associated with comparable levels of government expenditure. Privatization and the elimination of subsidies needed for funding chronically under-capitalized government enterprises should enable the public sector to free up funding for areas whose programs have the greatest economic impact—smaller industries and rural development, and energy. Hopefully, also the funding requirements of the government will decline once the government is out of the position of covering the deficits of the public enterprises. Lower fiscal deficits should also aid private-sector investment. Still, the success of the government's economic reforms will hinge on the ability of the authorities to address several essential issues.

Policy Coordination and Implementation

Liberalization, deregulation, and new incentives can foster industrial development when the provincial authorities participate fully in the new course of industrial revitalization. Without a significant increase in the resources of the concerned provincial authorities that are in charge of providing infrastructural facilities, the practical implementation of new incentives may be difficult. The government's intent is to ensure the supply of infrastructural facilities within sixty days of the approval of an industrial project. This necessitates provincial cooperation to mobilize the local machinery in charge of these facilities.

Some progress has been made toward better provincial/federal cooperation. To reduce regional tensions, the government has forged the first agreement in the country's history for equitable sharing of river waters among the four provinces and has framed a new arrangement for the sharing and expenditure of government income (Crossette 1991). This, for example, would let the North West Frontier Province (NWFP) keep more of the income from hydroelectric power, a long-standing demand of nationalists in the region. Similarly, Baluchistan would accrue a greater share of its gas revenues.

Because the geographical distribution of industry is uneven in Pakistan, balanced regional industrialization is, therefore, a major objective of the industrial strategy of the government. An array of fiscal concessions and investment incentives granted by the federal government favors locating industrial enterprises in backward areas. Unfortunately, the provincial governments still view the issue differently. The provinces seek solutions to regional imbalances within the context of their specific needs, and often put forward the formula of provincial autonomy for regional balance in industrialization.

Despite this, the federal government is expanding the coverage of investment incentive programs. These could undermine ongoing efforts to reduce policy-induced distortions and broaden the domestic tax base. In addition to the existing programs that provide tax holidays (for four to eight years) and duty free imports of (noncompeting) machinery for new undertakings in backward areas, the government recently introduced new incentives. They include (IBRD 1991, 2728): an enhanced and extremely generous incentive package granted the Gadoon Amazi (NWFP) Industrial Estate and a new package of industrial incentives extending a three year tax holiday for all new products, and the Rural

Industrialization Program, which covers most of Pakistan and provides a five year tax holiday, credit at eight percent, and duty free access to imported machinery. The government is also trying to attract money obtained from illegal sources into rural industrialization by declaring that no questions will be asked regarding the source of funds going into new investments.

In general, these programs tend to be grossly abused and do not achieve the intended objectives because of a general lack of infrastructure and skilled labor, and they often suffer from being great distances from markets. The proliferation of these measures could undermine the government's efforts to reform the corporate tax system. Such programs should be phased out, and for regional development, emphasis should shift to the provision of infrastructure and human resource development services.

As expected, the privatization program is seen as an important test for the success of the new economic policies. While the government says its plans are on schedule, a lukewarm response from investors because of a host of worries about the program has raised concerns that the program may be slowing. The government could raise around Rs 150 billion, the value of paid-up capital for all public-sector holdings, including factories, development finance institutions, and services. As one might imagine, the profitability of these companies is low—running between 1.5 to 1.8 percent of annual turnover. Potential investors appear hesitant because asking prices are higher than the productive worth of many of these units.

There is the suspicion that the balance sheets of many units are flawed, giving a misleading assessment of their financial liabilities. Other conditions such as the requirement that workers should not be laid off during an initial twelve-month period is also discouraging investors (Bokhari 1991). There are also fears that a new government might renationalize.

The pace of privatization may be slower than anticipated by the government. There are a number of powerful vested interests within the bureaucracy, who feel that the government is not receiving enough for the companies, and the unions, who fear job loss, are likely to put up considerable opposition (Banker 1991, 51).

Perhaps a more fruitful strategy in the long run will be that of attracting new capital formation directly into areas such as energy and infrastructure that have been traditionally in the public sector. An example of this is a new power project agreement recently signed by the government and a consortium of Western companies (Gray 1991). The project worth $1.3 billion will increase the country's electricity capacity by 18 percent. The World Bank is helping finance the complex through the private-sector energy development fund (PSEDF) aimed at providing long-term finance to attract private-sector investment in power and energy projects in Pakistan.

Incompatible Fiscal Policies

The government's decision to increase revenue sharing with the provinces will facilitate implementing the public-sector's infrastructure program. In addition it will be a move in the direction of bringing infrastructure to those areas where it is most needed and to those activities where it is most productive.

The greatest threat to the government's liberalization program will be its fiscal policies—both on the revenue and expenditure side. In Part III certain inconsistencies in the government's revenue and expenditure programs are identified. These generally involve defense trade-offs with infrastructural allocations, high fiscal deficits, and a growing debt problem. As the government's fiscal deficits have generally exceeded the planned magnitudes, the credit to private-sector borrowers tended to be further restricted. This crowding out of the private sector has been a particular problem for potential industrial exporters. The banks, for risk and profit considerations, prefer to lend the limited amount of available credit to established firms (Lee and Iwasaki 1991, 39).

Tax policy is improving but has far to go. Rates have traditionally been so high that few people paid. In fact, tax evasion is endemic, and all attempts mounted to date to make taxation more efficient have failed. A previous finance minister, Dr. Mahboobul Haq, maintained in 1986 that Rs 50 billion was lost each year through tax evasion, with a further Rs 40 billion stolen by state employees. It is estimated that as much as 80 percent of all corporate tax is paid by locally based foreign companies. In a country of 110 million people only around a million pay income tax. Of these, over half are salaried employees whose tax is deducted at the source (Hyman 1991, 108).

Beginning in July 1991 the government began attempts to deal with the problem. The top income tax has been dropped from 45 percent to 35 percent. New legislation also aims at simplifying the system. The country, however, remains saddled with a variety of indirect taxes, special levies, and relatively high rates that invite evasion and discourage legitimate business (Rosett 1991).

Despite these reforms, no new measures were introduced until June 1996 to tax the country's feudal landowners and farmers. The sector could provide a major source of revenues—it contributed more than 25 percent of the country's gross domestic product. In addition, it contributes directly or indirectly at least two thirds of the country's income from exports. It employs almost 51 percent of the country's labor force and 75 percent of the population. The government's position that the country's constitution prevents it from taxing the farms as agricultural taxation remains a provincial prerogative. Many observers, however, feel that in any case collecting an agricultural tax would be impossible (Bokhari, 1991a).

Financial Markets

While the government is taking some initial steps in its reform program to deal with the problem of segmentation in the financial system, the enormity of the problem means that it will be some years before the country has an efficient capital market. Currently while interest rates in the formal sector range between 6 and 14 percent per annum, those in the informal sector range from 24 to 30 percent. The lack of accessibility to formal credit by the new firms means they must resort to informal credit. Consequently, very little investment takes place in the nontraditional new manufactured export sector, while the established entrepreneurs continue to pursue low-return investments. Clearly the country's finance segmentation has serious implications for the long-term dynamism of the Pakistani industry (Lee and Iwasaki 1991, 39).

A related issue is that of illegally obtained funds. The government is trying to attract these questionable funds into rural industrialization by declaring that no questions will be asked regarding the source of funds going into new investments.

An important feature of the new industrial incentive system is the gradual phasing out of exemptions subsidies and the like. There has been an increase in the tax burden as a large number of industries previously exempted from sales tax are now subject to it. As a result of an increase in the tax burden, the corporate savings (and hence investment) rate is likely to remain stagnant for several years unless alternative sources of funding are developed.

CONCLUSIONS

After forty years of development experience, agencies such as the World Bank have concluded (IBRD 1991a) that a central explanation for success and failure in development lies in the mix of market competition and government intervention that countries have chosen to adopt (Thomas 1991). The new consensus is that governments must make significant progress in four areas (Prowse 1991):

1. *Investing in people.* Developing countries must spend more on primary education, basic health care and the like. In most countries, a stronger focus on human capital requires a sharp curbing of military spending.
2. *Improving the climate for enterprise.* Governments need to intervene less on industrial and agricultural pricing, deregulate entry to markets, and focus on improving infrastructure and the institutions such as the legal system underpinning businesses.
3. *Openly embrace of international trade and investment.* Developing countries should reduce tariffs substantially and impose fewer nontariff barriers to trade. A decisive move away from discretionary forms of control is needed.
4. *Firm macroeconomic policies.* Governments need to ensure fiscal deficits are low and that they are kept in check. Market-based incentives for saving and investment are essential to assure domestic resources will be available to finance development.

Seen in this context, the government of Pakistan has made significant progress in only the second, and to a much lesser extent the third, area. Even here, the reforms do not seem to go far enough in addressing the infrastructure and institutional framework needed to induce the private sector to make long-term real capital commitments.

Progress at the human capital and macro-economic level has lagged. The country's largely illiterate population will have a hard time taking advantage of any modern investments that may be attracted to the country. Ultimately, deficiencies in human capital together with shortages of infrastructure will retard productivity and the profitability of investment.

Given the country's high debt service ratios, low reserves, and declining remittances and aid, the financial capability of previous stabilization programs is absent. These programs failed under much better circumstances. The government seems unable to control defense expenditures or general consumption. There is no indication that tax reforms will be productive in containing the government's growing deficits.

2

Pakistan's Progress Toward Economic Freedom

INTRODUCTION

A short reasonably accurate definition of economic freedom is that it exists when persons and their rightfully owned property, that is "things" acquired without the use of force, fraud, or theft, are protected from assault by others. An individual's private ownership right includes the right to trade or give rightfully acquired property to another. Protection from invasion by others and freedom of exchange are the cornerstones of economic freedom. Economic freedom can thus be distinguished from political freedom which focuses on political and civil liberties (Gwartney, Lawson et al. 1996).

The purpose of this chapter is to extend the discussion of the previous chapter by examining Pakistan's progress toward the attainment of economic freedom: What gains have been made to date and in what areas? How has progress in the country compared to that attained in other parts of the world? What are the implications for the country's future growth?

CONCEPTUAL ISSUES

Economic freedom is at the same time a straightforward and subtle concept (Economist 1996, 21). Clearly the essence of economic freedom cannot be captured merely by looking at the size of public spending relative to the GDP, or the extent of state ownership of industry, or at the level of trade barriers. It is a combination of these and many other factors that leaves room for debate about the different elements of the mix (and their subsequent weighting in any index).

As noted above, stripped to its essentials, economic freedom is concerned with property rights and choice. Individuals are economically free if property that they have legally acquired is protected from invasions or intrusions by others, and if they are free to use, exchange, or give away their property so long as their actions do not violate other people's similar rights.

It follows that to measure freedom one must find appropriate measures of the ways in which it is restricted by governments. Gwartney and associates chose seventeen such measures in four broad areas (Table 2.1):

1. *Money and Inflation.* Does government protect money as a store of value and allow it to be used as a medium of exchange? This measure includes the volatility of inflation; monetary growth relative to the potential growth capacity of an economy; and citizens' rights to hold foreign currency accounts at home and bank accounts abroad.

2. *Government Operations and Regulations.* Who decides what is produced and consumed? The measures of this include public spending as a share of GDP; the size of the state-controlled sector; price controls; freedom to enter markets; and controls on borrowing and lending rates.

3. *Discriminatory Taxation.* Are the country's citizens free to earn, and to keep their earnings? Measures of this include subsidies and transfer payments.

4. *International Exchange.* Are citizens free to exchange goods and money with foreigners? Measures of this include taxes on international trade, any differences between an official and a black-market exchange rate, the actual size of a country's trade relative to the expected size and restrictions on capital flows.

In the Gwartney study, 102 countries were rated on each of these measures on a scale of 0–10, in which zero means that a country is completely unfree and ten means its is completely free. Such scores were given for 1974, 1980, 1985, 1990 and 1993–95 (depending on the latest figures available).

Having obtained such ratings, however, a major problem remains in the construct of an aggregate summary index. Do all of the measures matter equally? Any method is inherently arbitrary. The authors used three methods: (1) with each component having an equal impact (Ie); (2) with weights determined by a survey (Is1) of "knowledgeable people," defined as economists familiar with the problem; and (3) with weights derived from a survey (Is2) of experts on specific countries.

While Gwartney and associates feel method two above is the best measure, one can easily make the case that a more objective measure might provide additional, if not superior, insights. The factor analysis developed below is one such measure. Using the three summary measures together with the four broad components of economic freedom, one can trace Pakistan's progress in recent years.

PATTERNS OF ECONOMIC FREEDOM

Pakistan's summary economic freedom rating (Is1) improved from a very low 2.3 in 1975 to 5.4 in 1993-95. Most of the improvement came in the 1990s. In terms of the rankings, Pakistan moved from ninety-third in 1975 to fiftieth in the mid-1990s. The improvement in the country's economic freedom rating can be attributed to a few components in the index. First, top marginal tax rates have been reduced from 61 percent in 1975 (and 60 percent in 1985) to the cur-

Table 2.1
Components of the Index of Economic Freedom

I. Money and Inflation (Protection of money as a store of value and medium of exchange)

Average Annual Growth Rate of the Money Supply During the Last Five Years Minus the Potential Growth Rate of Real GDP
Standard Deviation of the Annual Inflation Rate During the Last Five Years
Freedom of Citizens to Own a Foreign Currency Bank Account Domestically
Freedom of Citizens to Maintain a Bank Account Abroad

II. Government Operations and Regulations

Government General Consumption Expenditures as a Percent of GDP
The Role and Presence of Government-Operated Enterprises
Price Controls—The Extent that Businesses are Free to Set Their Own Prices
Freedom of Private Businesses and Cooperatives to Compete in Markets
Equality of Citizens Under the Law and Access of Citizens to a Nondiscriminatory Judiciary
Freedom from Government Regulations and Policies that Cause Negative Real Interest Rates

III. Taxing and Discriminatory Taxation (Freedom to keep what you earn)

Transfers and Subsidies as a Percent of GDP
Top Marginal Tax rate (and income threshold at which it applies)
The Use of Conscripts to Obtain Military Personnel

IV. Restraints on International Exchange (Freedom of exchange with foreigners)

Taxes on International Trade as a Percent of Exports Plus Imports
Difference Between the Official Exchange Rate and the Black Market Rate
Actual Size of Trade Sector Compared to the Expected Size
Restrictions on the Freedom of Citizens to Engage in Capital Transactions with Foreigners

---

Source: (Gwartney, Lawson et al. 1996, 16)

rent 38 percent. A significant liberalization of the exchange rate system has reduced the black-market exchange rate premium from a high of 27 percent in 1980 to zero (and a rating of 10) in 1993–94. Some of the increase in the summary rating for 1993–95 may reflect the fact that the taxes on international trade (Iva) datum was not available for Pakistan in that year. In all the previous periods, this component received a zero rating. Its absence in the most recent period may have artificially inflated the summary rating slightly.

Summing up, it is clear there has been a slight move toward economic liberalization in Pakistan over the last two decades. This improvement has allowed Pakistan to report modest, if unremarkable, annual growth of per capita GDO of approximately 2.5 percent. For Pakistan to make the move into the modern market economy like Malaysia, Thailand, and Singapore, it must improve its regulatory environment that restricts citizens from holding bank accounts abroad, restricts prices and market entry, fails to treat citizens equally before the law, and interferes with capital transactions with foreigners.

As noted above, theory suggests that a sustained increase in economic freedom will enhance growth and a decline will retard it. Thus, one would expect countries with an expanding amount of economic freedom to have higher growth rates than those with a contracting amount of freedom. However, as Gwartney and associates stress (Gwartney, Lawson et al. 1996, 97), the immediate impact of a change in economic freedom is likely to be small—particularly in the case of an expansion in freedom. The reason is simple. There will be a lag between the time when institutional arrangements and policies become more consistent with economic freedom and when they began to exert their primary impact on economic growth.

The nations with the largest increase in economic freedom (Is1) during the 1975–90 period registered an average growth in per capita GDP of 2.7 percent during 1980–90. Their growth rate during the most recent ten years (1985–94) was even higher, 3.1 percent. All seventeen of these countries achieved a positive growth rate during 1980–94 and 1985–94. The growth of the nonindustrial countries that moved toward liberalization was particularly impressive. The per capita real GDP of eight (Chile, Malaysia, Portugal, Turkey, Singapore, Mauritius, Thailand, and Indonesia) of the twelve nonindustrial nations with the largest increases in economic freedom grew at three percent or more during the last decade. The average growth of per capita GDP for the twelve nonindustrial nations—the eight listed above plus Jamaica, Pakistan, Egypt, and Costa Rica—was 3.8 percent (Gwartney, Lawson et al. 1996, 99–100).

The economic record of the countries that restricted economic freedom during the 1975–1990 is in sharp contrast to that of those liberalizing their economies. These countries experienced (Gwartney, Lawson et al. 1996, 100) a decline in average real per capita GDP at an annual rate of 0.7 percent during 1980–1990 (and by 0.6 percent during 1985–94) in the sixteen countries for which the index of economic freedom fell the most. The economic decline was widespread. Twelve of the sixteen countries experienced reductions in real per capita GDP during the 1980–90 period. None were able to achieve a growth rate of more than 1.1 percent, a rate less than one-half the average growth rate for those that moved toward economic freedom.

As Gwartney and associates contend, maintenance of an increase in economic freedom is vitally important. Countries that shift back and fourth between liberal and restrictive policies will lose credibility, which will weaken the positive effects of their more liberal policies. Therefore, if we want to isolate the real impact of economic freedom, we need to consider the performance of economies that both increase and maintain a higher freedom rating. Interestingly, in addition to Pakistan only eight countries achieved at least a one unit increase in economic freedom (as measures by the (Is1 index) during 1975–1985 and maintained the increase into the 1990s. These economies were clearly freer throughout 1985–1995 than they were in 1975.

These countries' economies expanded at an annual rate of 3.1 percent during the 1980s and at a 3.5 percent rate during 1985–1994 up from 2.2 percent during 1975-85. During the last decade, the slowest growth rate among the nine was the 1.8 percent rate of the United Kingdom. Seven of the nine were classified as less developed by the World Bank at the beginning of the period. These seven—Mauritius, Chile, Portugal, Jamaica, Singapore, Pakistan and Turkey— grew at an average annual rate of 3.9 percent during the 1985–1994 period.

Again in contrast, those countries with the Is1 economic freedom rating declined by one unit or more during 1975–85 experienced poor economic performance. On average, the real GDP of these countries fell at an annual rate of one percent or more. During 1980–90, eight of nine regressors experienced reductions in per capita real GDP. None was able to achieve a growth rate of more than 0.65 percent during either 1980–90 or 1985–94. Clearly, the growth rates of the countries with a one unit or more reduction in economic freedom were persistently and substantially less than those with a one unit increase (Gwartney, Lawson et al. 1996, 103).

ANALYSIS

The indices provided by Gwartney provide valuable insights. There are, however, other logical ways to construct indices of economic freedom that may allow deeper insights as to the underlying patterns between government policy and economic performance. One method, factor analysis has the chief advantage of being independent of the choice of experts. This method also automatically generates objective indices that, in turn, can be used as inputs in further statistical analysis. More specifically, the basic assumption of factor analysis is that a limited number of underlying dimensions (factors) can be used to explain complex phenomena. The resulting data reduction produces a limited number of independent (uncorrelated) composite measures. In the current example, measures such as government consumption, inflation, negative interest rates, and the like will produce a composite index or factor of government.

Factor Analysis

Formally, as an initial step in exploratory data analysis, factor analysis has three objectives (Frane 1987, 3–4): (1) to study the correlations of a large number of variables by clustering the variables into factors such that variables within each factor are highly correlated, (2) to interpret each factor according to the variables belonging to it, and (3) to summarize many variables by a few factors.

The usual factor analysis model expresses each variable as a function of the factors common to several variables and a factor unique to the variable:

$$z_j = a_{j1}F_1 + a_{j2}F_2 + \quad + a_{jm}F_m + U_j$$

Where

z_j = the jth standardized variable
m = the number of factors common to all the variables
U_j = the factor unique to variable zj
a_{ji} = factor loadings

The number of factors, m, and the contribution of the unique factors should both be small. The individual factor loadings, a_{ji}, for each variable should be either very large or very small so each variable is associated with a minimal number of factors.

To the extent that this factor analysis model is appropriate for the problem at hand, the objectives stated above can be achieved. Variables with high loadings on a factor tend to be highly correlated with each other, and variables that do not have the same loading patterns tend to be less highly correlated. Each factor is interpreted according to the magnitudes of the loadings associated with it.

Perhaps more importantly for the problem at hand, the original variables can be replaced by the factors with little loss of information. Each case (firm) receives a score for each factor; these factor scores can be computed as

$$F_i = b_{i1}z_1 + b_i2_{z2} + \quad + b_{ip}z_p$$

where b_{ij} are the factor score coefficients. Factor scores are in turn used in the discriminant analysis that follows. In general, these factor scores have less error and are, therefore, more reliable measures than the original variables. The scores express the degree to which each case possesses the quality or property that the factor describes. The factor scores have a mean of zero and standard deviation of one.

Operationally the computations of factors and factor scores for each industry were performed using a principle components procedure (BMDP 1992, 311-337).   In addition to the data presented by Gwartney and associates socioeconomic indices and external debt figures from the World Bank (IBRD 1995) and defense expenditures from The United States Arms Control and Disarmament Agency (ACDA 1996) were added to the analysis.

The first factor exercise included a basic set of variables depicting the various aspects of economic freedom. To avoid year-to-year variations and missing values for specific years, the series were averaged over the 1974–94 period. In addition several general economic variables, the GDP, population, and area were added from the World Bank data set. For the total sample of countries (Table 2.2) four major trends appear to be present. The first reflects basic economic freedom. This measure of economic freedom is comprised of: (1) freedom to maintain bank balances abroad, (2) freedom to own foreign currency, (3) marginal tax rates, and (4) freedom to compete in the marketplace.

The next most important dimension can be characterized as reliance on market solutions and consists of (1) freedom from negative interest rates, (2) country-imposed price controls, (3) black-market exchange premium, (4) freedom to engage in capital transactions with foreigners, and (5) the size of government enterprises as a share of the economy. The negative sign on the black-market exchange rate stems from the fact that the actual values of the overvaluation were used (in contrast to the zero-to-ten scale for the other measures). Higher values for the exchange rate therefore, reflect a loss of economic freedom.

The third dimension consists largely of economic size variables. Clearly larger countries are, in terms of population, area, and GDP, less dependent on international trade. Finally, the last dimension consists of government consumption and taxes on the exports.

Omitting the developed countries from the analysis produced a similar pattern with several important differences (Table 2.3). First, the dimensions are clearer with freedom to engage in capital transactions with foreigners shifting to the basic freedom dimension (away from market solutions). Second, economic size becomes a separate dimension with trade and government consumption forming a separate independent factor. The results suggest (Tables 2.3–2.7) that Pakistan rates relatively low on basic economic freedoms and trade but has made progress toward market solutions.

To assess the stability of the underlying factor analysis as well as identifying several important linkages between economic freedom and various economic dimensions, additional variables were added to the basic factor analysis for developing countries (Table 2.3). First, since development assistance has been fairly important to the Pakistani economy, several measures of economic assistance, official development assistance as a percentage of GDP in 1993 (ODAY93), and per capital official development assistance in 1993 (ODAP93) were added to the analysis. The resulting patterns (Table 2.4) suggest that as a share of GDP, development assistance tends to flow to countries that have lagged in their progress toward market reforms. On a per-capita basis, this assistance is highly correlated with government consumption. While no causation is implied by this analysis one must conclude that countries lagging in reform simply "need" more foreign assistance (rather than assistance being a reward for inaction). On the other hand, it is apparent that much of this assistance allows countries to maintain a higher level of government consumption than would otherwise be possible.

Adding in average defense expenditures as a share of the GDP over the 1980 to 1993 period (MEY8093), as well as the average defense expenditure share of the central government budget (MEG8093), sharpened (Table 2.5) the role of aid as helping to finance increased levels of government consumption (of which defense is often a large component).

Finally, several measures of foreign capital flows as a proportion of net resource flows were added to the factor model. These included (1) official grants, POG93, (2) foreign direct investment (PFDI93), and (3) portfolio equity capital (PPEF93). Along with the addition of the growth in GDP (GDPG8093), this inclusion produced several additional insights (Table 2.6):

1. Portfolio equity capital flows (PPEF93) appear more influenced by the overall economic size of a country rather than any particular progress at economic reform.
2. While foreign direct investment (PFDI93) tends to shy away from countries with high levels of government consumption and defense expenditures, official grants are associated with relatively high expenditures in these areas.
3. While official development assistance as a share of GDP tends to be lower in countries that have made progress toward market solutions, the overall rate of growth of GDP tends to be higher in these environments.
4. For Pakistan, the pattern remains of relatively low attainment of economic freedom, above-average economic size, relatively high defense expenditures, good progress toward market solutions, and relatively low integration into the world economy.

The last result is in conformity with the growing body of literature (Gold and Ruffin 1993; Barro 1990; Henderson 1996) stressing the links between economic market liberalization and accelerated economic growth.

Discriminant Analysis

Progress of the advanced countries is often a standard held up for developing countries. In the area of economic freedom, there are some notable contrasts. These are most easily seen through a discriminant analysis. Here we are interested in determining the extent to which developing and developed countries can be profiled as separate groups, based on their attainment of economic

Table 2.2
Economic Freedom Factor Analysis, Total Sample

Factor Loadings	Factor 1 Basic Freedoms	Factor 2 Market Solutions	Factor 3 Economic Size	Factor 4 Public Sector
BANK	0.89610*	0.11204	0.06823	-0.09835
CUR	0.85060*	0.06915	0.11493	0.15639
MTR	0.69506*	-0.24122	-0.19131	-0.28758
MARKET	0.67068*	0.22742	0.24919	0.29122
NIR	0.01881	0.83195*	-0.04449	0.03896
PRICE	0.36213	0.62019*	0.08436	0.22275
BMEX	0.09641	-0.61424*	0.00706	-0.07219
CTF	0.56692	0.59757*	-0.02742	0.26627
RGENT	0.51552	0.55773*	-0.10127	-0.13781
AT	0.00649	0.31392	-0.76622*	0.11954
AMET	0.05449	0.30364	-0.65909*	-0.10109
AREA93	0.16292	0.16919	0.61477*	-0.08844
GDP93	0.18198	0.41871	0.58638*	0.08755
POP93	-0.21254	0.19279	0.54583*	-0.46455
GC	-0.18252	0.07651	-0.02584	0.82057*
TAXT	-0.35955	-0.37126	0.13197	-0.66947*

(Average Values 1974–1994)
* = factor loading greater than 0.50.
(MTR) Marginal tax rate; (BANK) Freedom to maintain bank balances abroad; (CUR) Freedom of residents to own foreign currencies; (MARKET) Freedom to compete in the marketplace; (CTF) Freedom to engage in capital transactions with foreigners; (NIR) Freedom from negative interest rates; (RGENT) Size of government enterprises as share of economy; (PRICE) Extent countries imposed price controls on various goods; (BMEX) Black market exchange rate premium; (AT) Actual trade (exports plus imports divided by GDP); (TAXT) Taxes on trade as a percent of exports plus imports; (AMET) Actual minus expected trade; (GC) Government consumption as a percent of GDP; (AREA) Geographical area, 1993; (GDP) Gross Domestic Product, $ US dollars, 1993; (POP) Population, Millions, 1993

Table 2.3
Economic Freedom Factor Analysis, Developing Countries

Factor Loadings	Factor 1 Basic Freedoms	Factor 2 Market Solutions	Factor 3 Trade Patterns	Factor 4 Economic Size
BANK	0.89103*	0.09190	-0.11904	-0.05437
CUR	0.88716*	-0.04344	-0.01136	-0.06731
MTR	0.81327*	0.01362	0.17195	0.03063
MARKET	0.73390*	0.12918	-0.02248	0.18006
CTF	0.55730*	0.39095	0.41524	-0.03758
NIR	-0.13633	0.82724*	0.04688	-0.15610
RGENT	0.42499	0.63917*	0.13395	-0.16542
PRICE	0.30286	0.62226*	0.03258	-0.06315
BMEX	0.13722	-0.50193*	-0.30763	-0.24339
AT	-0.02210	0.30035	0.74738*	-0.19875
TAXT	-0.32429	0.06622	-0.72208*	0.07625
AMET	-0.03481	0.22104	0.60757*	-0.08925
GC	-0.27171	-0.38512	0.52702*	-0.20730
AREA93	0.03302	-0.18902	-0.11072	0.88469*
GDP93	0.16405	-0.09143	-0.08171	0.87943*
POP93	-0.21814	0.15559	-0.35321	0.62029*

Country Scores				
South Asia				
Pakistan	-0.68237	0.63286	-1.29994	0.03759
India	-1.59076	1.44320	-2.07671	3.34935
Sri Lanka	-0.95055	1.01865	-0.99323	-0.56178
Bangladesh	-0.78013	0.31672	-1.94414	-0.53139
Middle East				
Egypt	-0.24041	-0.54112	-0.33064	-0.29160
Israel	0.13462	-2.38636	1.65368	-0.13031
Jordan	-0.41073	-0.51516	1.65630	-0.39980
Turkey	0.12700	-0.26181	-0.37166	0.54591

Note: See Table 2.2 for listing of variables.
* = factor loading greater than 0.50.

Table 2.4

Factor Analysis With Economic Freedom and Aid Dimensions

Factor Loadings	Factor 1 Basic Freedoms	Factor 2 Economic Size	Factor 3 Market Solutions	Factor 4 Trade Patterns	Factor 5 Fiscal
CUR	0.87647*	-0.00079	0.13341	-0.04507	-0.05454
BANK	0.85651*	-0.04821	0.07354	-0.00929	0.25003
MTR	0.82334*	0.03368	-0.01720	0.17179	0.06954
MARKET	0.72157*	0.14521	0.28240	-0.13137	0.03381
CTF	0.57778*	-0.11096	0.30898	0.42277	0.06037
RGENT	0.46585*	-0.38124	0.45463	0.14824	0.20936
GDP93	0.12678	0.87258*	0.11329	-0.09508	0.11531
AREA93	0.02016	0.86764*	-0.11908	-0.10601	0.13460
POP93	-0.30158	0.56179*	0.14807	-0.18337	0.29337
BMEX	-0.12745	-0.13643	-0.82770*	-0.04342	0.09849
ODAY93	-0.27010	-0.31376	-0.70508*	0.02449	-0.05025
NIR	-0.16261	-0.36754	0.66638*	0.15350	0.34643
PRICE	0.27839	-0.19737	0.51920*	0.16211	0.27620
AMET	-0.03113	-0.08199	-0.02110	0.84844*	0.11765
AT	-0.01800	-0.20221	0.24089	0.82143*	-0.15489
TAXT	-0.45147	0.06025	0.01978	-0.55485*	0.29990
GC	-0.16327	-0.12035	-0.07145	0.12403	-0.89076*
ODAP93	-0.08388	-0.25915	-0.10276	-0.02230	-0.81229*

Country Scores South Asia					
Pakistan	-0.84004	-0.00192	0.66920	-0.97086	0.68485
India	-2.02850	2.76101	1.35955	-1.06380	1.38600
Sri Lanka	-1.07563	-0.74751	0.56062	-0.47693	0.80970
Bangladesh	-0.80281	-0.81789	-0.69189	-1.53348	1.29370

Note: See Table 2.2 for listing of main variables. ODAP93 = official development assistance per capita, 1993; ODAY93 = official development assistance share of GDP, 1993.
* = factor loading greater than 0.50.

Table 2.5
Factor Analysis With Military and Aid Dimensions

Factor Loadings	Factor 1 Basic Freedoms	Factor 2 Defense Expenditure	Factor 3 Market Solutions	Factor 4 Economic Size	Factor 5 Trade Patterns
CUR	0.88026*	0.12233	0.13933	0.00627	-0.04593
BANK	0.84600*	-0.22736	0.12961	-0.02114	-0.01112
MTR	0.81787*	-0.12053	-0.01584	0.01560	0.18548
MARKET	0.72998*	0.02959	0.26580	0.16687	-0.13146
CTF	0.57063*	-0.02885	0.34428	-0.08535	0.41213
MEY8093	-0.06140	0.95573*	-0.07563	-0.00176	0.12065
GC	-0.13957	0.75123*	-0.23652	-0.24770	0.14818
MEG8093	0.04354	0.72778*	0.12275	0.10229	0.00035
ODAP93	-0.06456	0.67629*	-0.22545	-0.37286	-0.01075
NIR	-0.17540	-0.26853	0.75007*	-0.26373	0.12894
BMEX	-0.14521	-0.06119	-0.71097*	-0.15416	-0.05608
ODAY93	-0.28671	-0.03887	-0.64069*	-0.36494	0.02803
PRICE	0.27016	-0.20996	0.57883*	-0.12215	0.14710
RGENT	0.45604	-0.09487	0.55457*	-0.29984	0.12266
GDP93	0.14728	-0.04769	0.01498	0.87736*	-0.08213
AREA93	0.03468	-0.16054	-0.22437	0.84050*	-0.08362
POP93	-0.29338	-0.06016	0.17936	0.64296*	-0.21539
AMET	-0.04879	0.01945	0.08590	-0.03814	0.82283*
AT	-0.02516	0.17781	0.26087	-0.19693	0.81172*
TAXT	-0.45129	-0.07504	0.11712	0.15350	-0.59564*
Country Scores South Asia					
Pakistan	-0.81495	0.75330	1.13092	0.46493	-1.15018
India	-1.97630	0.08627	1.58548	3.27581	-1.30281
Sri Lanka	-1.10604	-0.61033	0.75799	-0.55282	-0.50460
Bangladesh	-0.85336	-0.74212	-0.16227	-0.53674	-1.66047

Note: See Table 2.2 for listing of main variables. MEY8093 = average share of defense expenditures in GNP 1980–93; MEG8093 = average share of defense expenditures in the central government budget, 1980–93.

Table 2.6
Factor Analysis With Military, Aid and Capital Flow Dimensions

Factor Loadings	Factor 1 Basic Freedoms	Factor 2 Economic Size	Factor 3 Defense Expenditures	Factor 4 Market Solutions	Factor 5 Trade Patterns
CUR	0.87605*	0.10608	0.00336	0.11892	-0.02708
BANK	0.86932*	0.07166	-0.14320	0.10550	0.02306
MTR	0.85998*	0.01176	0.00295	-0.14364	0.02431
MARKET	0.70761*	0.24657	0.00419	0.19009	-0.18512
CTF	0.64310*	-0.06058	-0.03751	0.27010	0.21155
GDP93	0.06460	0.91075*	-0.00502	-0.06078	-0.05804
PPEF93	0.09728	0.81220*	-0.01470	0.14569	0.15829
AREA93	-0.01546	0.74688*	-0.04302	-0.31491	-0.12894
ODAP93	-0.17646	-0.65616*	0.17515	-0.16337	0.23393
POP93	-0.30859	0.54044*	0.05112	0.12137	-0.34417
PFDI93	0.02360	0.06026	-0.92282*	0.02578	-0.07985
POG93	0.04298	-0.08762	0.90748*	-0.00288	0.09966
MEY8093	-0.14699	-0.10201	0.87502*	-0.11678	0.17622
MEG8093	0.01421	0.08070	0.74953*	0.02539	-0.12128
GC	-0.21188	-0.44719	0.46105*	-0.21056	0.40917
NIR	-0.09316	-0.21956	-0.09102	0.78967*	0.02363
BMEX	-0.18789	-0.18446	-0.05171	-0.66720*	-0.07511
PRICE	0.31574	-0.06407	-0.18378	0.55727*	-0.07409
RGENT	0.53912	-0.20949	0.07585	0.54859*	0.02783
ODAY93	-0.31302	-0.38924	-0.02312	-0.54596*	0.07445
GDPG8093	-0.28197	0.36361	-0.02206	0.53721*	0.28168
AMET	-0.05366	0.00616	0.10210	0.12138	0.74837*
AT	-0.07791	-0.44028	0.30064	0.17548	0.71948*
TAXT	-0.46003	0.09053	0.11577	0.13740	-0.64810*
Pakistan	-0.82880	0.38409	0.81435	0.99967	-1.39683
India	-1.89173	2.29386	0.55254	1.07938	-2.21769

Note: See Table 2.2 for listing of main variables. PFDI93 = net foreign investment as a share of net resource flows, 1993; POG93 = government grants as a share of net resource flows, 1993; PPEF93 = portfolio equity flows as a share of net resource flows, 1993; and GDPG8093 = growth in real GDP, 1980–93.

freedom. Specifically, which of the main factors identified in Table 2.2 are significant in a statistical sense in distinguishing developed from underdeveloped economies?

For this purpose a discriminant analysis was undertaken in an attempt to see if by simply knowing the extent of economic freedom one could predict whether a sample country was developed or underdeveloped. First an examination of the means of each of countries on the main factor dimensions shows some important differences (Table 2.7), with the developed countries consistently scoring higher on each of the four main dimensions: basic dimensions, market solutions, economic size, and public sector.

The discriminant analysis indicated that each dimension was statistically significant in distinguishing whether a country was developed, with the most important dimension being factor 2, market solutions, followed by factor 4, public sector, factor 3, economic size, and finally factor 1, basic economic freedoms. The standardized coefficients of these variables show that factors 2 and 4 are about equal in strength, with both about twice as important as factors 1 and 3.

Overall, the model produced good results with the sixty-eight of the seventy-two countries for which data was available being correctly classified (Table 2.7). Pakistan, with a highly negative discriminant score of -1.4785 (Table 2.8) was classified as a developing country with a probability of 99.91 percent of being in that category. In other words, given Pakistan's reforms to date, the country has a very long way to go before it reaches the levels of economic freedom often associated with the developed world.

Regression Analysis

One of the main advantages of discriminant analysis is the generation of a discriminant function for latter use. In the case at hand, the discriminant function score allows groupings to be made on the basis of what in essence is an overall economic freedom index. For example, countries such as the United States have a very high score (5.77, Table 2.8), whereas countries such as Pakistan come inconsiderably lower (-1.47, Table 2.8).

If we group the countries on the basis of their discriminant function score, say into one group with a high average degree of economic freedom (discriminant function scores greater than one) and one group with low degrees of economic freedom (discriminant function scores less than one), several additional patterns of interest emerge. As noted earlier, the literature continually stresses the positive link between increased economic freedom and economic growth. The factor analysis described above found this pattern (Table 2.6), but it was somewhat weak—a standardized regression coefficient of growth on market solutions of only 0.537, and actually a negative standardized regression coefficient of -0.28 on basic economic freedoms.

Table 2.7
Discriminant Analysis: Developed and Developing Countries

	Factor 1 Basic Freedoms	Factor 2 Market Solutions	Factor 3 Economic Size	Factor 4 Public Sector
Country Scores				
Bangladesh	-0.94106	-0.44376	0.74389	-1.29102
India	-2.14448	1.25601	2.78387	-3.42604
Pakistan	-0.88967	-0.02568	0.48250	-1.20698
Sri Lanka	-1.12802	0.36740	-0.06404	-0.74093
Group Means				
Developed	-0.13087	-0.31236	-0.16146	-0.30748
Underdeveloped	0.36506	0.87133	0.45038	0.85770

Stepwise Introduction of Discriminating Variables

Step	Variable	Wilks' Lambda	Significance
1	Factor 2	0.72399	0.0000
2	Factor 4	0.45656	0.0000
3	Factor 3	0.38282	0.0000
4	Factor 1	0.33437	0.0000

Standardized canonical discriminant function coefficients
Factor 1	0.45512
Factor 2	0.94754
Factor 3	0.55397
Factor 4	0.93822

Classification results

Group	Actual	Predicted	
		Developing	Developed
Developing	53	49	4
		92.5%	7.5%
Developed	19	0	19
		0.0%	100.0%

Percent of grouped cases correctly classified: 94.44 percent

Based on analysis in Table 2.2.

Table 2.8
Country Placement and Discriminant Scores

Country	Classified	Discriminant Score	Probability of Placement	
			Developing	Developed
United States	2.00	5.77823	0.00000	1.00000
Canada	2.00	2.91608	0.00106	0.99894
Australia	2.00	2.49503	0.00398	0.99602
Japan	2.00	2.76249	0.00171	0.99829
New Zealand	2.00	1.95639	0.02140	0.97860
Austria	2.00	1.19494	0.19476	0.80524
Belgium	2.00	1.48231	0.08896	0.91104
Denmark	2.00	3.20413	0.00043	0.99957
Finland	2.00	2.19033	0.01034	0.98966
France	2.00	1.93397	0.02293	0.97707
Germany	2.00	3.22002	0.00040	0.99960
Ireland	2.00	1.36439	0.12409	0.87591
Italy	2.00	1.52467	0.07870	0.92130
Netherlands	2.00	1.89896	0.02554	0.97446
Norway	2.00	1.79162	0.03548	0.96452
Spain	2.00	1.28897	0.15237	0.84763
Sweden	2.00	3.42077	0.00021	0.99979
Switzerland	2.00	0.88736	0.38973	0.61027
England	2.00	2.83650	0.00136	0.99864
Argentina	1.00	-1.09484	0.99701	0.00299
Bolivia	1.00	-0.38934	0.97292	0.02708
Brazil	1.00	-0.75508	0.99130	0.00870
Chile	2.00*	1.06377	0.26790	0.73210
Honduras	1.00	-0.79647	0.99236	0.00764
Columbia	1.00	-0.51493	0.98162	0.01838
Costa Rica	1.00	0.46345	0.70881	0.29119
Ecuador	1.00	-1.62821	0.99944	0.00056
Jamaica	1.00	-0.02979	0.92031	0.07969
Mexico *	1.00	-0.71879	0.99026	0.00974
Nicaragua	1.00	-1.48194	0.99912	0.00088

* = misclassified by model.

Table 2.8 continued

Country	Classified	Discriminant Score	Probability of Placement	
			Developing	Developed
Panama	2.00*	1.25104	0.16848	0.83152
Paraguay	1.00	-2.26867	0.99993	0.00007
Peru	1.00	-1.10661	0.99712	0.00288
Trinidad	1.00	0.10196	0.88398	0.11602
Guatemala	1.00	-0.51531	0.98164	0.01836
El Salvador	1.00	-0.23051	0.95606	0.04394
Uruguay	1.00	-0.00992	0.91558	0.08442
Venezuela	1.00	-1.42929	0.99896	0.00104
Egypt	1.00	-1.56955	0.99933	0.00067
Greece	2.00*	0.81567	0.44468	0.55532
Hungary	1.00	-1.20530	0.99789	0.00211
Israel	2.00*	1.27737	0.15716	0.84284
Jordan	1.00	-0.45776	0.97806	0.02194
Poland	1.00	-3.33347	1.00000	0.00000
Portugal	1.00	0.52301	0.66855	0.33145
Turkey	1.00	-0.43863	0.97673	0.02327
Bangladesh	1.00	-1.90668	0.99977	0.00023
India	1.00	-1.74260	0.99961	0.00039
Indonesia	1.00	-1.16898	0.99763	0.00237
Malaysia	1.00	-0.33029	0.96755	0.03245
Pakistan	1.00	-1.47850	0.99911	0.00089
Philippines	1.00	-1.64985	0.99948	0.00052
Singapore	1.00	-0.19933	0.95174	0.04826
South Korea	1.00	-0.25107	0.95871	0.04129
Sri Lanka	1.00	-0.95939	0.99542	0.00458
Thailand	1.00	-0.72162	0.99034	0.00966
Botswana	1.00	-0.22010	0.95466	0.04534
Cameroon	1.00	-1.70275	0.99956	0.00044
Congo	1.00	-1.21601	0.99796	0.00204
Ivory Coast	1.00	-1.67086	0.99951	0.00049
Gabon	1.00	-0.73134	0.99063	0.00937

* = misclassified by model.

Table 2.8 continued

Country	Classified	Discriminant Score	Probability of Placement	
			Developing	Developed
Ghana	1.00	-2.52589	0.99997	0.00003
Kenya	1.00	-0.81903	0.99288	0.00712
Malawi	1.00	-0.72336	0.99039	0.00961
Morocco	1.00	-1.17349	0.99766	0.00234
Nigeria	1.00	-2.25414	0.99992	0.00008
Senegal	1.00	-1.08138	0.99688	0.00312
South Africa	1.00	0.20373	0.84676	0.15324
Tunisia	1.00	-1.35801	0.99869	0.00131

* = misclassified by model

The empirical literature has had less to say on the linkages between economic freedom and investment, although again, the link is implicitly assumed to be positive. To test the link between economic freedom and growth and that between economic freedom and investment, a simple model was developed.

The growth equation posits a simple link between investment and the expansion in GDP. In addition and following an extensive literature (Looney 1991a); (Looney 1991), government expenditure in the form of the defense burden (the share of defense expenditures in GNP) is assumed to be a drag on the economy reducing growth, and changes in economic freedom (the Is1 measure) are assumed to stimulate higher rates of economic expansion. The estimated equation is a variant of the form originally proposed by Benoit (Benoit 1973; (Frederiksen and Looney 1985). As a basis of comparison the Gwartney study found (1996, 109) growth to be a function of the level of economic freedom, the change in economic freedom, and the share of investment in GDP. In that study, however, the level of economic freedom was barely significant at the 95 percent level, suggesting that using a somewhat different sample of countries might result in this variable being insignificant.

The second equation, the growth of investment was also assumed to respond to growth in the previous period (1970–80) and the change in economic freedom (again the change in Is1). The results are similar to those reported in Gwartney with several notable exceptions (Table 2.9).

Table 2.9
Factors Affecting Growth and Investment

Total Sample
Gross Domestic Product
GDPG8093 = 1.81 + 0.30 GDIG8093 + 0.07 MEY8093 + 0.20 ΔIS2
         (6.42) (8.21)   (1.08)   (1.49)
Adjusted R Square = 0.551; df = 76; F = 33.33

Investment
GDIG8093 = -0.09 + 1.55 ΔIS2 + 0.05 GDPG7080
         (-0.05)   (3.75)
Adjusted R Square = 0.157; df = 75; F = 8.16

Countries With Discriminant Scores > 0
Gross Domestic Product
GDPG8093 = 1.56 + 0.35 GDIG8093 + 0.02 MEY - 0.01 ΔIS2
        (3.98) (6.57)   (0.32)   (-0.04)
Adjusted R Square = 0.666; df = 23; F = 18.31

Investment
GDIG8093 = 2.65 + 0.98 ΔIS2 - 0.62 GDGPG7080
        (1.13) (1.52)   (-1.19)
Adjusted R Square = 0.103; df = 24; F = 2.49

Countries With Discriminant Scores < 0
Gross Domestic Product
GDPG8093 = 1.99 + 0.27 GDIG8093 + 0.12 MEY8093 + 0.63 ΔIS2
        (4.36) (5.34)   (1.03)   (3.11)
Adjusted R Square = 0.62658; df = 37; F = 23.32

Investment
GDIG8093 = 1.50 + 1.99 ΔIS2 - 0.24 GDPG7080
        (0.92) (3.29)   (-0.86)
Adjusted R Square = 0.181; df = 38; F = 5.43

Note: Two-stage least squares estimates. GDPG8093 = growth in GDP, 1980–93; GDPG7080 = growth in GDP, 1970–80; GDIG8093 = growth in investment, 1980–93; ΔIS2 = change in economic freedom 1974–1994 (Is2 measure); MEY8093 = average share of defense expenditures in GNP, 1980–93.

When the total sample of countries was included in the analysis, the change in economic freedom has a positive sign but is insignificant at the 95 percent level. The change in economic freedom is, however, positive and statistically significant in the investment function. The same analysis on individual groupings of countries, those with high and low degrees of economic freedom based on their discriminant function score, suggests that countries already enjoying relative high levels of economic freedom do not have much scope for expanding growth or investment through additional reforms.

For countries already enjoying high degrees of economic freedom, changes in economic freedom were statistically insignificant on affecting either the growth in GDP or in investment. On the other hand, positive changes in economic freedom in those countries possessing relatively low levels of economic freedom produce strong and positive stimulus to further growth and expansion in investment.

From these results we conclude that improvements in economic freedom, while no doubt desirable in and of themselves, experience diminishing returns when evaluated in terms of their ability to quantitatively improve economic performance. Countries with very low initial levels of economic freedom can expect fairly dramatic improvements in economic performance from liberalization.

CONCLUSIONS

In recent years a large body of literature has emerged concerning the benefits of increased political (Pourgerami 1992) and economic freedom. Results on the benefits of increased political freedom are mixed, with some studies linking it to subsequently improved economic performance (Pourgerami and Assane 1992a; Feng 1995) and others suggesting that it may impede governments from undertaking difficult economic reforms (Huntington 1995; Barro 1994, 1994a). On the other hand the benefits of increased economic freedom are seldom questioned (Messick 1996; Greenwood and Ogus 1994), although the methods used to attain economic freedom are sometimes debated (Ijaz 1996).

As Chaudhry has rightly noted (1995, 190), despite the high pay-off to economic liberalization the fact remains that the process in Pakistan has proceeded unevenly across the various sectors. Clearly shaky governments (Brauchli 1995) and powerful interests have caused the reform process to proceed at an uncertain pace (Dahlburg 1994). Except for the removal of input subsidies, practically nothing but mere lip-service has happened in agriculture, although the government's recent tax efforts in that sector may signal a change (Bokhari 1996, 1996a).

The findings in this chapter confirm the opportunities that exist for and the benefits that should stem from increased economic freedom in Pakistan. Given the government's current financial crisis, this may be the only viable option available to the authorities for restoring continued economic expansion.

Part II

SECTORAL ANALYSIS

3

Sources of Growth

INTRODUCTION

The sources of growth in any country can be examined from several different perspectives, each suggestive of policy actions undertaken by government authorities.

1. The factors of production—the relative contribution of labor capital and the like to overall output.
2. The major sources of output demand—consumption, investment, and exports.
3. Sectoral contribution to growth—the contribution to output made by agriculture, manufacturing, and so forth.

Regarding the sectoral contributions to growth in Pakistan, Burney (1986) found over the 1960–85 period commodity-producing sectors (agriculture and manufacturing) accounted for more than 40 percent of the growth in GDP. The major crops were the main source of the varying contribution of agriculture. In the case of manufacturing, the large-scale sector's output accounted for more than 60 percent of the contribution.

The economy has gone through a number of major changes since 1985. In particular, but especially from 1988 onwards, progress has been particularly strong in the area of freeing the private sector from regulation and artificial price distortions. In addition, a complementary privatization program was launched to reduce the role of the public sector in manufacturing and services. As a side benefit the program was seen as alleviating the government's financial and administrative burden and creating new opportunities for the private sector.

While growth in large-scale manufacturing output has not accelerated in recent years (nor has its overall contribution to GDP growth increased) there is hope (particularly among official policy makers) that this activity is finally beginning to play the classic role of a leading sector. However, for manufacturing to be a true leading sector it must be shown that its expansion tends to create a number of direct linkages with other key sectors such as construction, agriculture, and the like. Since these sectors also have numerous linkages with the rest of the economy, an increase in manufacturing would set in motion a broad-based cumulative expansion of the economy.

The purpose of this chapter is to explore these issues. What areas of the economy appear to respond to increased manufacturing output. Does manufacturing appear to be largely exogenous or is it affected to a large extent by output in other areas of the economy?

Leading Sectors

As noted, a main thrust of the government's post-1988 program has been to accelerate the rate of growth in manufacturing in the hope that this sector will act as a leading sector through imparting its growth momentum to other areas of the economy. Here it is instructive to compare the relative percentage contribution made to the GDP growth over time by manufacturing. For large-scale manufacturing, the picture is somewhat mixed (Table 3.1). For the 1988–92 period, manufacturing's average contribution to GDP growth was 13.25 percent That is, 13.25 percent of GDP growth was accounted for by the expansion in large-scale manufacturing. However, if we leave out 1988, this average increases to 15.59, which compares favorably to 11.24 percent for the 1974–92 period as a whole. It is, however, still below the 16.85 percent for the 1980-85 period.

The patterns for small-scale manufacturing are more stable (Table 3.2). During the 1988–92 period this sector contributed an average of 7.51 percent to GDP growth, up slightly over the 7.26 percent for the 1974–92 period as a whole. However, the growth of this sector is considerably above its average of 4.53 percent for the 1980–85 period.

In short, there does not appear to be a major shift in recent years in growth-generating capability to the manufacturing sector. The simple growth comparisons presented above do not, however, tell the whole story. The true test of whether manufacturing is evolving into a leading sector is its causal relationship with the GDP (and other sectors).

According to Currie, leading sectors have two critical characteristics: An unexploited or latent demand that can be actualized, and a sufficiently large demand as to cause its satisfaction to have a significant impact on the whole economy. Another qualification is that an increase in the sector's growth can be exogenous and occur independently of the current overall rate of growth of the economy (Burney 1986, 576). It follows that one could conclude that the manufacturing sector is beginning to assume the role of a leading sector if it can be shown that its recent performance reflects an increasing level of exogenous growth. To be a true leading sector, this growth must have a significant and positive impact on the country's overall economic expansion.

Table 3.1
Pakistan: Contribution of Large-
Scale Manufacturing to GDP Growth, 1974–1992

Year	Growth in GDP	Share of GDP	Growth	Contribution to GDP	
				(absolute)	(%)
1974	7.42	11.02	7.33	0.81	10.90
1975	5.68	11.39	9.21	1.02	17.87
1976	3.28	11.02	-0.04	-0.01	-0.16
1977	1.08	10.63	-2.48	-0.27	-25.31
1978	6.36	10.46	4.62	0.49	7.72
1979	8.04	10.19	5.23	0.55	6.80
1980	6.66	10.89	13.97	1.42	21.36
1981	6.96	11.08	8.87	0.97	13.87
1982	7.81	11.33	10.24	1.14	14.54
1983	6.89	11.37	7.30	0.83	12.00
1984	3.85	12.16	11.02	1.25	32.56
1985	8.66	11.73	4.82	0.59	6.76
1986	6.20	11.76	6.45	0.76	12.20
1987	5.72	12.00	7.87	0.92	16.16
1988	6.45	12.19	8.16	0.98	15.16
1989	4.64	11.82	1.48	0.18	3.90
1990	4.65	12.32	9.12	1.08	23.16
1991	8.11	12.34	8.26	1.02	12.55
1992	6.28	12.29	5.85	0.72	11.49
Averages					
AV 74-92	6.04	11.47	6.70	0.76	11.24
AV 74-79	5.31	10.79	3.98	0.43	2.97
AV 80-92	6.38	11.79	7.96	0.91	15.06
AV 80-85	6.81	11.43	9.37	1.03	16.85
AV 86-92	6.01	12.10	6.74	0.81	13.52
AV 88-92	6.03	12.19	6.57	0.80	13.25

Note: Computed from World Bank Data. Sectoral contribution to growth rate iscomputed by weighing the sectoral growth rates by the previous year's sectoral share of GDP. AV = average; VA = variance.

Table 3.2
Pakistan: Contribution of Small-
Scale Manufacturing to GDP Growth, 1974–1992

Year	Growth in GDP	Share of GDP	Growth	Contribution to GDP	
				(absolute)	(%)
1974	7.42	3.31	7.20	0.24	3.21
1975	5.68	3.72	19.06	0.63	11.09
1976	3.28	3.89	7.92	0.03	8.99
1977	1.08	4.14	7.49	0.29	26.99
1978	6.36	3.96	1.86	0.08	1.21
1979	8.04	4.00	8.98	0.36	4.42
1980	6.66	4.10	9.43	0.38	5.66
1981	6.96	4.03	5.22	0.21	3.07
1982	7.81	3.80	1.53	0.06	0.79
1983	6.89	3.91	10.01	0.38	5.52
1984	3.85	3.97	5.57	0.22	5.66
1985	8.66	4.17	14.09	0.56	6.47
1986	6.20	4.52	14.91	0.62	10.04
1987	5.72	4.66	9.12	0.41	7.20
1988	6.45	4.60	5.14	0.24	3.72
1989	4.64	4.80	9.04	0.42	8.97
1990	4.65	5.08	10.72	0.51	11.05
1991	8.11	5.12	9.16	0.46	5.73
1992	6.28	5.30	9.92	0.51	8.09
Averages					
AV 74-92	6.04	4.27	8.76	0.36	7.26
AV 74-79	5.31	3.84	8.75	0.31	9.32
AV 80-92	6.38	4.47	8.76	0.38	6.30
AV 80-85	6.81	4.00	7.64	0.30	4.53
AV 86-92	6.01	4.87	9.72	0.45	7.83
AV 88-92	6.03	4.98	8.80	0.43	7.51

Note: Computed from World Bank Data. Sectoral contribution to growth rate is computed by weighing the sectoral growth rates by the previous year's sectoral share of GDP. AV = average; VA = variance.

AN ALTERNATIVE THEORY

In rejecting the notion that manufacturing has acted as a leading sector in Pakistan's recent economic expansion, James and Naya (1990) contend that the high rates of economic growth achieved in Pakistan were not due to a manufacturing-led expansion, but simply facilitated by the external circumstances that relaxed the balance of payment constraints. As these external circumstances worsened in the mid-to-late 1980s, underlying macroeconomic imbalances emerged and the growth slowed.

In part the growth that occurred in the late 1970s could be attributed to recovery from the recession and the economy's adjustment to the traumas of the early 1970s. However, the fact that rapid real GDP gains were sustained year after year into the late 1980s indicates a fundamental acceleration in the growth trend that occurred in the late 1970s.

More specifically, they argue that improvement in growth performance has been associated with higher manufacturing and agricultural growth. Increasingly, the orientation of the trade, the exchange rate, and the industrial policies have been to exports and competitive markets. Regulatory restrictions on businesses have been relaxed and an expanded role given to the private sector. These positive changes may help explain the high growth rate from 1977–87. The assessment of how much the partial liberation of policies influenced productivity and growth is tempered by the realization that a number of special circumstances also influenced the income (James and Naya 1990, 203):

1. The sharp increases of worker's remittances from the Middle East after 1979
2. Large inflows of foreign aid in response to the invasion of Afghanistan

As James and Naya note, both of these fortuitous factors allowed the economy to grow at a faster rate than warranted by the domestic savings rate. After a decade of growth (averaging almost 7 percent between 1987 and 1990), real growth of the GDP fell to an average of about 5 percent, indicating that some of the favorable factors for growth have receded. At the same time a number of serious macroeconomic imbalances have arisen, and these demand corrective measures that could further reduce growth. The imbalances include wide deficits in the budget and trade accounts, the low and declining saving-rate, rising inflation, and an increasing debt service burden.

An important part of the government's growth strategy was an effort to increase investment efficiency. Raising the investment ratio through the encouragement of the private sector became a major component of the high growth strategy adopted by the government after 1977. The continued high level of public investment was to complement the private investment expansion. The government investment program would concentrate on infrastructure, private investment on productive sectors—agriculture, industry, and services. The government was successful in raising the share of private investment between 1978 and 1988 from 30 percent to 50 percent. Yet the growth of total investment has been so slow that between 1978 and 1988 the investment rate fell slightly as a percentage of the GDP. A remarkable feature of the high growth since the late 1970s is that it has been accomplished with relatively low investment levels.

Increased public deficits and low saving rates suggest that reforms are needed to increase the revenues and reduce the expenditures. However, the structure of government expenditure may show little room for the government to cut expenditure. A large portion of the expenditure is for defense and interest payments—which together accounted for over half of government current expenditure. Development expenditures, including investment and spending on social and economic service, declined from 8 percent of GDP in the early 1980s to under 7 percent of the GDP in 1988. Clearly this share could not be reduced any further. Consequently, the improvement of budgetary deficits from the expenditure side will rely heavily on reducing subsidies and improving performance of public enterprises.

Another factor that would seem to cast suspicion on any leading-sector role attributed to manufacturing is the manner in which the government has affected that sectors competitive position in international markets. Rostow (1990, ch.18) and other writers have stressed that in many cases export markets can provide the impetus for rapid expansion in manufacturing output.

According to the factor proportions theory of international trade, a priori, one would expect a labor-surplus, agrarian country like Pakistan to specialize in the production and export of labor-intensive and agribased goods (James and Naya 1990, 211–215). Given the scarcity of domestic savings, the country would tend to import goods intensive in various forms of capital–both physical and human. This pattern appears to fit Pakistan's foreign trade.

Still, Pakistan's export performance during the period 1971–77 was relatively poor. The share of nontraditional (mainly labor-intensive) exports was stagnant. Manufactured exports between 1970 and 1985 in nominal terms averaged only 10 percent per annum growth; this is less than half the average for all developing countries. During much of the 1970s—a period of relatively robust growth in world trade compared to the 1980s—trade and industrial policies in Pakistan were erratic.

After 1977, efforts were made to rationalize policies to some degree to establish more effective incentives to exports, substitute domestic production for imports and promote efficiency in stimulating industrial growth. Perhaps the most significant change was the adoption of more flexible and aggressive exchange rate management beginning in the early 1980s.

Several studies (Lewis 1970, Guisinger and Scully 1989; Naqvi and Kemal 1991) have evaluated the structure of protection and the effects of various promotion policies on Pakistan's industries (James and Naya 1990, 212–214):

1.   Comparatively, Pakistan's domestic markets been heavily protected. Among developing countries in Asia the early 1980s, Pakistan had one of the highest average

tariff levels. Not only were tariffs high, but imports were all subject to quantitative restrictions. Nevertheless, over time it appears that the overall level of protection in Pakistan has been reduced.

2. One of the most significant features of trade protection and industrial promotion policies in Pakistan is the unevenness of incentives across activities and even within industries according to size or location of firms. This unevenness is amply demonstrated by studies of "effective protection" and industrial policies. These irregularities arise for a variety of reasons—including variations in tariffs, differences in treatment of import licenses, varying rates of indirect taxes (including excises and export duties) and subsidies and differences in access to the government bureaucracy itself.

3. The variations in rates of protection often produce unintended, even bizarre, results. Examples are high protection of inefficient industries; negative protection of efficient and export-oriented industries; encouragement of capital intensive, large-scale firms; and discouragement of efficient and small- and medium-scale enterprises.

4. The existing studies indicate that protection in Pakistan in the early 1980s was strongly biased against export activities in which the country had comparative advantage.

5. By 1981, more and more commentators were speculating that the rupee was highly overvalued (Dawn 1981). The exchange rate overvaluation coupled with the high average tariffs, restrictive quota licenses on imports and deployment of indirect taxes on imports, and exports (some partially offset by duty drawbacks and subsidies) created a strong overall bias in favor of import-substituting industries. This situation also encouraged firms to produce for domestic (protected) markets over all foreign markets.

6. The system of protection also had negative effects on employment and distribution by unduly favoring investment in large inward-looking industries.

7. In a sense the import quotas and bans along with tariff restrictions were necessitated by efforts to overcome short-term disturbances and crises manifested in foreign exchange shortfalls. The pernicious longer term consequences of discretionary controls were rarely considered. The objectives of protecting domestic industries in sectors with comparative advantage, and thereby eventually attaining a stronger export and import-competing industrial base, were undermined.

8. The businesses that received the licenses for imports and allocations of foreign exchange concentrated on collecting rents resulting from excess demand and cultivating bureaucrats rather than efforts to increase efficiency in their plants so that they could compete in external markets.

These features have delayed the diversification of exports and have hamstrung the development of labor-intensive manufacturing activities with export potential. Clearly these policies have stifled whatever leading-sector capabilities manufacturing might otherwise have developed. On the other hand, the policies introduced to liberalize markets may be working in the direction of integrating manufacturing with other main branches of economic policy.

The general problem of liberalization can be simply expressed as one of revising incentives so that it is roughly equally profitable to produce goods for foreign and domestic markets.

The opening up of Pakistan's economy to foreign trade and investment has been at best a gradual process. Moreover, liberalization measures have not been introduced as part of a well thought-out program, but rather piecemeal often under the prodding of international donors. Despite this haphazard approach, some of the changes introduced have been substantial (James and Naya 1990, 212–214):

1. Since the early 1980s, Pakistan has broadly followed a combination of policies to move toward a more neutral trade regime. Despite the partial nature of trade liberalization in Pakistan, the trend has been comparatively clear in the 1980s *vis a vis* the previous decade. The average level of tariffs and the dispersion has been reduced. By the late 1980s, the tariff level averaged 30 percent, compared to 70 percent in 1979.

2. The reduction in import controls has also been noticeable. Export incentives have also improved. Among these has been an aggressive, flexible exchange rate management. From 1981 to 1989 the rupee has depreciated against the Special Drawing Right (SDR) by 135 percent. Imports have been liberalized by expanding the open general license for imported equipment and industrial raw materials.

3. Export subsidies have included not only duty drawbacks but also export credit facilities. The procedures for collecting rebates for exporters were streamlined and focused on nontraditional (new manufactured goods).

4. The World Bank has estimated that the share of industries where imports have been liberalized (in the sense of being on the free list or under Open General License) has expanded from only one-third in 1980 to two-thirds or more. Tariffs above 50 percent are imposed on only about one-fifth of total imports.

THE ISSUE OF CAUSATION

It is quite possible these reforms may have enabled manufacturing to begin stimulating growth in other sectors. In this regard, the issue of causation is an integral element in Currie's view of the critical elements needed by an activity to be a leading sector (Currie 1974, 6). That is, growth in of the leading sector must be exogenous and, in turn, lead the expansion in output of other major areas of the economy. Has expanded manufacturing output occurred independently of the GDP? In turn has this expansion in manufacturing output created through demand linkages sufficient to stimulate other areas of economic activity?

It follows that before drawing any definitive conclusions as to the impact of the government's recent policy packages toward the private sector, one must satisfactorily address the issue of causation. Fortunately, several statistical tests using regression analysis for this purpose are gaining wider acceptance. The original and most widely used causality test was developed by Granger (1969).

According to this test, increased manufacturing output causes say growth in the construction sector, if rates of expansion in the construction sector can be predicted more accurately by past values of manufacturing output than by past growth rates in construction value added. To be certain that causality runs from manufacturing to construction, past values of manufacturing must also be more accurate than past values of construction in predicting the observed rates of growth in manufacturing output over time.

The results of Granger causality tests depend critically on the choice of lag length. If the chosen lag length is less than the true lag length, the omission of relevant lags can cause bias. If the chosen lag is greater than the true lag length, the inclusion of irrelevant lags causes estimates to be inefficient. While it is possible to choose lag lengths based on preliminary partial autocorrelation methods, there is no *a priori* reason to assume lag lengths equal for all types of economic activity. To overcome the difficulties noted above, we used the Hsaio (1981) method to identify the optimal lags (Thornton and Batten 1985).

Four cases are possible:

1. *Manufacturing Growth causes Nonmanufacturing Sectoral Growth.* This occurs when the prediction error for nonmanufacturing decreases when manufacturing is included in the growth equation. In addition, when nonmanufacturing output is added to the manufacturing equation, the final prediction error should increase.

2. *Nonmanufacturing Growth causes Manufacturing Growth.* This is present when the prediction error for nonmanufacturing increases when manufacturing is added to the regression equation for nonmanufacturing, and is reduced when nonmanufacturing is added to the regression equation for manufacturing.

3. *Feedback.* This pattern takes place when the final prediction error decreases when manufacturing is added to the sectoral output equation, and the final prediction error decreases when nonmanufacturing output is added to the manufacturing equation.

4. *No Relationship.* This exists when the final prediction error increases both when manufacturing is added to the nonmanufacturing output equation and when non-manufacturing output is added to the manufacturing equation.

Summing up, the main questions of interest are Has the expansion in manufacturing initiated an overall expansion in other key sectors of the economy? And if so which areas? Has this pattern changed over time? Here again we are especially interested in examining the impact of the post 1988 reform program.

RESULTS

Using Word Bank data (IBRD 1991, 1992, and 1993), the linkages between large-scale manufacturing and GDP have appeared to change over time (Figure 3.1) with changes in the GDP providing a strong stimulus to manufacturing growth during the earlier (1974–88) period.

Figure 3.1
Pakistan: Patterns of Growth, GDP, and Manufacturing

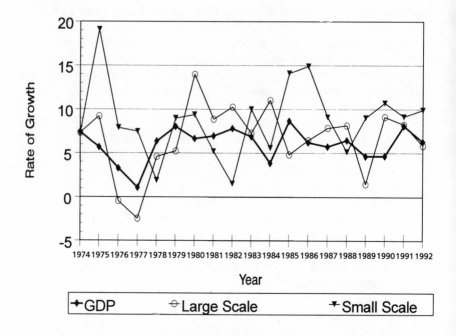

The average impact was rapid, with the optimal lag averaging two years. For the latter period (1978–92), however, large-scale manufacturing provided a very weak stimulus to GDP. The impact was also very rapid, averaging one year. These patterns merged into a feedback relationship for the period as a whole (1974–92). Again over this interval, the impact of GDP on large-scale manufacturing was quite strong, but that of manufacturing on GDP was very weak. There were no statistically significant patterns between small-scale manufacturing and the GDP. Several interesting patterns (Table 3.3) occur between the individual sectors and manufacturing:

Table 3.3
Pakistan: Manufacturing/Sectoral Causality Patterns

Sector	Direction of Causation	Optimal Lag (Years)	Impact	Relative Strength
Large-Scale Manufacturing/Agriculture				
1974–1992	Feedback	3,4	+,-	s,w
1974–1988	Ag-->Mfg.	2	+	s
1978–1992	Feedback	3,4	+,-	s,m
Small-Scale Manufacturing/Agriculture				
1974–1992	Mfg.-->Ag	3	(-)	m
1974–1988	Mfg.-->Ag	3	(-)	m
1978–1992	Mfg.-->Ag	3	(-)	m
Large-Scale Manufacturing/Mining				
1974–1992	No Relationship	---	---	---
1974–1988	No Relationship	---	---	---
1978–1992	No Relationship	---	---	---
Small-Scale Manufacturing/Mining				
1974–1992	Mfg.-->Mining	1	+	w
1974–1988	Mfg.-->Mining	1	+	w
1978–1992	Mfg.-->Mining	1	+	w
Large-Scale Manufacturing/Construction				
1974–1992	No Relationship	---	---	---
1974–1988	Const-->Mfg.	4	+	m
1978–1992	No Relationship	---	---	---
Small-Scale Manufacturing/Construction				
1974–1992	Const-->Mfg.	2	(-)	m
1974–1988	Const-->Mfg.	2	(-)	m
1978–1992	Mfg.-->Const	2	+	w

Note: See text for a description of the computational method. In the case of feedback, the first term refers to the impact from Sector --->Manufacturing. The second term depicts the relationship from Manufacturing --->Sector. All variables are defined in terms of their year-to-year rate of growth. Strength assessment based on size of the regression coefficient(s) and the improvement in r^2.

Table 3.3 continued
Pakistan: Manufacturing/Sectoral Causality Patterns

Sector	Direction of Causation	Optimal Lag (Years)	Impact	Relative Strength
Large-Scale Manufacturing/Transportation				
1974–1992	Feedback	2,2	+,-	w,w
1974–1988	Feedback	4,2	+,-	w,w
1978–1992	No Relationship	---	---	---
Small-Scale Manufacturing/Transportation				
1974–1992	No Relationship	---	---	---
1974–1988	Mfg.-->Trans	1	(-)	w
1978–1992	No Relationship	---	---	---
Large-Scale Manufacturing/Commerce				
1974–1992	Feedback	4,1	-,+	m,m
1974–1988	Feedback	2,1	+,+	m,m
1978–1992	Feedback	1,1	-,+	w,w
Small-Scale Manufacturing/Commerce				
1974–1992	Feedback	1,2	+,+	w,w
1974–1988	Feedback	1,2	+,+	w,m
1978–1992	Mfg.-->Comm	4	+	w
Large-Scale Manfacturing/Ownership of Dwellings				
1974–1992	OD-->Mfg.	2	+	w
1974–1988	No Relationship	---	---	---
1978–1992	OD-->Mfg.	3	+	w
Small-Scale Manufacturing/Ownership of Dwellings				
1974–1992	Mfg.-->OD	1	(-)	w
1974–1988	Feedack	2,1	+,-	w,w
1978–1992	Mfg.-->OD	3	(-)	w

Note: See text for a description of the computational method. In the case of feedback, the first term refers to the impact from Sector --->Manufacturing. The second term depicts the relationship from Manufacturing --->Sector. All variables are defined in terms of their year-to-year rate of growth. Strength assessment based on size of the regression coefficient(s) and the improvement in r^2.

Table 3.3 continued
Pakistan: Manufacturing/Sectoral Causality Patterns

Sector	Direction of Causation	Optimal Lag (Years)	Impact	Relative Strength
Large-Scale Manfacturing/Finance				
1974–1992	No Relationship	---	---	---
1974–1988	Mfg.-->Fin	2	+	m
1978–1992	No Relationship	---	---	---
Small-Scale Manufacturing/Finance				
1974–1992	No Relationship	---	---	---
1974–1988	Fin-->Mfg.	4	+	m
1978–1992	No Relationship	3,2	-,+	w,m
Large-Scale Manufacturing/Public Admin/Defense				
1974–1992	Mfg.-->PubAdm	3	+	m
1974–1988	Mfg.-->PubAdm	3	+	s
1978–1992	Feedback	2,3	-,+	m,m
Small-Scale Manufacturing/Public Admin/Defense				
1974–1992	PubAdm-->Mfg.	3	+	m
1974–1988	PubAdm-->Mfg.	3	+	m
1978–1992	PubAdm-->Mfg.	4	+	m
Large-Scale Manufacturing/Other Services				
1974–1992	Feedback	2,1	+,+	s,m
1974–1988	Feedback	2,4	+,+	s,w
1978–1992	Feedback	2,2	+,+	w,m
Small-Scale Manufacturing/Other Services				
1974–1992	No Relationship	---	---	---
1974–1988	No Relationship	---	---	---
1978–1992	No Relationship	---	---	---

Note: See text for a description of the computational method. In the case of feedback, the first term refers to the impact from Sector --->Manufacturing. The second term depicts the relationship from Manufacturing --->Sector. All variables are defined in terms of their year-to-year rate of growth. Strength assessment based on size of the regression coefficient(s) and the improvement in r^2.

1. As one might have anticipated, the links between small and large-scale manufacturing and other sectors of the economy differ considerably. This pattern holds across nearly all the main sectors of the economy.

2. Concerning agriculture, causation appears to flow largely from agriculture to large-scale manufacturing. This pattern is consistent with the notion that expanded production in agriculture tends to lower raw material costs and thus raise profitability in manufacturing. It is also consistent with several of the linkage mechanisms developed in the context of the Green Revolution (Kaneda 1971; Child and Kaneda 1975).

3. Surprisingly, expansion in small-scale manufacturing has a consistently (and moderately strong) negative impact on agriculture. One possible explanation for this pattern is the occurrence of labor shortages in agriculture as small rural-based industries deplete the local labor pool. The increasing labor costs to farmers reduce profitability and hence future output levels.

4. Expanded large-scale manufacturing provides no real stimulus to the mining sector. However, increased small-scale manufacturing does a short-run, albeit weak, increase in the demand for mining output. No doubt this effect is felt most in the metal working areas of manufacturing.

5. There are few positive links from manufacturing to construction. Here, the only significant links involve an often negative one from construction to manufacturing. Again this negative relationship may originate in construction related shortages in local labor markets.

6. One interesting development in recent years is that of a positive linkage between small-scale manufacturing and the construction sector. It should be noted, however, that this link is still quit weak. Also of importance is that the long-run trend in construction growth is declining while that of manufacturing is increasing. Clearly, the negative links between construction and (particularly large-scale) manufacturing are not significant impediments to increased industrial activity.

7. Increases in transportation and communications appear to produce a weak stimulus to large-scale manufacturing (while manufacturing in turn impacts negatively on transportation). Again, there is little evidence here that manufacturing is assuming the role of a leading sector.

8. The financial sector has responded positively to increased output in large-scale manufacturing. However, this pattern seems to have broken down in the last four or five years.

9. Both in terms of strength and consistency, the major linkages between manufacturing and the economy appear to be in the areas of public administration/defense and other government services. In all cases, manufacturing has made a moderate to strong impact. That is, increased manufacturing activity appears to place pressure on or provide the means for the government to expand services.

10. It should be noted, however, that the longer run trend in growth in public administration and defense and in other public services is downward. That is, the average growth rate of each is experiencing a secular deceleration. Clearly the potential of manufacturing to lead a service-led expansion in growth has been limited.

CONCLUSIONS

Earlier we speculated that the economic reforms introduced in the 1980s might have enabled manufacturing to play a more critical role through stimulating growth in other sectors. Drawing on Currie's conceptual framework, we tentatively defined a leading sector as one whose growth is largely exogenous and, in turn, initiates an expansion in output in other major areas of the economy (Currie 1974, 6). The shift in the pattern of causal growth from one of GDP to large-scale manufacturing in an earlier period to the more recent one of manufacturing stimulating GDP suggests that the reforms may be creating an environment whereby manufacturing is able to play a greater role in initiating economic growth.

On the other hand, however, the absence of any major links (or evidence of movement in that direction) between large-scale manufacturing and other sectors of the economy suggests that this conclusion is premature. It is apparent from the analysis above that the positive linkages from manufacturing to the overall economy stem largely from the relationship between manufacturing and public services. In the Pakistani context, expanded manufacturing appears to elicit more of a response from the government (in terms of providing more services/bureaucracy, etc.) than it creates real demand for other commodities. Given the budgetary policies facing the government and that the long run growth trend in services is downward, it would appear that the growth model developed over the last twenty or so years is self-terminating.

Noman has best articulated the inability of large-scale manufacturing to develop links with other sectors: "In the 1980s private manufacturing has continued the shift toward ore sophisticated intermediate and capital goods. Nonetheless, industrial diversification has been stunted. Industry has been found wanting in developing forward and backward linkages." (Noman 1991, 854)

Like many observers, Noman attributes the poor performance of large-scale manufacturing to inappropriate government policies—overvalued exchange rate, excessive protection, and low taxes—factors that tend to increase or maintain high rates of profit while providing no incentives for efficiency or use or links with other sectors.

One bright spot is the performance in small-scale manufacturing. While it is well known that the sector is extremely labor intensive and its growth has aided in expanding the nonagricultural labor force, a number of other attributes have made this sector a powerful force for growth. As documented by Hamid (1983), small-scale industry is an efficient user of capital and investment in that it adds more value added than it does in large-scale industry. Also, small-scale industry uses domestically produced machinery; therefore, its growth, on the one hand, generates feedback and further strengthens the country's capital goods manufacturing capability, and, on the other hand, requires little foreign exchange and thus relaxes an important constraint on the country's growth (Hamid 1983, 67).

The analysis above suggests another role played by small-scale industry—that of forging a number of positive, although weak, linkages with construction, finance, and commerce. Traditionally, small-scale firms have not had access to foreign exchange, nor have they had the financing (and incentive) to import foreign equipment. Perhaps the recent trade reforms will divert a larger proportion of large-scale manufacturing inputs to the domestic market. That would clearly be a favorable development and would redirect growth in that sector to a broader based sectoral expansion.

Admittedly, by themselves, the causation results presented above do not identify the underlying reasons for the differential performance of large- and small-scale firms. However, the differential performance of small-scale manufacturing is consistent with several, albeit overlapping, mechanisms: (1) these firms face different factor-price incentives and, therefore, utilize resources differently than their larger counterparts, or (2) their size enables them to be more flexible and adaptable to changing conditions.

Concerning the first, further research should examine the extent to which large- and small-scale manufacturing firms face different government-created incentives, and the extent to which these incentives direct demand toward or away from other domestic producers. Regarding the second interpretation, a productive area to explore would be that of flexible specialization. Briefly stated, flexible specialization at the macro level "encapsulates the move from a dominant mass production system, where stable markets, factor-cost reductions, and economies of scale were key variables to more diversified and ever-changing markets, products and production processes, where flexibility and innovation occupy center stage" (Rasmussen, Schmitz et al. 1992, 6). Nabi (1988) found several case studies where flexible specialization was an important factor distinguishing large from small firms in Pakistan. To what extent has the flexibility of smaller Pakistani firms contributed to their superiority in generating links with other productive sectors? And is this induced by the government's more favorable policies for larger scale firms?

4

Public-Sector Deficits and Private Investment

INTRODUCTION

An important aspect of Pakistan's post-1988 stabilization programs has been the attention given to supply side policies. The privatization program and additional steps to liberalize domestic economic activities are important elements in the authorities' strategy to enhance the productive side of the economy. Expanded privatization is being accompanied by the opening of new activities (such as utilities assurance) to the private sector, further simplification of the investment regime, and the removal of remaining price distortions.

In addition, the authorities hoped that private investors would respond along the lines originally suggested by Hirschman (1958), taking advantage of the cost-reducing effects of infrastructure. Through this mechanism, public investment was to assume a leading role in financing expanded capital formation in productive investment, especially manufacturing.

However, the patterns of public and private investment have been paradoxical. That is, contrary to the unbalanced infrastructure-led (compare Looney and Frederiksen 1981) development model postulated by Hirschman, several recent studies have found that public investment has played a passive role in stimulating follow-on private investment (Looney 1992a, 1992c; Looney and Winterford 1992). Specifically, public facilities appear to have largely expanded in response to the needs created by expanded private investment in manufacturing, rather than strongly initiating the capital formation process.

Clearly if the economy is to sustain high rates of overall growth in the future, the government must find ways of encouraging the private sector to play a more active role. Does this mean a shift away from infrastructure and toward other programs more effective in encouraging private investment? Has the failure of infrastructure-led growth been due to a general unwillingness of the private sector to invest, despite the incentives created by infrastructure, or has expanded infrastructure investment created an offsetting set of factors associated with "crowding out" or the preemption of investment funds (or driving up borrowing rates) thus discouraging private investment?

The purpose of this chapter is to assess whether this public-sector crowding out of investment in manufacturing has been a major factor affecting the pattern of private capital formation in that sector. Has crowding out occurred? If so, was the crowding out financial or real? Was crowding out associated with public sector-fiscal deficits, or with the manner in which these deficits were financed? Based on the answers to these questions, several implications are drawn for macroeconomic policy.

THE CROWDING OUT HYPOTHESIS

The issue of crowding out has been discussed at length in the literature.
As Blejer and Khan note (1985, 219), one could argue with some justification that crowding out may be a common phenomenon in the developing world. *Although* casual observation of the experiences of most developing countries would support this view, the mechanism or mechanisms through which such crowding out occurs, if it does, are still being debated, and there is no unanimity of opinion (Gupta 1992) .

If budgetary deficits cause a displacement of private investment a link should exist between budget deficits and interest rates with rising interest rates leading to the crowding out of private investment expenditures. As Burney and Yasmeen note (1989, 917) , the empirical evidence on this point has been inconclusive. For example they cite a number of studies (Cebula 1988; Deleuw and Holloway 1985; Hoelscher 1986; Khan 1986) that have found evidence linking deficits to higher interest rates. On the other hand, (Dewald 1983; Dwyer 1982; Evans 1982; Hoelscher 1983; Makin 1983; Mascaro and Meltzer 1983; McMillin 1986; Motley 1983; Plosser 1982) have found that deficits do not have a significant impact on interest rates. It should be noted, however, that all these studies focus almost exclusively on conditions in the developed countries.

Previous Studies

Several studies have attempted to identify the existence of crowding out in the Pakistani context. Ahmad (1994), tests for this phenomenon over the period from 1970–1991. He also examines the hypothesis that the real interest rates are adversely influenced by the expected rate of inflation. Pakistan has experienced a host of structural changes during this period, especially in the financial sector. For example, a partial interest-free banking system was introduced in 1981. Pakistan also announced a policy of delinking the Pakistan rupee from the U.S. dollar and dropped a floating exchange rate system in 1981. This led to a sharp depreciation of the Pakistani currency and subsequently increased workers' remittances at an unprecedented rate.

After testing an IS-LM model with interest rates related to real government spending, real government budget deficits, real money stock, and the expected rate of inflation, he finds that none of the explanatory variables exert a significant influence on the nominal rate of interest. The real rate of interest is adversely affected by the expected rate of inflation. From this, he concludes that there is no support for the crowding out hypothesis. This suggests that monetary and fiscal policies have no impact on interest rates and, therefore, stabilization policies can be used in Pakistan, within reasonable limits, without worrying about their adverse effect on economic growth.

In contrast, Burney and Yasmeen's study focuses on possible budgetary links with interest rates. Their findings (1989, 976) suggest that the overall government budget deficit in Pakistan does not have any significant impact on the nominal interest rates. However, when assumed that people can predict the future rate of inflation accurately, the overall deficit is found to have a significant impact on the nominal interest rate. Although they do not directly examine the impact on private investment, it is noted that there may be (Burney and Yasmeen 1989, 976) an inverse relationship between investment and nominal interest rates. If this is the case, their results suggest that an increase in the overall deficit is likely to crowd out private investment expenditure in Pakistan. Burney and Yasmeen (1989, 977) feel that budget deficits if financed through borrowing from the banking system are likely to result in higher nominal interest rates and hence may end up crowding out private investment and consumption expenditures. This being the case, the government's efforts to boost investment in the economy by increasing the share of the public sector, particularly by borrowing, is likely to fall short of its objectives. As Burney and Yasmen note, this may also lead to a slowing down of the economy.

However, in the case of Pakistan, there is ample reason to believe that the usual crowding mechanisms involving rising interest rates (stemming from increased public domestic borrowing) are a minor factor in suppressing private investment compared to credit rationing (Kemal 1991) in an environment of financial repression. A. Khan (1988a), for instance, has convincingly identified the presence of financial repression in the country's capital markets.

Similarly, Khan, Hasah and Malik (1992) find the real interest rate exerted a positive and significant effect on the national savings rate. A 1-percent increase in the real interest rate is likely to increase the savings rate by 0.07 percent. They conclude that this positive and significant effect of the real interest rate on the savings rate confirms the existence of financial repression in Pakistan.

Conceptual Problems

Because the interest rate mechanism does not play nearly as active an allocative role in Pakistan and many other developing countries, the mechanisms responsible for possible crowding out are not as well established. Still, one could argue with some justification that, in view of the significant share of the public sector in total capital formation, the degree and magnitude of the administrative controls over the financial system, and the limited access to international capital markets by private borrowers, the government would still exercise a relatively strong influence over private investment.

The absence of a flexible interest rate mechanism means that reduced form type equations are more applicable for estimating possible crowding out. Here crowding out can be broadly defined to include both financial and real crowding out (Blejer and Khan 1985).

Financial Crowding Out

Financial crowding out stemming from fiscal deficits can be examined in within the framework (FitzGerald 1980, 1979; Looney and Frederiksen 1987) of one of three macroeconomic theories: (1) conventional crowding out, (2) What FitzGerald calls Keynesian crowding out, and (3) the monetary approach to the balance of payments (Khan and Iqbal 1991).

1. *Conventional Crowding Out.* This effect occurs when the deficit is financed by selling bonds. The price of bonds is bid down (because of oversupply) which is equivalent to an increase in interest rates. The higher interest rates cause investment to decline, or to be crowded out as a result of the higher deficit. Neither savings (s) nor the external balance is affected since these depend on income and relative price levels, respectively.
2. *The Monetary Approach.* Here emphasis is on the case where the deficit is monetized, creating an excess supply of money. Since interest rates are (for most smaller countries) determined internationally, savings and investment are unchanged. Thus there is either a capital outflow or an increase in imports—the full effect of the deficit is felt by the worsening of the external balance (B).
3. *Keynesian Crowding Out.* This approach assumes that any increase in the deficit is paid for through increases in private savings. This is the same as a decrease in or the crowding out of private consumption.

While seemingly straightforward, when applied to developing countries, crowding out has often led to conflicting findings. For example, Fitzgerald (1979, 1980) found that public deficits displaced, or crowded out, private consumption in Mexico. In this context, private savings increased to finance the deficit. Furthermore, the increase in savings came at the expense of private consumption rather than private investment. This finding suggests that under certain circumstances the fiscal deficit may actually mobilize savings for increased levels of investment and thus growth. However, in their examination of Mexico, Looney and Frederiksen (FitzGerald 1980) found a more Keynesian result: increases in the deficit were accompanied by increases in consumption. In addition, private investment was adversely affected by inflation (in turn probably stemming from government deficits).

Several studies have examined these issues in Pakistan. Bilquees (1989), for example, examined the relevance of the monetary approach to the balance of payments and suggested that the theory's strong assumptions concerning homogeneity and openness make its relevance questionable for Pakistan. Consistent with this, his empirical study finds that the monetary approach to balance of payments fails to explain the flows of foreign reserves in Pakistan (and India), where monetary policy is restrictive and the foreign exchange and capital markets are controlled (Bilquees 1989, 202).

On the other hand Khan and Iqbal (1991) found no evidence of either conventional or Keynesian crowding out effects. Instead, they find that the deterioration of the fiscal deficit has been worsening the current account balance, a finding that is in line with the monetary approach to the balance of payments.

In addition, their findings suggest that increases in the fiscal deficit have reduced private savings and, therefore, investment and growth in Pakistan. Besides the existence of financial repression (low or negative real interest rates) and lack of financial development (few financial institutions and the availability of few financial instruments), the fiscal deficit appears to be an important factor in accounting for such low savings. In short, their findings suggest that government savings are a substitute for private savings.

Khan and Iqbal's findings also imply a positive association between the price levels and private consumption, therefore, confirming the dominance of income effects. Since the increase in price level increases private consumption, it must reduce private savings and private investment.

In another study, Haque and Montiel (1991) note that the macroeconomic consequences of fiscal deficits in Pakistan have apparently been quite different from those in other developing countries experiencing deficits of a comparable magnitude. Specifically, Pakistan has experienced neither hyperinflation nor debt rescheduling. As measured by the official figures, growth has remained quite strong through the last two decades, inflation has not been high, and the current account deficit has averaged about 2.5 percent of the GNP, remaining largely capable of being financed and not posing debt servicing problems for the country. They argue that to some extent growth has itself accounted for this since the associated expansion of the base for both conventional taxes and seigniorage has made it possible to finance "equilibrium" deficits that are significantly larger than would have been possible to finance in a slow-growth economy.

They warn nevertheless that since the early 1980s fiscal deficits have been financed by recourse to domestic nonbank borrowing, resulting in increasing ratios of domestic public debt to GNP and to rising interest rates on such debt. Their model simulations suggest that while relying on this source of finance may have mitigated the inflationary consequences of the deficits, this may have been done at the expense of some crowding out of private investment and has thus implied slower growth than would otherwise have been observed. Controlling the deficit over this period would have contributed to more favorable macroeconomic outcomes—at least with respect to growth and the external accounts—but not if the deficit reduction had been brought about in a manner commonly relied upon both in Pakistan and elsewhere—that is, through reducing public investment.

Real Crowding Out

In addition to the financial factors noted above, private investment may have experienced real crowding out. This could occur if government expenditures preempt scarce physical resources that would otherwise be available to the private sector.

As with financial crowding out, however, the results of studies testing for real crowding out have been mixed (Galbis 1979; Sundararajan and Thakur 1980; Wai and Wong 1982; Looney 1992; Taylor 1988). No doubt a complicating factor here stems from the fact that government expenditures can cause real "crowding in" as well as nominal "crowding out." As Noman (1991a, 783–784) observes, recent research has emphasized that private investment and public expenditures can be not only substitutes but also complements. Thus, certain public investments, for example, on infrastructure can "crowd in" à la Hirschman rather than crowd out private investment. As he warns, however, "ultimately though unsustainably large fiscal deficits, even if they are not crowding out the private sector for extended periods, force adjustment and if that is excessively delayed lead to a macroeconomic crisis" (Noman 1991a, 783).

Areas for Study

Clearly a case can be made that some form of crowding out of private investment has occurred in Pakistan. The real issue seems to come down to the manner in which crowding out has taken place. To pin down these mechanisms, additional analysis needs to be undertaken:

1. In the studies noted above, the direction of causation has implicitly been assumed to go from government deficits to expanded domestic borrowing to interest rate increases and/or credit rationing and ultimately reduced private investment. One could just as easily argue that increased levels of private investment have placed pressure on the government to expand facilities, especially in energy. The government,

wishing to aid private investment while simultaneously lacking adequate funding for major infrastructural programs, may first grant the private sector various forms of relief such as tax holidays followed by modest increases in public investment. The outcome of this process would be expanded deficits, but not necessarily the crowding out of private investment in the classical sense. The causation issue must be addressed before any definitive conclusion can be made concerning crowding out.

2.   As a related issue, the timing of these impacts needs to be identified. Many effects associated with government deficits are likely to have a delayed impact on private investment decisions. Again because the timing of these effects has not been spelled out, the patterns of causation are unclear.

3.   If we assume that interest rate effects are only one factor associated with the government deficit as it pertains to private investment, the theory of crowding out becomes unclear as to the relevant form of the budgetary deficit. If the interest rate mechanism is not perfect, are private investors more concerned or affected (through perhaps credit rationing) by the actual deficit, some sort of expected deficit, unanticipated changes in the deficit, or even deviations in the deficit from some longer run budgetary trend?

4.   The environment in which deficits exist needs to be identified. Obviously, if deficits stem largely from increased government consumption or defense, their negative impact on private investment will be greater than if they had stemmed simply from increased infrastructural investment.

5.   The financing of the public-sector deficit and government capital formation needs to be examined in detail. Have the deficits been associated with government investment or consumption? How have the deficits been financed as between domestic and foreign borrowing? Do the impacts of domestic versus foreign borrowing vary with regard to their effect on private industrial investors?

6.   One reason for these inconclusive results is due to the failure to separate out real from financial crowding out. In this regard, Blejer and Khan (1984, 1985) have argued that public investment involves both the development of infrastructure, which likely would be complementary with private investment, and other types of noninfrastructural investment that competes with private investment either through absorbing limited physical resources or thorough the production of marketable output. Taken together these effects of the infrastructural and noninfrastructural components can offset each other, thereby yielding the impression that the impact of total government investment on the level of private investment is weak or insignificant. Their work has shown that once the two aspects of public investment are recognized and a distinction is made along functional lines involving infrastructural and noninfrastructural investment, much stronger statements can be made on the role of governmental investment in private capital formation.

THE ISSUE OF CAUSATION

As noted, a major issue in the analysis of the role of government deficits in Pakistan's post 1971 development centers around the direction of causation: do deficits affect private-sector investment in manufacturing as suggested by the crowding out school, or do deficits simply respond to the needs created by an expanding economy?

It follows that before drawing any definitive conclusions as to the impact of the public sector deficit, one must satisfactorily address the issue of causation. Fortunately, as noted in Chapter 3, several statistical tests given in the appendix using regression analysis for this purpose are gaining wider acceptance. The original and most widely used causality test was developed by Granger (1969, 1980, 1986, and 1988). According to this test, deficits (DEF) affect, say, growth of private-sector investment in manufacturing (PIM) if this series can be predicted more accurately by past values of deficits than by past (investment) growth patterns. To be certain that causality runs from deficits to PIM, past values of the public deficit must also be more accurate than past values of private investment at predicting increases in the deficit.

Following the general framework given in the Appendix, depending on the value of the final prediction errors, four cases are possible: (1) "Fiscal policies (deficits, borrowing, expenditures) cause private investment" when the prediction error for private investment decreases when the fiscal action is included in the growth equation. In addition, when private investment is added to the fiscal equation, the final prediction error should increase; (2) "Private investment causes a fiscal response" when the prediction error for private investment increases when fiscal actions are added to the regression equation for private investment, and is reduced when private investment is added to the fiscal regression equation; (3) "Feedback" occurs when the final prediction error decreases when a fiscal policy is added to the private investment equation, and the final prediction error decreases when private investment is added to the fiscal equation; and (4) "No relationship" exists when the final prediction error increases both, when fiscal policies are added to the private investment equation and when private investment is added to the fiscal equation.

OPERATIONAL PROCEDURES

The data used to carry out the causation tests was derived from The International Monetary Fund (IMF) (1995 and 1994) and the World Bank (IBRD) (1993, 1992, 1991, and 1983). Unit root tests (Doornik and Hendry 1994) indicated the lograthemetic constant price form was the correct specification (see also Sakr 1993).

To assess the robustness of our findings and whether the results were sensitive to the definition of key variables, various measures of the deficit were examined. These included the actual, or realized, deficit; the expected deficit, the predicted value obtained by regressing each year's deficit on its value for the previous year; and the unexpected deficit, the difference between each year's actual deficit and that anticipated based on past patterns. *A priori* we might expect that unanticipated increases in the fiscal deficits or in domestic borrowing would have a stronger effect of private investment. Presumably, unanticipated increases in these variables signify more of an emergency borrowing situation and thus making it more difficult for the private sector to realize its borrowing needs.

Besides the financial variables (fiscal deficits, and public-sector borrowing) traditionally used in used in crowding out analysis to test for real crowding out, several types of government expenditure were also examined. Infrastructure investment was defined as general government investment (consisting of federal, provincial, and local investment). Noninfrastructural public investment consists largely of investment in public enterprises and was defined as total public investment minus general (infrastructural) investment.

Ceteris paribus infrastructure investment should have a positive (crowd in) affect on private investment since it is most likely to reduce the costs of private-sector manufacturing and thus stimulate capital formation in that sector. On the other hand, noninfrastructural investment is assumed, *ceteris paribus* to result in "real" crowding out of private investment.

As a basis of comparison, government consumption (and in several cases defense expenditures) was also included in the analysis. Since this type of expenditure is not likely to compete with the private sector for resources, real crowding out was assumed not to be a factor in affecting private investment. On the other hand, the manner in which government consumption was financed might cause either financial crowding out or a Keynesian demand-induced expansion in private investment.

To sum up, the expected impact of governmental financial and expenditure policies on private investment in manufacturing are as follows:

Fiscal Policy		Expected Impact	Mechanism
Financial			
	Fiscal Deficits	-	financial crowding out
	Domestic Borrowing	-	financial crowding out
	Foreign Borrowing	+	increased foreign exchange
Expenditure			
	Infrastructure	+	real crowding in
	Non-infrastructure	-	real crowding out
	Consumption	?	net outcome real/financial

Using this framework,

1. We examined both the financial and real impacts of fiscal policy on private investment in manufacturing.
2. Because we would expect large manufacturing units to be more dependent on outside financing, separate tests were carried out for large and small firms.
3. As a basis of comparison similar tests were performed on: (a) total private non-manufacturing investment, (b) private investment in housing, and (c) private investment in transport/communications.

4.   To assess whether specific public expenditures were financed in a particular way
     (e.g., general deficit or internal/external borrowing), we examined the links between
     the government's expenditures and its fiscal accounts.

RESULTS

This analysis produced a number of interesting findings (Tables 4.1–4.7).
First, regarding the impact and interaction of the government's finan-
cial/expenditure policies on private investment in large-scale manufacturing
(Table 4.1):

The pattern of government expenditures and private investment expenditures on private investment in large-scale manufacturing also produced several
interesting insights:

1.   Both the infrastructural and noninfrastructural components of public investment re-
     sponded to the needs produced by expanded private investment (Table 4.1, equa-
     tions 7 and 8). That is, private investment in large-scale manufacturing induced a
     follow-on increase in government investment. Infrastructure was the more respon-
     sive component of government investment, with private investment inducing a
     strong and rapid (optimal lag of one year) governmental response.
2.   Increased government consumption provides (equations 9 and 12) a fairly strong
     stimulus to private investment in large-scale manufacturing. Because of its strength
     in both realized and unanticipated forms, consumption probably stimulates private
     investment through a Keynesian demand linkage mechanism.
3.   The link between private investment in large-scale manufacturing and unexpected
     public investment varied by type of investment. Unexpected infrastructure
     investment (equation 10) appears to be a response to the needs of the private sector.
     No doubt, this expansion in infrastructural facilities tends to be largest during peri-
     ods of acceleration in private investment.
4.   Noninfrastructural investment appears to crowd out a certain amount of private
     investment in large-scale manufacturing (equation 11). A feedback mechanism oc-
     curs here whereby increases in private investment also encourage a further expan-
     sion of noninfrastructural investment.

As noted above, tests were also undertaken for unanticipated private investment in large-scale manufacturing. Our logic here was that this measure of
private investment, rather than its level, might be more sensitive to sudden shifts
in financial conditions. This assumption was not, however, completely borne
out:

1.   No statistically significant patterns exist between unexpected private investment
     (Table 4.1, equation 13) in large-scale manufacturing and unanticipated fiscal defi-
     cits.
2.   Unexpected increases in domestic borrowing did (equation 14), however crowd out
     a certain amount of private investment, although this effect was rather weak.

Table 4.1
Pakistan: Causal Patterns:
Private Investment in Large-Scale Manufacturing

Relationship	Direction of Causation	Impact	Relative Strength
Private Investment/Financial Policies			
(1) Realized Fiscal Deficit	Feedback	-,+	w,w
(2) Realized Public Domestic Borrowing	Feedback	-,+	m,w
(3) Realized Public Foreign Borrowing	No Relationship		
(4) Unexpected Fiscal Deficit	Feedback	-,+	m,w
(5) Unexpected Domestic Borrowing	Feedback	-,+	m,w
(6) Unexpected Public Foreign Borrowing	No Relationship		
Private Investment/Expenditure Policies			
(7) Realized Public Infrastructure Invest.	Private -->Public	+	s
(8) Realized Public Non-Infst. Investment	Private -->Public4	+	w
(9) Realized Public Consumption	Public -->Private4	+	s
(10) Unexpected Infrastructure Invest.	Private -->Public	+	w

Notes: See text for a description of the estimation methods. The dominant pattern is that with the lowest final prediction error. All variables estimated in logarithmic form. The signs (+,-) represent the direction of impact. In the case of feedback the first term is the impact of fiscal policy on private investment; the second is the impact of private investment on fiscal policy. Strength assessment (w) weak, (m) moderate, and (s) strong made on the basis of the improvement in r^2 and the size of the standardized regression coefficient.

Table 4.1 continued
Causal Patterns:
Private Investment in Large-Scale Manufacturing

Relationship	Direction of Causation	Impact	Relative Strength
Private Investment/Expenditure Policies			
(11) Unexpected Non Infrastructural Invest.	Feedback	-,+	s,w
(12) Unexpected Public Consumption	Public -->Private	+	s
Unexpected Private Investment/Fiscal Policies			
(13) Unexpected Fiscal Deficit	No Relationship		
(14) Unexpected Domestic Borrowing	Public -->Private	-	w
(15) Unexpected Public Foreign Borrowing	No Relationship		
(16) Unexpected Infrastructure Invest.	Private -->Public	+	m
(17) Unexpected Non Infrastructural Invest.	Feedback	-,-	s,w
(18) Unexpected Public Consumption	No Relationship		

Notes: See text for a description of the estimation methods. The dominant pattern is that with the lowest final prediction error. All variables estimated in logarithmic form. The signs (+,-) represent the direction of impact. In the case of feedback the first term is the impact of fiscal policy on private investment; the second is the impact of private investment on fiscal policy. Strength assessment (w) weak, (m) moderate, and (s) strong made on the basis of the improvement in r^2 and the size of the standardized regression coefficient.

3.   On the other hand the patterns between unexpected government investment in infrastructure and private investment were quite strong, with private investment again inducing a follow-on amount of infrastructure expansion.

4.   Links with noninfrastructural investment were of a feedback type increase in noninfrastructural investment strongly suppressing private investment. In turn, unexpected expansions in private investment lowered future increases in noninfrastructural investment. This final effect, however, was relatively weak.

5. Apparently, the demand increases associated with unexpected increases in public consumption (equation 18) are not considered significant enough to warrant a response by private large-scale manufacturing investors.

For the purposes of this study, the patterns associated with private investment in small-scale manufacturing (Table 4.2) were in sharp contrast to those found to characterize large-scale manufacturing. Again, we were looking mostly for evidence of crowding out of private investment:

1. In contrast to the negative impact on private investment in large-scale manufacturing produced by fiscal deficits, private investment in small-scale industries increased with the size of the deficit (Table 4.2, equation 2). This pattern also characterized unexpected domestic borrowing (equation 5)
2. In addition, the fiscal deficit appears to have almost no impact on investment in small-scale manufacturing. Instead, increases in this type of investment encourage follow-on public expenditures (equations 7 and 8) which, in turn, causes the government to accelerate expenditures relative to revenues (equations 1 and 4)
3. A final contrast occurs with respect to unexpected public consumption. Instead of stimulating further private investment, this form of public expenditure suppresses (equation 12) further private investment
4. Finally the results using unexpected private investment in small-scale manufacturing produced little in the way of firm evidence for crowding out, either of the financial or real type. In fact, unanticipated increases in domestic borrowing were associated with further increases in private investment (equation 14)

Private investment in nonmanufacturing activities produced another distinctive pattern (Table 4.3):

1. Overall evidence exists of crowding out, financial or real. Instead, the dominant pattern is one of feedback between both public-sector financial and expenditure activities and private investment (equations 1, 2, 4, 5, 7, and 8)
2. The impacts of this feedback are strongest in the direction of public to private. The one exception is the relatively strong impact of increased private investment on government infrastructural investment (equation 7)
3. The only negative impact was between unexpected increases in private investment and unexpected increases in noninfrastructural investment. However, from these results alone it is impossible to identify the source of this pattern, that is whether for example the private sector was able to crowd out the public sector by outbidding it for resources

The results for private investment in: housing, agriculture, and transport and communications mirrored those of total non-manufacturing. Again, there was no evidence of either financial or real crowding out of private investment in these activities.

Table 4.2
Pakistan: Causal Patterns:
Private Investment in Small-Scale Manufacturing

Relationship	Direction of Causation	Impact	Relative Strength
Private Investment/Financial Policies			
(1) Realized Fiscal Deficit	Private-->Public	+	m
(2) Realized Public Dom. Borrowing	Feedback	+,+	m
(3) Realized Public Foreign Borrowing	No Relationship		
(4) Unexpected Fiscal Deficit	Private-->	+	w
(5) Unexpected Domestic Borrowing	Feedback	+,+	m,w
(6) Unexpected Public Foreign Borrowing	No Relationship		
Private Investment/Expenditure Policies			
(7) Realized Public Infrastructure Invest.	Private-->Public	+	w
(8) Realized Public Non-Infst Investment	Feedback	+,+	w,w
(9) Realized Public Consumption	Public -->Private		+ w
(10) Unexpected Infrastructure Invest.	Feedback	-,+	w,w
(11) Unexpected Non-Infrastructural Invest.	No Relationship		
(12) Unexpected Public Consumption	Public-->Private	-	w

Notes: See text for a description of the estimation methods. The dominant pattern is that with the lowest final prediction error. All variables estimated in logarithmic form. The signs (+,-) represent the direction of impact. In the case of feedback the first term is the impact of fiscal policy on private investment; the second is the impact of private investment on fiscal policy. Strength assessment (w) weak, (m) moderate, and (s) strong made on the basis of the improvement in r^2 and the size of the standardized regression coefficient.

Table 4.2 continued
Pakistan: Causal Patterns:
Private Investment in Small-Scale Manufacturing

Relationship	Direction of Causation	Impact	Relative Strength
Unexpected Private Investment/Fiscal Policies			
(13) Unexpected Fiscal Deficit	Private-->Public	1	(-)m
(14) Unexpected Domestic Borrowing	Feedback	+,-	w,m
(15) Unexpected Public Foreign Borrowing	No Relationship		
(16) Unexpected Infrastructure Invest.	No Relationship		
(17) Unexpected Non-Infrastructural Invest.	Private-->Public	-	w
(18) Unexpected Public Consumption	Public-->Private	-	w

Notes: See text for a description of the estimation methods. The dominant pattern is that with the lowest final prediction error. All variables estimated in logarithmic form. The signs (+,-) represent the direction of impact. In the case of feedback the first term is the impact of fiscal policy on private investment; the second is the impact of private invest-ment on fiscal policy. Strength assessment (w) weak, (m) moderate, and (s) strong made on the basis of the improvement in r^2 and the size of the standardized regression coeffi-cient.

Table 4.3
Pakistan: Causal Patterns:
Private Nonmanufacturing Investment

Relationship	Direction of Causation	Impact	Relative Strength
Private Investment/Financial Policies			
(1) Realized Fiscal Deficit	Feedback	+,+	m,w
(2) Realized Public Domestic Borrowing	Feedback	+,+	w,w
(3) Realized Public Foreign Borrowing	No Relationship		
(4) Unexpected Fiscal Deficit	Feedback	+,+	s,m
(5) Unexpected Domestic Borrowing	Feedback	+,+	m,w
(6) Unexpected Public Foreign Borrowing	No Relationship		
Private Investment/Expenditure Policies			
(7) Realized Public Infrastructure Invest.	Feedback	+,+	w,m
(8) Realized Public Non-Infst. Investment	Feedback	+,+	w,w
(9) Realized Public Consumption	Feedback	+,+	w,w
(10) Unexpected Infrastructure Invest	Private-->Public	+	w

Notes: See text for a description of the estimation methods. The dominant pattern is that with the lowest final prediction error. All variables estimated in logarithmic form. The signs (+,-) represent the direction of impact. In the case of feedback the first term is the impact of fiscal policy on private investment; the second is the impact of private investment on fiscal policy. Strength assessment (w) weak, (m) moderate, and (s) strong made on the basis of the improvement in r^2 and the size of the standardized regression coefficient.

Table 4.3 continued
Pakistan: Causal Patterns:
Private Nonmanufacturing Investment

Relationship	Direction of Causation	Impact	Relative Strength
Private Investment/Expenditure Policies			
(11) Unexpected Non-Infrastructural Invest	Private-->Private	+	w
(12) Unexpected Public Consumption	No Relationship		
Unexpected Private Investment/Fiscal Policies			
(13) Unexpected Fiscal Deficit	Public-->Private	+	w
(14) Unexpected Domestic Borrowing	No Relationship		
(15) Unexpected Public Foreign Borrowing	No Relationship		
(16) Unexpected Infrastructure Invest	No Relationship		
(17) Unexpected Non-Infrastructural Invest	Feedback	+,-	w,m
(18) Unexpected Public Consumption	No Relationship		

Notes: See text for a description of the estimation methods. The dominant pattern is that with the lowest final prediction error. All variables estimated in logarithmic form. The signs (+,-) represent the direction of impact. In the case of feedback the first term is the impact of fiscal policy on private investment; the second is the impact of private investment on fiscal policy. Strength assessment (w) weak, (m) moderate, and (s) strong made on the basis of the improvement in r^2 and the size of the standardized regression coefficient.

These findings suggest that crowding out may be largely confined to one, albeit a very important, area of investment: private investment in large-scale manufacturing. Here crowding out appears to be largely associated with increased fiscal deficits and associated domestic borrowing. However, unanticipated increases in public investment in noninfrastructural activities may cause some real crowding out.

The issue of real versus financial crowding out is complex, and the results obtained so far for private investment in large-scale manufacturing are only suggestive. As noted in Table 4.1 increases in both unexpected domestic borrowing and in unexpected non-infrastructural investment reduced unexpected increases in private sector in large-scale manufacturing. In short, the observed real crowding out of this type of private investment may simply reflect a spurious correlation between noninfrastructural investment and increased public borrowing in the domestic capital markets.

To examine the links between public-sector expenditures a causal analysis was undertaken similar to that performed on private investment. Here we are interested in assessing the patterns and timing of government expenditures and the public sector's financial actions. As a basis of comparison, total government expenditures and defense expenditures were added to public investment and consumption. For the patterns associated with public expenditure and the fiscal deficit (Table 4.4)

1. Realized increases in all major expenditure categories expanded the fiscal deficit. The strongest links were between the increases in government consumption and the deficit (equation 3), followed by infrastructure investment (equation 1), and finally, non-infrastructural investment (equation 2).
2. Several feedback effects were also present. In the case of realized consumption, increased deficits tended to retard further expansion in expenditures. However, in the case of increases in non-infrastructural investment increased deficits were associated with a further expansion in expenditures.

The patterns associated with noninfrastructural investment seem to suggest that once the government decides to move ahead with noninfrastructural investment, largely in public-sector enterprises, it also commits itself to a series of follow-on expenditures over time. Apparently, given the inflexibility of the country's tax system, this translates into growing deficits. The short-run nature of government consumption, however, apparently allows the government to cut back on this type of expenditure once deficits reach unacceptable levels.

These patterns shift (Table 4.4, equations 4–6) when the analysis shifts to unanticipated values for expenditures and deficits.

1. No feedback effects occur with unanticipated deficits.
2. Unexpected increases in noninfrastructural investment (equation 4) stem from an expansion in unanticipated deficits. That is, increases in unanticipated deficits produce an enlargement in unanticipated investment in noninfrastructural projects. This pattern occurs with an optimal lag of two years.
3. *Ceteris paribus* higher levels of consumption tended (equation 6) to increase the likelihood of higher than anticipated deficits. Again, however, no feedback mechanism links these deficits to future levels of consumption.
4. However, as with expected deficits, causation still runs (equation 4) from infrastructure investment to deficits. This pattern was quite strong with unanticipated increases in infrastructure, having an optimal lag of two years in affecting the deficit.

Table 4.4
Pakistan: Causal Patterns in the Public Sector

Relationship	Direction of Causation	Impact	Relative Strength
Realized Fiscal Deficits and Public Expenditures			
(1) Infrastructure Invest.	Inv. -->FD	+	m
(2) Noninfrastructural Invest.	Feedback	+,+	w,w
(3) Government Consumption	Feedback	+,-	s,m
Unexpected Fiscal Deficits and Public Expenditures			
(4) Unexpected Infrastructure Invest.	Inv. -->FD	+	s
(5) Unexpected Noninfrast. Invest.	FD -->Inv.	+	m
(6) Unexpected Govt. Consumption	Cons. -->FD	+	s
Realized Government Domestic Borrowing and Public Expenditures/Deficits			
(7) Infrastructure Invest.	Inv. -->GB	+	m
(8) Noninfrastructure Invest.	Feedback	+,+	w,s
(9) Government Consumption	Cons. -->GB	+	m
(10) Fiscal Deficit	Feedback	+,+	w,w
Unexpected Government Domestic Borrowing and Public Expenditures/Deficits			
(11) Unexpected Infrast. Invest.	Inv. -->GB	+	m
(12) Unexpected Noninfrast. Invest.	GB -->Inv.	+	w
(13) Unexpected Govt. Consumption	Cons. -->GB	+	m
(14) Unexpected Fiscal Deficits	Feedback	+,+	w,w

Notes: See Table 4.3. GB = Government Domestic Borrowing; FD = Fiscal Deficit; EB = Government External Borrowing.

Table 4.4 continued
Pakistan: Causal Patterns in the Public Sector

Relationship	Direction of Causation	Impact	Relative Strength
Realized Govt. External Borrowing and Public Expenditure/Fiscal Policies			
(15) Infrastructure Invest.	No Relationship		
(16) Noninfrastructural Invest.	Inv. -->GB	+	w
(17) Government Consumption	Feedback	+,-	w,m
(18) Fiscal Deficits	Feedback	+,-	w,w
(19) Domestic Borrowing	GB -->EB	+	w
Unexpected Government External Borrowing and Public Expenditure/Fiscal Policies			
(20) Infrastructure Invest.	No Relationship		
(21) Noninfrast. Invest.	Inv. -->Borrowing	+	m
(22) Unexpected Fiscal Deficits	No Relationship		
(23) Domestic Borrowing	GB -->Foreign	+	w

Notes: See Table 4.3. GB = Government Domestic Borrowing; FD = Fiscal Deficit; EB = Government External Borrowing.

5. The patterns of causation from consumption and infrastructure to increased deficits were quite robust, and that leading from deficits to noninfrastructural investment was only moderately strong.

As noted above, deficits per se are not necessarily associated with financial crowding out. Crowding out occurs when the deficits are financed domestically. The question here, therefore, is whether the government systematically borrows in the domestic or foreign markets to finance a particular type of expenditure. For realized values in the domestic markets (Table 4.4, equations 7–10):

1. It appears that increases in all categories of government expenditure place pressure on the authorities to borrow in the domestic markets.
2. The fiscal deficit itself results (equation 10) in increased domestic borrowing. However, the positive feedback effect from expanded domestic borrowing may reflect the fact that the authorities see further increases in the deficit capable of being financed from this source.
3. The same is true for noninfrastructural investment. Expanded expenditures in this area appear to force the government to tap domestic markets for increased funding. This borrowing, in turn, may convince the authorities that additional noninfrastruc-

tural expenditures can be easily financed from this source. This effect from borrowing to investment is quite strong, and that from noninfrastructural investment to domestic borrowing is quite weak.

4. In contrast, increased domestic borrowing does not appear to induce the government to allocate additional amounts to infrastructure or public consumption.

For the unexpected components of expenditures and borrowing (Table 4.4, equations 11–14):

1. The fiscal deficit-domestic borrowing (equation 14) is the same as the one observed for the realized magnitudes of these variables. Also as with the realized values, the feedback effects in both directions are rather weak, suggesting that fiscal deficits are directly translated into a domestic borrowing strategy.
2. Again, causation flows largely from public consumption (equation 14) and infrastructural investment (equation 11) to domestic borrowing. However, unexpected increases in noninfrastructural investment stem largely from unanticipated increases in the government's domestic borrowing program.

As a frame of reference, the same causal tests were performed for public borrowing in the external markets (Table 4.4, equations 15–23). Again, several interesting patterns emerged:

1. Overall, public-sector borrowing in the domestic markets (equation 19) appears to spill over into the external capital markets. This relationship occurs with an optimal lag of about three years.
2. While no statistically significant links occur between infrastructural investment and external borrowing, increases in both noninfrastructural investment (equation 16) and public consumption (equation 17) expanded the government's borrowing from foreign sources.
3. In turn, increased external borrowing may have placed some constraints on further increases in government consumption (equation 17), that is, the feedback effect from increased external borrowing to consumption was negative. This pattern also characterized the relationship between external borrowing and the fiscal deficit (equation 18).

For unanticipated magnitudes of these variables (Table 4.4, equations 20–23):

1. A clear pattern exists from increases in noninfrastructural investment to a subsequent expansion in external borrowing (equation 21). This pattern takes place over a fairly long period—the optimal lag is four years.
2. As with the realized values, it appears that expanded domestic borrowing eventually spills over into the external markets.

Based on these patterns it appears that our conclusion that noninfrastructural investment may cause real crowding out is valid—there does not appear to be evidence on increased noninfrastructural investment, placing strong pressure on the domestic capital markets. Instead, noninfrastructural investment may simply be either accommodated by favorable borrowing conditions in the domestic markets or successful placement in the external markets.

CONCLUSIONS

The accumulation of real physical capital stock in manufacturing has long been regarded as one of the major factors in economic development. Fluctuations in investment also have a significant impact on the functioning of an economy. From the viewpoints of both development planning and demand management, the question of what determines investment behavior in Pakistan is an important one. However, when one tries to establish an empirical investment function for Pakistan, several problems arise. The lack of data on capital stock makes it difficult to observe the stock adjustment mechanism upon which most investment theories for developed countries are based. Historically the observable interest rates in that country have not, because of regulations and other imperfections, reflected the true scarcity of capital.

Still, several factors suggest that private investment in Pakistani manufacturing, especially in the larger firms, should be positively related to government investment. First, if resources are not fully employed, an increase in government investment would increase income directly and indirectly through the multiplier effect so that private investors would be encouraged to invest more since their profitability would tend to increase with the observed or expected demand for final products. Second, the country has a large component of government investment concentrated on infrastructure projects. The creation of special infrastructure facilities by the government for transport, communications, electric power, and irrigation should reduce the cost of production or the returns to scale and thus increase the profitability for private investors. Third, even where government investment is in secondary or tertiary industries, the establishment of new factories will increase the demand for related products and thus induce a higher level of private investment. It is also possible for government investment to act as an important catalytic agent through reducing certain costs of production.

Unfortunately as many studies on developing countries have found, these potentially beneficial effects of public investment are often offset by adverse developments in financial markets—the so-called crowding out effect. Similarly increased public-sector investment may preempt resources that might otherwise be available at reasonable prices for private investment—real crowding out. Our main assumption was that for the financial crowding out hypothesis to be valid for Pakistan, a pattern should occur whereby increased public expenditures expand the size of the fiscal deficit. In turn, the enlarged deficit is financed through additional domestic borrowing rather than alternative sources of funding (taxes, foreign borrowing). Our assumption was that real crowding out might be inferred if two conditions were present: (1) causation was from public investment to private investment and its impact was negative, and (2) causation was not from increased public investment to increased government borrowing in the domestic markets.

The causality tests suggest that expanded public investment in infrastructure has not played an important role in stimulating private investment in industry. If anything, the results suggest that it is private investment that has stimulated a follow-on expansion in infrastructure. Instead of crowding in (i.e., a positive feedback effect) additional private investment, however, infrastructure investment appears to have led to larger deficits and domestic borrowing. In turn, these financial developments have dampened the flows of private capital into the important large-scale manufacturing sector.

To sum up, financial crowding out of private investment in large-scale manufacturing is a distinct possibility, but it may not be a simple straightforward process. The results obtained above also suggest that private investment in large-scale manufacturing has suffered from real crowding out associated with the government's non-infrastructural investment program. Finally, it should be noted that neither financial nor real crowding out seems to occur in other areas of private investment. Clearly further research should be undertaken to determine why the large-scale manufacturing sector is unique in this regard.

5

The Textile Sector: Competitive Pressures

INTRODUCTION

The textile industry in Pakistan is one of great significance in terms of its contribution to employment and exports. The production of cotton textiles predominates, despite the existence of a large jute industry and the increasingly important carpet and synthetic textiles industries. Although the share of textiles in manufacturing value added fell from 32.4 percent in 1977 to around 15 percent in recent years, the industry currently employs 28 percent of the total labor force and accounts for around 60 percent of the country's total exports (UNIDO 1990, 53). Capital investment in the sector accounts for around 28 percent of total national investment (and 37 percent of foreign currency investment in 1991).

The purpose of this chapter is to examine recent trends in the industry. What have been the main patterns of growth, changes in the composition of output, and government policies to encourage production and export? In addition, given the relative efficiency of textiles, it is of some interest to examine the structural differences between that sector and other lines of manufacturing. Are there any discernible differences between textiles and other main areas of manufacturing with regard to factors associated with relative efficiency? Do these factors vary by ownership pattern, that is, public versus private? What are the links between efficiency, ownership, and the degree of protection received by firms? Based on our findings, several policy implications are drawn.

RECENT DEVELOPMENTS

The textile industry in Pakistan experienced phenomenal growth during the 1950s and 1960s, but it started encountering problems in the 1970s. The production and export stagnated and a large part of the industry became "sick." In addition just when new investments were needed, the owners shied away and generally let the capital stock run down. Things started improving gradually around 1979, with a number of positive changes taking place since that time (Haque 1992).

Growth of the Cotton Textile Industry

The growth record of Pakistan's textile industry shows a reverse trend, especially in the weaving capacity of the mill sector in which the install capacity of looms, shrank from 24,000 in 1984 to 15,000 (Table 5.1) in 1992 (Memon 1993). The number of actual working looms was reported to be only 8,000 in 1992. Clearly the sector made an all-out shift toward cotton spinning and almost completely gave up efforts to develop and modernize the weaving sector. By the end of 1992, the spinning capacity increased to 6.1 million spindles, from 4.3 million in 1988. As a result, cotton consumption increased at an average rate of 14.6 percent per annum during the 1988–92 period (Table 5.2).

Corresponding to this expansion in equipment, the textiles sector has also accelerated its contribution to the overall gross domestic product (GDP). In the period 1982–88 textiles accounted for only 2.15 percent of expanded GDP. By 1989–92 this had more than doubled to 4.67 percent (Table 5.3). Although detailed data on the country's manufacturing only gores through 1988, the increased contribution over time of textiles (Table 5.4) to the overall rate of growth in manufacturing is also apparent. For the period as a whole textiles contributed 4.6 percent to the overall expansion in manufacturing. This increased to 15.3 and 19.6 percent for the 1982–87 and 1985–87 periods respectively.

The corresponding contributions of apparel and ginning are more erratic. For the period as a whole, apparel contributed 2.6 percent to the overall growth in manufacturing. However, this increased to 5.3 percent during the 1985–87 period. Ginning contributed 6.6 percent to the growth in manufacturing over the 1977–87 period. This fell to 5.2 percent in the 1985–87 period.

While the expansion in textiles is encouraging, it has not been regionally balanced in recent years. Nearly 73 percent of new investment has been flowing into the Punjab (Table 5.5).

The spinning sector operates in an environment of considerable uncertainty. In addition to the law and order problems in the Sind, there are the usual concerns with fluctuation demand, erratic prices in export markets, quota restrictions on export at home, movements in raw cotton prices, cost push inflationary pressures, frequently changing tax policy of the government, adverse impact on production from power breakdowns, labor problems, and so forth. During the past three years, prices of cotton yarn increased from 22 to 52 percent in the local market, creating concern for the producers of value added products in the manufacturing sectors.

The share of the coarse and medium varieties of yarn has been constant at

Table 5.1
Pakistan: Cotton Textile Production

Year	Number of Reporting Mills	Installed Capacity		Hours Worked (millions)	
		No. of Spindles (000)	No. of Looms (000)	Spindles	Looms
1970	107.0	2,379.0	31.0	16,964.0	197.1
1971	113.0	2,605.0	30.0	18,505.0	202.8
1972	131.0	2,848.0	30.0	19,629.0	188.5
1973	150.0	3,226.0	29.0	22,606.0	190.6
1974	155.0	3,308.0	29.0	23,617.0	192.7
1975	143.0	3,392.0	29.0	20,438.0	179.2
1976	127.0	3,478.0	29.0	20,095.0	167.4
1977	135.0	3,544.0	29.0	18,118.0	138.6
1978	140.0	3,560.0	26.0	19,776.0	110.5
1979	152.0	3,704.0	27.0	20,456.0	95.0
1980	149.0	3,731.0	26.0	21,468.0	99.1
1981	158.0	3,983.0	25.0	22,217.0	90.5
1982	155.0	4,180.0	25.0	22,924.0	85.1
1983	158.0	4,265.0	24.0	23,011.0	78.6
1984	162.0	4,224.0	24.0	23,683.0	91.6
1985	158.0	4,396.0	23.0	33,274.0	69.8
1986	160.0	4,422.0	19.0	24,620.9	64.7
1987	187.0	4,293.0	17.0	26,836.0	57.8
1988	197.0	4,330.0	16.0	29,823.0	66.2
1989	219.0	4,790.0	17.0	32,089.0	67.9
1990	236.0	5,195.0	16.0	36,170.0	67.5
1991	247.0	5,493.0	15.0	39,542.0	60.2
1992	271.0	6,141.0	15.0	43,606.0	58.8
Growth					
1970-92	4.3	4.4	-3.2	4.4	-5.3
1970-79	4.0	5.0	-1.5	2.1	-8.4
1980-92	5.1	4.2	-4.5	6.1	-4.3
1988-92	8.3	9.3	-1.6	10.1	-2.9

Source: Government of Pakistan, *Economic Survey 1992-93* (Islamabad: Finance Division, Economic Adviser's Wing, 1993), p. 75.

Table 5.2
Pakistan: Cotton Textile Demand

Year	Consumption of Cotton (000 kg)	Total Yarn Produced (000 kg)	Surplus Yarn (000 kg)	Total Production of Cloth (000 sq. mtr)
1970	334,693.0	273,236.0	175,396.0	606,545.0
1971	360,006.0	303,791.0	205,431.0	658,295.0
1972	407,147.0	335,702.0	236,917.0	628,189.0
1973	463,118.0	376,122.0	286,242.0	588,606.0
1974	475,348.0	379,460.0	283,404.0	592,172.0
1975	420,608.0	351,200.0	363,097.0	555,855.0
1976	419,735.0	349,653.0	265,710.0	520,338.0
1977	343,194.0	282,640.0	217,188.0	408,287.0
1978	355,986.0	297,894.0	242,730.0	391,347.0
1979	387,581.0	327,798.0	276,581.0	339,442.0
1980	428,554.0	362,862.0	324,952.0	342,335.0
1981	444,611.0	374,947.0	331,670.0	307,882.0
1982	501,009.0	430,154.0	387,530.0	325,021.0
1983	516,699.0	448,430.0	397,867.0	335,537.0
1984	506,458.0	431,581.0	396,610.0	296,596.0
1985	558,714.0	431,731.0	375,223.0	271,831.0
1986	553,599.0	482,186.0	436,330.0	253,480.0
1987	697,719.0	586,371.0	549,960.0	237,879.0
1988	779,738.0	685,031.0	643,465.0	281,620.0
1989	871,978.0	757,903.0	720,303.0	269,862.0
1990	1,054,144.0	911,588.0	864,469.0	294,839.0
1991	1,197,451.0	1,041,248.0	1,001,033.0	292,911.0
1992	1,342,819.0	1,170,736.0	1,134,716.0	307,933.0
Growth				
1970-92	6.5	6.8	8.8	-3.0
1970-79	1.6	2.0	5.2	-6.2
1980-92	10.0	10.3	11.0	-0.9
1988-92	14.6	14.3	15.2	2.3

Source: Government of Pakistan, *Economic Survey 1992-93* (Islamabad: Finance Division, Economic Adviser's Wing, 1993), p. 75.

Table 5.3
Pakistan: Summary of Sectoral
Contributions to GDP Growth, 1989–1992

Sectors	Average 82-88	1989	1990	1991	1992 89-92	Average
Agriculture	1.07	1.77	0.79	1.31	1.64	1.38
Wheat	0.06	0.44	-0.04	0.10	0.01	0.13
Rice	0.00	0.02	0.02	0.05	-0.11	-0.01
Cotton	0.35	-0.06	0.04	0.52	1.23	0.41
Sugar Cane	0.00	0.24	-0.01	0.04	-0.08	0.02
Livestock	0.41	0.44	0.46	0.38	0.45	0.44
Mining	0.04	0.01	0.05	0.06	0.02	0.04
Mfg.	1.44	0.67	1.00	1.11	1.36	1.03
Large-Scale	1.09	0.29	0.06	0.07	0.94	0.63
Food	0.15	0.03	0.04	0.03	0.02	0.08
Textiles	0.14	0.09	0.28	0.26	0.38	0.25
Fertilize	0.09	0.02	0.03	-0.02	-0.04	-0.01
Petroleum	0.04	-0.03	0.03	0.09	0.00	0.02
Cement	0.02	0.00	0.01	0.01	0.01	0.01
Pig-Iron	0.05	-0.02	-0.01	0.03	0.01	0.00
Auto	0.05	0.03	0.04	0.00	0.03	0.02
Other	0.57	0.16	0.17	0.31	0.35	0.25
Small-Scale	0.36	0.38	0.40	0.41	0.42	0.40
Construction	0.22	0.01	0.13	0.24	0.25	0.18
Electricity	0.21	0.37	0.44	0.34	0.24	0.35
Transport	0.73	-0.41	0.61	0.52	0.66	0.35
Commerce	1.26	0.87	0.58	0.91	1.25	0.90
Finance	0.21	0.08	0.09	0.08	0.04	0.07
Public Adm.	0.40	0.57	0.02	0.24	0.13	0.28
Other Serv	0.69	0.77	0.78	0.78	0.79	0.78
GDP	6.51	4.79	4.67	5.59	6.38	5.35
Textile Contribution %						
	2.15	1.88	6.00	4.65	5.96	4.67

Source: Computations based on data provided by the Federal Bureau of Statistics. Note: Sectoral contribution to growth rate are computed by weighting the sectoral growth rates by the previous years sectoral share (in GDP).

Table 5.4
Pakistan: Contribution of Textiles
to the Growth in Manufacturing Value Added, 1977–1988

Year	Growth in Mfg. (%)	Textiles			
		Share (%)	Growth (%)	Contribution to Manuf	
				Absolute	%
1977	15.30	22.2	4.9	1.2	7.9
1978	11.50	19.8	-0.2	0.0	-0.3
1979	3.84	17.8	-6.9	-1.4	-36.5
1980	21.56	17.4	18.5	3.3	15.3
1981	3.36	15.9	-5.2	-0.9	-27.2
1982	10.11	15.9	10.0	1.6	15.7
1983	3.09	16.1	4.4	0.7	23.2
1984	9.55	14.2	-3.5	-0.6	-5.9
1985	9.66	15.9	22.7	3.3	33.5
1986	3.80	15.5	1.5	0.2	6.1
1987	17.02	16.1	21.1	3.3	19.3
1988	0.35	17.4	8.1	1.3	520.8
AV 7787	9.9	17.0	6.1	1.0	4.6
AV 7782	10.9	18.1	3.5	0.6	-4.2
AV 8287	8.9	15.6	9.4	1.4	15.3
AV 8587	10.2	15.8	15.1	2.2	19.6
VA 7787 34.7	7.7	93.9	2.4	407.4	
VA 7782 40.0	8.9	77.6	2.5	418.6	
VA 8287 21.5	0.7	81.4	1.8	157.1	
VA 8587 29.4	0.5	79.1	1.7	125.3	

Source: Computed from data in Government of Pakistan, *Economic Survey* (Islamabad: Finance Division, Economic Adviser's Wing) various issues. Note: Sectoral contribution to the growth rate in manufacturing is computed by weighing the sectoral growth rates by the previous years sectoral share of GDP. AV = Average; VA = Variance.

Table 5.5
Investment Approved for the Textile Sector, 1991

(Rs. million)

Province	Local Currency	%	Foreign	%	Total	%
Sindh	2,541.1	13.3	1,502.6	23.8	4,043.8	15.9
Punjab	14,356.2	75.1	4,140.3	65.6	8,496.9	72.7
NWFP	1,149.4	6.0	346.5	5.5	1,495.9	5.9
Balochistan	146.9	0.8	19.8	.9	266.7	1.1
Azad Kashmir	933.3	4.9	203.9	3.2	1,137.2	4.4
Total	19,126.9	100.0	6,613.1	100.0	25,440.5	100.0
Total Investment (all industries)	73,254.8		17,861.4		91,116.2	
Share of Textiles in Total Invest	26.1		37.0		27.9	

Source: *Pakistan & Gulf Economist* (April 10/16. 1993), 13.

about 82 percent in recent years. The share of blended yarn has, however, almost doubled while that of fine and super fine yarn has fallen from 7.3 percent in 1987 to only 2.4 percent in 1992. On the other hand, the production of fine blends of cloth, by the mill sector has declined, while that of coarse cloth has increased. It is clear that without an improvement in the quality of yarn, quality improvements in cloth production are unsustainable.

Some indication of the relative importance of the wearing apparel sector can deduced from the country's export statistics. The textile product exports increased their share in total textile export from 55.5 percent in 1990 to 59.9 percent in 1992. Export earnings from the export of canvas knitwear, woven garments, towels, and other made-ups increased from about US $1.1 billion to over US $1.6 billion during this period. Further growth is limited, however, by increased competition in international markets and the low productivity of the domestic industry.

Pakistan's textile industry had to consolidate its leading position as an exporter of yarn in addition to catering to the domestic demand for low-quality yarn for the domestic hosiery goods manufacturing industry and power looms, most of which have been geared to the production of gray cloth for export.

The industry's revival in recent years was largely caused by the sharp rise in the demand for yarn and other textile goods in Japan and other foreign markets. The boom was a response to the improvement in the quality of yarn, hence the expansion in new spinning units in recent years. It should be noted that the boom in cotton yarn also stems from the withdrawal of South Korea from export markets. That country has diverted its attention to the expansion and modernization of the cloth-manufacturing sector.

Exports

While textiles have led Pakistan's recent export surge, the industry has not established a real niche in export markets, even at the lower end of the quality scale. Exports in 1992 amounted to US $6.9 billion. Pakistan has lost ground, particularly during the 1970s, to South Asian countries. Korea's textile exports currently earn US $17 billion.

Both cotton yarn and cotton cloth may be considered as export-oriented industries—since export shares are significantly higher than world production shares. As far as yarn is concerned, this represents an important structural weakness of the textile industry: Pakistan is unable to domestically utilize a large share of its yarn for the production of higher value-added textile products. Thus, the country loses out to its main competitors at the higher end of the world textile markets.

On the other hand the quality of raw cotton produced in the country has gradually improved. Pakistani short- and medium-staple cotton is of high quality. But this cannot be used for the production of the count yarn and superior quality fabrics. Ginning quality is very poor, and foreign matter is often present in the ginned cotton. Clearly the modernization of the ginning sector should be a high priority in investment.

Policy Incentives

To encourage exports of textiles, the Pakistani government has experimented with a variety of financial incentives and institutions. The most significant incentive involved cash compensatory rebates. This incentive, introduced in 1973, was intended to cover domestic taxes not included in the duty draw back. Because of abuses and losses in revenue to the government, these incentives were withdrawn in 1988. In retrospect it appears that the incentives (Haque 1992, 12) created these effects:

1.   Provided a substantial boost to textile exports. In the first year after introduction of the rebates, yarn and fabric exports increased by 60 percent and 20 percent in vol-

ume terms. In value terms, yarn and fabric exports increased by 46 percent while garments, hosiery etc. increased by about 35 percent

2.   Had a minimal impact on unit values, although this was a major aim
3.   Did not induce growth of value-added products—the differentials between various product groups were not sufficiently large
4.   Allowed inefficient and sick mills to survive
5.   Encouraged abuse

Presently the following incentives are available to exporters (Haque 1992, 12):

1.   Export finance scheme
2.   Rebates of customs and excise duties on refund of sales tax
3.   Income tax concessions on export earnings
4.   Special licensing facilities for export industries
5.   Import facilities for modernization
6.   Programs to encourage locally manufactured machinery

To encourage export of higher quality yarn, an import exemption has been allowed under the new Trade Policy of 1992–93 for the import of machinery designed for yarn of this make-up. Under the new procedures, a 5 percent surcharge and a 6 percent license fee is charged. At the same time, the surcharge can be deferred for two years. The export duty on higher quality yarn has been drastically reduced. The intent of this incentive is to increase the production of these products in the hope that increased production of this type of yarn will also increase the production of higher valued added textile products for export. Shifts of this type are the only way to increase the value of textile exports to quota markets such as the United States and Western Europe.

Impediments to Growth

Pakistan enjoys domestic availability of cotton that greatly exceeds the domestic demand. However, the textile industry is functioning in an international trade environment that is increasingly subject to protectionism. The export of textile products is restrained in the larger markets, such as the United States, European Economic Community (ECC), Canada, Sweden, and Finland, within the framework of the Multifibre Agreement (MFA) and bilateral agreements. In addition, the industry suffers from

1.   A narrow production base
2.   Outdated industrial structure
3.   Low stage of technology
4.   Lack of attention to research and development (R&D)
5.   Severely selective markets (e.g., more than 64 percent of the yarn market is Japan)
6.   Limited product range
7.   Increasing quality consciousness in the importing countries

In addition to these difficulties, the textile industry faces a number of problems in the area of design. There is no design institute in the country that can help the manufacturers design products suitable for highly competitive international markets. Moreover, Pakistan in spite of being a cotton/textile-oriented economy does not have a single university offering a curriculum focused on the industry.

To counter these problems Pakistan is in the process of developing a long-term textile strategy. The First National Textile Conference (P&GE 1989) held in April 1989 made the following recommendations:

1. Establish a federal textile ministry
2. Abandon the old MFA negotiating strategy followed by Pakistan in the past (the major concern of which was achieving a marginal increase in quotas)
3. Develop target markets
4. Encourage direct foreign investment especially in the quality product areas

Pakistan will hopefully be able to strike a balance between maintaining a domestic demand-oriented, labor-intensive industry producing cheap and durable products for low-income groups and the need to rapidly expand the production of quality textiles and wearing apparel. To achieve the latter, rationalization incentives need to be implemented. Fashion and design centers need to be developed, and possibilities for extensive collaboration with international firms (particularly those based in Southeast Asia) should be explored. Although raw cotton exports are a major source of foreign exchange, they are mainly destined to countries whose cotton textile exports compete with those of Pakistan (UNIDO 1990, 55).

FACTORS RELATING TO EFFICIENCY

Another option open to the government is that of privatizing public-sector textile firms. On the surface there would appear to be a number of cases where a shift from public to private ownership could be expected to increase efficiency output. The most notorious of the public firms is a joint project between the governments of Pakistan and Iran—the Pak-Iran Textile project in Baluchistan (Ali 1992).

This plant is Pakistan's largest and most modern textile complex, with 100,000 spindles and 2,200 looms capable of producing 66.58 million yards of cotton and blended fabrics plus 5.38 million pounds of marketable yarn. However, the plant, has been out of production for the last nine years, with the government paying over Rs 500 million in salaries to the idle workers (Ali 1992). There are about 3,000 such workers getting money without any work at Pak-Iran Textile Miles, one at Baleli and another at Uthal. These mills with 50,000 spindles and 1,100 looms each, equipped with ultra modern machinery for mercerizing, sanforizing, bleaching, dyeing, printing, and other finishing facilities, went into production in 1981. But just two years later, these mills were declared sick because of bribery, corruption inefficiency, and mismanagement.

Since then these Pak-Iran Textiles Mills with large defaulted loans from public sector banks are defunct. These mills became neither productive, despite the heavy investment by Pakistan and Iran, nor paid taxes and utility bills. They also failed to provide employment, and production or export of textile goods.

Clearly, Pak-Iran is an extreme example. However, the country's privatization program is predicated on the assumption that public firms are on average less efficient than their private counterparts. Is this assumption correct for the textile industry? Does the situation in textiles vary from that in other sectors and, if so, in what manner?

As is well known, ownership is only one factor entering into a firms efficiency. A number of World Bank reports have noted correctly that perhaps a more important source of efficiency/inefficiency lies in the type of incentives provided by government. Based on a World Bank research project, this section analyzes the incentive regimes in textiles. As a basis of comparison, two other subsectors, chemicals and engineering are also examined.

For purposes of this study the Domestic Resource Cost (DRC) concept is used to measure the efficiency of a particular manufacturing activity. A DRC coefficient over 1 indicates inefficient production conditions. The efficiency profile with the three subsectors (Table 5.6) is then contrasted with the economic incentives resulting from the trade regime, as measured by the Effective Rate of Protection (EPR).

On average the three industrial subsectors—textiles, chemical, engineering—are facing domestic resource costs that are close to international standards and thus not operating particularly inefficiency. However, the DRCs in the chemical and engineering sectors are just above unity. On the level of individual product classes the picture is very mixed. There are many items that are manufactured at domestic opportunity costs that are significantly above the cost of importing the respective products.

Similarly, current average effective protections levels seem moderate but conceal vast differences among product groups. For example in the chemical subsector (average EPR = 20 percent) industrial chemicals, fertilizers, and synthetic fibers are highly protected. In the engineering sector (average EPR = 12 percent) basic metals and mechanical products enjoy high rates of effective protection, whereas electrical and electronic products are negatively protected. Among textile products (average EPR = 13 percent) it is weaving and finishing activities as well as woolen and jute products that are heavily protected, whereas protection levels for cotton spinning and made-ups are low.

Overall it appears that textile industry in Pakistan is the most efficient subsector (DRC = 0.92) within the manufacturing sector. Efficiency is, however, far from uniform with DRC estimates at the product group level varying from 0.72 for cotton spinners to 2.20 for wool products.

Table 5.6
Pakistan: Impact of Trade Reform
on Effective Protection and Profitability

	Existing Rates		
	DRC	EPR	Private Returns
Textiles			
Cotton Spinners	0.72	-5.0	20.0
Weaving and Finishing	1.22	45.0	16.0
Cotton Made-ups	0.87	9.0	18.0
Woolen Products	2.20	93.0	6.0
Jute Products	1.07	38.0	16.0
Subsector	0.92	13.0	17.0
Chemical			
Paper Products	0.86	-8.0	12.0
Basic Indust Chem	1.69	70.0	9.0
Fertilizers	1.08	23.0	14.0
MMF	1.30	29.0	9.0
Other Chemicals	0.76	10.0	27.0
Rubber & Plastics	1.03	19.0	13.0
Glass and Ceramics	1.03	6.0	11.0
Subsector	1.04	20.0	14.0
Engineering			
Basic Metals	1.33	2.0	7.0
Metal Products	1.10	19.0	12.0
Mechanical Machinery	1.25	58.0	19.0
Electrical Machinery	0.76	-13.0	14.0
Electronics	0.92	-31.0	2.0
Transport Equipment	1.07	-1.0	7.0
Subsector	1.07	12.0	11.0

Source: World Bank.

In general, the industry is most efficient in the spinning of locally secured fiber (cotton) and the use of the same in make-up items. It is relatively less efficient in the conversion of spun short staple and filament yarn into cloth and is least efficient in the conversion of imported fiber into both yarn and cloth. Internationally the textile industry is characterized by large-scale integrated operations employing very sophisticated technology to produce an increasingly more demanding product. Both the weaving and finishing industry and the woolen industry in Pakistan are characterized by small-scale, nonintegrated units employing very simple, relatively labor-intensive technology to produce a product of questionable quality.

The industry as a whole operates within a largely neutral assistance regime (EPR = 13 percent), earning average private financial returns of 17 percent which are approximately equal to the estimated public economic return of 18 percent. This picture is, however, highly misleading. Some 25 percent of domestic resources are employed in industries which are very efficient and negatively protected. These industries are all characterized by the use of man-made fiber and are unable to pass-on an average 24 percent distortion in input prices to their customers because of competition from a close substitute—pure cotton textiles—which is generally priced domestically at or near the world price. Such a situation is hardly conducive to the growth of the man-made fiber (MMF) section of the industry, which is necessary if Pakistan is to develop a more balanced profile relative to international demand trends.

In contrast to textiles, the development of Pakistan's chemical industry is based on import substitution, and is largely restricted to the manufacture of common chemicals and a range of relatively simple final products. The production of basic industrial chemicals and man-made fibers stand out a particularly inefficient and generate the lowest returns in the industry, even with the highest rates of protection.

Finally, Pakistan's engineering industry is characterized by a bimodal industrial structure with either the production of simple shapes and components or the assembly of complex industrial products. It currently meets some 50 percent of demand for engineering products utilizing labor-intensive techniques with low levels of productivity. The recent export performance of the subsector is very poor, with only surgical instruments achieving any significant penetration of export markets. Not surprisingly the product group currently most exposed to competition—electrical machinery (DRC = 0.76) is the most efficient while the product group least exposed to competition is the least efficient—base metals (DRC 1.32). Within the electrical machinery industry, transformer and switch gear manufacturers sell the bulk of the output to the Water and power Development Authority (WAPDA) against international tenders; domestic appliance manufacturers compete against smuggled goods; and the fan industry is intensely competitive with 250 to 400 manufacturing enterprises.

Within this framework the next section attempts to assess the critical manner in which public and private firms differ. Specifically, we are interested in determining if efficiency is one area where these firms systematically diverge.

METHODOLOGY

In Pakistan differences between public- and private-sector industrial firms take many forms: variations in capital labor ratios, size, efficiency of resource use, productivity of capital, and the like. Unfortunately, there is little consensus on the most meaningful way to depict these differences. There is even less agreement on the best way to define these differences. Should size be defined in terms of the number of workers per firm or the value of fixed assets per establishment? Which measure best depicts efficiency: output per worker, or value added per unit of capital? As it turns out, each measure provides a somewhat different picture.

Elements Distinguishing Private- and Public-Sector Firms

One away to get around this problem is to compile an extensive data set of the most widely used industrial statistics and measures of manufacturing output, costs, and performance. Clearly, many of these measures will overlap and thus be redundant. Factor analysis, however, can identify the main dimensions of firm diversity.

More specifically the basic assumption of factor analysis is that a limited number of underlying dimensions (factors) can be used to explain complex phenomena. The resulting data reduction produces a limited number of independent (correlated) composite measures. In the current example, measures such as employment, sales, value added, capital stock will produce a composite index or factor depicting the relative size of the sample firms. One advantage of indexes formed in this manner is that it avoids the problem of selecting one measure of size, say fixed assets, over just as logical alternatives. Through this type of data reduction a clearer picture of firm differences can emerge.

Factor Analysis

Following the methodology used in Chapter 2, a factor analysis estimation was first performed. Operationally the computations of factors and factor scores for each industry were performed using a principle components procedure (BMDP 1992). The data was comprised of the industrial statistics provided in the annual Census of Manufacturing Industries for 1985–86 and 1986–87. The raw data by industry consists of the following:

1. Number of reporting establishments
2. Value of fixed assets at the end of the year
3. Changes in stocks
4. Average daily persons engaged
5. Average daily Employment including contract labor—number
6. Average daily Employment including contract labor—cost
7. Industrial cost during the year
8. Value of production during the year

9.   Value added during the year

For use in comparing firms across industries, several of these variables were transformed. In total, thirteen variables were created: value added per cost of labor, value added per unit of capital, value added per industrial costs, value added per worker, value added per firms, labor costs per firm, workers per firm, capital per firm, industrial costs per worker, industrial costs per firm, industrial costs per unit of capital, capital per labor costs, and capital per worker.

Each of these variables is identified first by region: total country, Punjab, Sind,   NWFP, or Baluchistan. They are then identified by ownership pattern: (a) individual ownership, (b) partnership, (c) private limited company, (d) public limited company, (e) cooperative society, (f) federal ownership, (g) corporation by act of national/provisional assembly, (h) provincial government establishment, (i) or local body government establishment. Individual ownership, partnership, and private limited companies were aggregated to obtain total private firms. The remaining firms were classified as public-sector entities.

Logistic Analysis

Identifying the main dimensions of the industrial data set is a first and necessary step in assessing the manner in which private and public enterprises vary in resource usage, productivity, and so on. The factor analysis and means of the resulting factor scores by ownership pattern provide some initial insights. As to the manner in which private and publicly held firms differ. Ultimately, however, a more rigorous test is needed to determine which of these factors are statistically significant in distinguishing public- from private-sector firms. Discriminant analysis and logistic regression analysis provide this tool.

If our hypothesis that each set of firms—domestic and foreign—have distinct and unique structural and performance characteristics that set them apart, the logistic analysis should classify with a high degree of probability each firm in its appropriate ownership category (SPSS 1992).

RESULTS

The analysis of the textile sub-sector over the 1976–87 period produced a number of interesting patterns (Tables 5.7–5.8):

1.   The dominant trend in characterizing textile plants was size (Factor 1), followed by the various measures of value added (Factor 2), capital intensity (Factor 3) and finally industrial costs (Factor 4).
2.   In terms of the main differences between private and public firms: (a) as measured by the composite value added factor score, private firms are somewhat more efficient than their public counterparts; (b) private firms are smaller; (c) use less capital per worker, and have relatively lower industrial costs per unit of capital/worker.

Table 5.7
Pakistan: Structural Characteristics,
The Textile Industry

Variable	Factor 1	Factor 2	Factor 3	Factor 4
	Size	Value Added	Capital	Indust Costs
Labor Costs/Firm	0.953*	-0.165	0.023	-0.194
VA/Firm	0.950*	0.135	0.063	-0.189
Indust. Costs/Firm	0.943*	0.059	0.047	0.215
Workers/Firm	0.924*	-0.183	-0.023	-0.190
Capital/Firm	0.862*	-0.138	0.307	-0.178
VA/Labor Costs	-0.053	0.932*	0.079	0.070
VA/Worker	-0.033	0.920*	0.153	0.062
VA/Capital	-0.162	0.675*	-0.522*	-0.002
Capital/Worker	0.092	0.107	0.939*	-0.004
Capital/Labor Costs	0.066	0.023	0.932*	-0.057
Indust. Costs/Worker	-0.157	0.310	0.042	0.875*
Indust. Costs/Capital	-0.144	0.170	-0.384	0.808*
VA/Indust. Costs	0.095	0.363	-0.151	-0.770*
Eigen Value	4.991	2.449	2.150	1.883

Profiles of Ownership

Efficiency Measure: Factor 1 > 0.5

Owner	Efficiency	Factor 1	Factor 3	Factor 4
Private	1.182	-0.509	-0.030	-0.031
Public	1.085	1.043	0.061	0.063
Total	1.150	0.000	0.000	0.000

Notes: Principal component factor analysis, oblique rotation. See *SPSS/PC+, Professional Statistics, version 5.0* (Chicago: SPSS Inc., 1992) for a description of the methods used. * = factor loadings greater than 0.50.

Table 5.8
Pakistan: Factors Affecting the Likelihood
of Ownership—Public versus Private, The Textile Sector

Efficiency Measure: Factor 1 > -0.5

Variable	Coefficient	Std Error	Significance
Efficiency	-0.852	0.647	0.1880
Factor 1	3.267	0.563	0.0000*
Factor 3	0.021	0.259	0.9342
Factor 4	0.317	0.244	0.1950
Constant	0.796	1.151	0.4892

Prediction—Overall Correct = 87.78 percent

	Private	Public	Percent Correct
Private	115.0	6.0	95.04
Public	16.0	43.0	72.88

Efficiency Measure: Factor 1 > 0

Variable	Coefficient	Std Error	Significance
Efficiency	-0.417	0.519	0.4221
Factor 1	3.331	0.588	0.0000**
Factor 3	0.014	0.262	0.9582
Factor 4	0.208	0.223	0.3509
Constant	-0.085	0.790	0.9140

Prediction—Overall Correct = 87.78 percent

	Private	Public	Percent Correct
Private	115.0	6.0	95.04
Public	16.0	43.0	72.88

Notes: Logistic Regression Analysis. See *SPSS/PC+, Advanced Statistics, version 5.0* (Chicago: SPSS Inc., 1992) for a description of the method used.   * = significant at the 99 percent level.

Table 5.8 continued
Pakistan: Factors Affecting the Likelihood
of Ownership—Public versus Private, The Textile Sector

Efficiency Measure: Factor 1 > 1.0			
Variable	**Coefficient**	**Std Error**	**Significance**
Efficiency	-1.770	0.811	0.0292*
Factor 2	3.702	0.672	0.0000**
Factor 3	0.007	0.284	0.9801
Factor 4	0.140	0.232	0.5456
Constant	1.501	1.040	0.1451

Prediction—Overall Correct = 89.44 percent

	Private	Public	Percent Correct
Private	117.0	4.0	96.69
Public	15.0	44.0	74.58

Notes: Logistic Regression Analysis. See *SPSS/PC+, Advanced Statistics, version 5.0* (Chicago: SPSS Inc., 1992) for a description of the method used. * = significant at the 95 percent level; ** = significant at the 99 percent level.

Although one might argue on the basis of these mean factor scores that private firms are more efficient than their public-sector counterparts, more rigorous statistical analyses need to be performed before any definitive conclusions can be drawn. To this end, logistic analysis looked at the potential roles of size (factor 1), value added per factor input (factor 2), capital intensity (factor 3), and industrial costs (factor 4) in differentiating public from private firms. That is, can we say with a high degree of statistical confidence whether private or public firms are likely to be larger, more capital intensive, and lower cost?.

Again several interesting patterns emerged:

1. Using a fairly broad definition of efficient firms (those firms with a factor 2 scores greater than -0.5 were coded with as 1.0 and those with those with factor 2 scores less than -0.5 coded as 2.0), only size was statistically significant in differentiating public from private firms. Simply knowing the size of a firm one could have classified a firm as private with a 95 percent chance of being correct. The corresponding value was slightly less than 73 percent for a public firm.

2. This same general pattern emerged as the definition of efficiency narrowed (factor 1 scores greater than 0. However, for very efficient firms (those with factor 1 scores over 1.0, efficiency became statistically significant (along with size) in distinguishing public from private firms.

3. The negative sign indicates that, private firms are more efficient than their public counterparts, and that this relative efficiency is a critical element in distinguishing public from private firms.
4. Based on the high cutoff for efficient/inefficient, over 96 percent of private firms would have been classified correctly on the basis of their size and efficiently rating. For public firms the corresponding percentage was 74.5 percent.

These results suggest that in a competitive industry such as textiles, public and private firms are both forced to utilize resources efficiently. If one simply divides efficient firms more or less in half (factor 2 scores greater or less than 0), there is no indication that private firms are more efficient than their public counterparts. On the other hand, if one demands a higher level of value added per factor input to be classified as efficient (factor 2 scores greater than 1.0), then private firms tend to be more efficient than their public counterparts—efficiency is a critical element (along with size) in distinguishing private from public firms.

As a basis of comparison, a similar analysis was undertaken on the chemicals industry. As noted above, this industry is on average somewhat less competitive than textiles. The results of this analysis provide an interesting contrast (Tables 5.9, 5.10):

1. Capital intensity (factor 1) is the dominant trend (Table 5.9) in the chemicals industry, followed by size (factor 2), efficiently (factor 3), and finally industrial costs per unit of inputs (factor 4).
2. Public and private firms differ in that public firms tend to be more efficient, have relatively greater capital intensity and size, and incur greater industrial costs per unit input.
3. In terms of the critical elements differentiating public from private firms, the logistic analysis (Table 5.10) suggests that all four factors are statistically significant in this regard. This pattern holds across a wide definition of efficiency.

The model is quite accurate in classifying public and private firms, with an average probability a firm being classified correctly on the basis of its efficiency and factor scores nearly 95 percent. The positive sign on the efficiency term suggests that public firms are more efficient than their private-sector counterparts.

For a final comparison, the least competitive subsector, engineering was selected. Because of the great diversity of the major subsectors in this industry, we focused on one main area of specialization, basic metals. Firms producing basic metals were selected because this industry appears to be one of the least competitive areas of the economy, thus providing a good contrast to the competitive environment characterizing textiles and chemicals.

Again, several interesting patterns emerged from the factor and logistic analysis (Tables 5.11 and 5.12):

Table 5.9
Pakistan: Structural Characteristics,
The Chemical Industry

Variable	Factor 1	Factor 2	Factor 3	Factor 4
	Capital	Size	Value Added	Indust. Costs
Capital/Worker	0.919*	0.087	0.309	0.181
Capital/Labor Costs	0.912*	0.436	0.208	-0.042
Capital/Firm	0.848*	0.374	0.202	0.037
VA/Capital	-0.637*	0.304	0.576	0.238
Workers/Firm	-0.008	0.970*	0.037	0.015
Labor Costs/Firm	0.175	0.955*	0.105	0.032
VA/Firm	0.133	0.859*	0.377	0.044
VA/Labor Costs	0.152	0.141	0.939*	-0.051
VA/Worker	0.357	0.117	0.845*	0.078
VA/Indust. Costs	0.132	0.203	0.571*	0.516*
Indust. Costs/Capital	-0.262	0.003	0.052	0.882*
Indust. Costs/Worker	0.547*	0.013	-0.005	0.795*
Indust. Costs/Firm	0.540*	0.319	-0.032	0.726*
Eigen Value	5.043	2.772	2.219	1.550

Profiles of Ownership Efficiency Measure: Factor 3 > 0				
Owner	Efficiency	Factor 1	Factor 3	Factor 4
Private	1.272	-0.252	-0.358	-0.029
Public	1.577	0.443	0.631	0.050
Total	1.383	0.000	0.000	0.000

Notes: Principal component factor analysis, oblique rotation. See *SPSS/PC+, Professional Statistics, version 5.0* (Chicago: SPSS Inc., 1992) for a description of the methods used.

* = factor loadings greater than 0.50.

Table 5.10
Pakistan: Factors Affecting the Likelihood of
Ownership—Public versus Private, The Chemical Industry

Efficiency Measure: Factor 3 > 1.0

Variable	Coefficient	Std Error	Significance
Efficiency	6.449	1.557	0.0000**
Factor 1	7.507	2.229	0.0008**
Factor 2	11.816	2.230	0.0000**
Factor 4	5.820	2.031	0.0042**
Constant	-3.766	1.437	0.0088
	Private	Public	Percent Correct
Private	121	4	96.80
Public	6	65	91.55

Efficiency Measure: Factor 3 > 0.5

Variable	Coefficient	Std Error	Significance
Efficiency	5.942	1.330	0.0000**
Factor 1	10.392	2.781	0.0002**
Factor 2	12.376	2.507	0.0078**
Factor 4	7.512	2.335	0.0013**
Constant	-3.329	1.183	0.0049**
Prediction—Overall Correct = 94.39 percent			
	Private	Public	Percent Correct
Private	121	4	96.80
Public	7	64	90.14

Efficiency Measure: Factor 3 > 0

Variable	Coefficient	Std Error	Significance
Efficiency	3.433	0.869	0.0001**
Factor 1	7.562	1.995	0.0002**
Factor 2	10.888	2.061	0.0000**
Factor 4	5.289	1.551	0.0006**
Constant	-1.754	1.141	0.1243*
Prediction—Overall Correct = 94.39 percent			
	Private	Public	Percent Correct
Private	123	2	98.40
Public	9	62	87.32

Notes: Logistic Regression Analysis. See *SPSS/PC+, Advanced Statistics, version 5.0* (Chicago: SPSS Inc., 1992) for a description of the method used. * = significant at the 95 percent level; ** = significant at the 99 percent level.

Table 5.11
Pakistan: Structural Characteristics,
The Basic Metals Industry

Variable	Factor 1	Factor 2	Factor 3	Factor 4
	Size	Value Added	Indust. Costs	Capital
Labor Costs/Firm	0.960*	-0.047	-0.194	-0.134
Capital/Firm	0.934*	-0.024	-0.123	0.206
Indust. Costs/Firm	0.930*	-0.037	-0.151	0.021
Workers/Firm	0.917*	-0.022	-0.291	0.150
Capital/Worker	0.900*	-0.034	-0.109*	0.348
VA/Firm	0.835*	0.108	-0.284	0.341
VA/Worker	0.072	0.927*	0.212	0.080
VA/Capital	-0.219	0.915*	0.214	-0.153
VA/Labor Costs	-0.015	0.716*	0.112	0.651*
VA/Indust. Costs	0.342	0.618*	-0.559*	0.280
Indust. Costs /Worker	-0.208	0.239	0.886*	-0.006
Indust. Costs / Capital	-0.408	0.333	0.725*	-0.171
Capital/Labor Costs	0.327	0.000	-0.187	0.913*
Eigen Value 6.695		3.090	1.284	0.931

Profiles of Ownership
    Efficiency Measure: Factor 2 > -0.5

Owner	Efficiency	Factor 1	Factor 3	Factor 4
Private	1.531	-0.411	0.236	-0.011
Public	1.929	0.940	-0.539	0.027
Total	1.652	0.000	0.000	0.000

Notes: Principal component factor analysis, oblique rotation. See *SPSS/PC+, Professional Statistics, version 5.0* (Chicago: SPSS Inc., 1992) for a description of the methods used. * = factor loadings greater than 0.50.

Table 5.12
Pakistan: Factors Affecting the Likelihood of
Ownership—Public versus Private, The Basic Metals Industry

Efficiency Measure: Factor 3 > 0.5				
Variable	**Coefficient**	**Std Error**	**Wald**	**Significance**
Efficiency	-3.116	4.153	0.56	0.4532
Factor 1	14.067	7.236	3.78	0.0519*
Factor 2	-3.254	1.768	3.38	0.0658*
Factor 4	0.835	2.439	0.12	0.7321
Constant	6.300	6.390	0.97	0.3242

Prediction—Overall Correct = 97.83 percent

	Private	Public	Percent Correct
Private	32	0	100.00
Public	1	13	92.86

Efficiency Measure: Factor 3 > 0				
Variable	**Coefficient**	**Std Error**	**Wald**	**Significance**
Efficiency	2.029	2.437	0.69	0.4051
Factor 1	15.315	7.824	3.83	0.0503*
Factor 2	-3.017	1.453	4.31	0.0379**
Factor 4	2.519	3.419	0.55	0.4604
Constant	-0.069	2.878	0.00	0.9810

Prediction—Overall Correct = 95.65 percent

	Private	Public	Percent Correct
Private	31	1	96.88
Public	1	13	92.86

Notes: Logistic Regression Analysis. See *SPSS/PC+, Advanced Statistics, version 5.0* (Chicago: SPSS Inc., 1992) for a description of the method used. * = significant at the 90 percent level; ** = significant at the 95 percent level.

Table 5.12 continued
Pakistan: Factors Affecting the Likelihood of
Ownership—Public versus Private, The Basic Metals Industry

Efficiency Measure: Factor 3 > -0.05

Variable	Coefficient	Std Error	Wald	Significance
Efficiency	12.172	81.681	0.02	0.8815
Factor 1	14.218	7.472	3.62	0.0570*
Factor 2	-4.079	2.741	2.21	0.1368
Factor 4	5.801	6.493	0.80	0.3709
Constant	-20.690	163.213	0.02	0.8991

Prediction—Overall Correct = 95.65 percent

	Private	Public	Percent Correct
Private	31	1	96.88
Public	1	13	92.86

Notes: Logistic Regression Analysis. See *SPSS/PC+, Advanced Statistics, version 5.0* (Chicago: SPSS Inc., 1992) for a description of the method used. * = significant at the 90 percent level.

1. Size (factor 1) is the most important factor (Table 5.11) characterizing these firms. This was followed by efficiently (factor 2), industrial costs per factor input (factor 3) and finally capital intensity (factor 4).
2. Based on the mean factor scores on the four main dimensions, it appears that public firms are on average considerably more efficient than their private counterparts. In addition they are larger, have lower industrial costs per factor input, and have greater capital intensity.
3. While public firms appear more efficient based on simple factor scores, logistic analysis found little evidence that efficiency differences were an important element in distinguishing firms by ownership type. For these firms relative size and industrial costs appear to be the critical factors in distinguishing private from public firms.
4. It should be noted that while the logistic model correctly classified public and private firms with a high degree of accuracy (over 95 percent), the statistical significance of the size and industrial cost firms was only marginal.

The basic metals case suggests that for industries with low levels of competitive pressures, there is no particular mechanism that forces either public or private firms to be relatively efficient. This finding is consistent with the extensive literature on X-Efficiency (Leibenstein 1966; Bergsman 1974).

CONCLUSIONS

The remarkable progress shown by the spinning sector is the result of government support policies, availability of sufficient finance, good quality cotton at low prices, low labor cost, and availability of technical and managerial personnel (Memon 1993, 14). Above all, the highly developed management skill in all phases of production together with a favorable international market have been responsible for the development of a strong spinning sector. This will serve as the main source of strength to the downstream industries like weaving, knitting, finishing garments and specialized textiles. The experience gained during the last forty-five years in manufacturing and marketing of cotton yarn should help the industry gain a stronger position in the international market.

At the present time the textile industry continues to be the largest industry in Pakistan, and still commands the strongest comparative advantages in resource utilization. It is also the largest foreign exchange earner. Presently Pakistan has a share of 28.9 percent in export in the world trade of cotton yarn, but only 6.5 percent in fabrics and 1 percent in garments.

The industry is one of the most efficient in Pakistan, but even here there is room for improvement. The analysis above suggests that private firms may be considerably more efficient than their public counterparts. Privatization of the remaining public firms in the industry would most likely lead to even greater improvements in efficiency and competitive strength in external markets.

In this regard, it is interesting to note that in all Pakistani industries subject to less competitive pressures, private firms do not appear to be any more efficient than their public counterparts. If anything, they may be less efficient. Clearly for these industries, a joint policy of reducing tariffs and other barriers to competition would be a necessary element for the privatization of public enterprises to result in marked improvements in overall sector efficiency.

6

Financial Development and Investment

INTRODUCTION

Along with a number of other market reforms the government of Pakistan has, in recent years, committed itself to a thorough and comprehensive reform of the country's financial sector. The program is aimed at allocating credit in response to market signals, improving the health and efficiency of the banking system and establishing a more efficient system to issue government debt. The main objectives of the reform program are to reduce segmentation of financial markets and develop capital markets by introducing a system of auctioning government debt, raising concessional rates of interest, and limiting directed credit schemes. The authorities are also attempting to strengthen the health of the banking system and increase competition by recapitalizing and privatizing the nationalized commercial banks, improving prudential regulations and bank supervision and allowing private domestic banks to enter the market.

The ultimate purpose of these programs is to aid the country in accelerating its mobilization of financial and real assets. In this regard a number of studies have suggested that a higher rate of financial growth is positively associated with real economic growth. In this regard the government's programs implicitly assume that financial liberalization will aid the private sector in mobilizing funds for investment in manufacturing. In this regard, a number of studies of financial liberalization in developing countries have verified that a higher rate of financial growth is positively associated with successful real growth.

Will financial liberalization in Pakistan accelerate real economic growth? In addition to overcoming a number of technical and administrative problems, the success of the government's program will largely depend on the direction of causation between financial development and real investment. Specifically, does financial development proceed and tend to create an environment conducive to increased private investment? Or, instead, does financial development tend to be more passive, simply increasing to accommodate the more complex asset needs of a growing economy? The purpose of this chapter is to shed light on these issues through identifying the direction of causation between finance and real growth. Based on these findings, several observations are made concerning the policies to increase the rate of private sector capital formation in manufacturing.

DEMAND-FOLLOWING AND SUPPLY-LEADING FINANCIAL DEVELOPMENT

Financial development has received increasing attention in the economic development literature. Traditionally the financial system has been assumed to accommodate—or to the extent that it malfunctions—it restricts growth of real per capita output. For example Joan Robinson (1952) notes that its seems to be the case that where enterprise leads finance follows.

Such an approach places emphasis on the demand side for financial services; as the economy grows it generates additional and new demands for these services, which bring about a supply response in the growth of the financial system. In this view, the lack of financial institutions in underdeveloped countries is simply an indication of the lack of demand for their services.

More formally Patrick (1989) notes that we may term as "demand following" the phenomenon in which the creation of modern financial institutions, their financial assets and liabilities, and related financial services is in response to the demand for these services by investors and savers in the real economy. In this case, the evolutionary development of the financial system is a continuing consequence of the pervasive, sweeping process of economic development. The emerging financial system is shaped both by changes in objective opportunities—the economic environment, the institutional framework—and by changes in subjective responses—individual motivations, attitudes, tastes, and preferences.

In this situation, the nature of the demand for financial services depends upon the growth of real output and upon the commercialization and monetization of agriculture and other traditional subsistence sectors. Patrick notes that more rapid the growth rate of real national income, the greater will be the demand by enterprises for external funds (the savings of others) and, therefore for financial intermediation, since under most circumstances firms will be less able to finance expansion from internally generated depreciation allowances and retained profits. The proportion of external funds in the total source of enterprise funds will rise. For the same reason, with a given aggregate growth rate, the greater the variance in the growth rates among different sectors or industries the greater will be the need for financial intermediation to transfer savings to fast-growing industries and from individuals. The financial system can thus support and sustain the leading sectors in the process of growth.

This school of thought stresses that the demand-following supply response of the growing financial system comes about more or less automatically. Here it is assumed that the supply of entrepreneurship in the financial sector is highly elastic relative to the growing opportunities for profit from provision of financial services, so that the number and diversity of types of financial institutions expand sufficiently; and a favorable legal, institutional, and economic environment exists.

While the demand-following approach implies that finance is essentially passive and permissive in the growth process, imperfections in the operation of the market mechanism may dictate an inadequate demand-following response by the financial system. The lack of financial services in many developing countries may thus restrict or inhibit effective growth patterns and processes (Patrick 1989, 204).

Less emphasis has been given in academic discussion to what is often termed the "supply-leading" phenomenon: the creation of financial institutions and the supply of their financial assets, liabilities and related financial services in advance of demand for them especially in the modern growth-inducing sectors.

Supply-leading has two functions: to transfer resources from traditional (nongrowth) sectors to modern sectors and to promote and stimulate an entrepreneurial response in these modern sectors. Financial intermediation that transfers resources from traditional sectors, whether by collecting wealth and savings from those sectors in exchange for its deposits and other financial liabilities or by credit creation and forced savings, is akin to the Schumpeterian concept of innovation financing.

New access to such supply-leading funds may in itself have substantial favorable expectational and psychological effects on the entrepreneurs. It opens new horizons as to possible alternatives, enabling the entrepreneur to conceptualize larger investment packages. This may be the most significant effect of all, particularly in countries where entrepreneurship is a major constraint on development (Patrick 1989, 204).

It cannot be said that supply-leading finance is a necessary condition or precondition for inaugurating self-sustaining economic development. Rather, it presents an opportunity to induce real growth through by financial means. It is likely to play a more significant role at the beginning of the growth process rather than later. It should be noted, however, that the supply-leading approach to developing a country's financial system also has its dangers; the use of resources, especially entrepreneurial talents and managerial skills, and the costs of explicit or implicit subsidies in supply-leading development must produce sufficient benefits to stimulate real economic development for this approach to be justified.

In actual practice there is likely to be an interaction of supply-leading and demand-following phenomena. Nevertheless, the following sequence may be postulated. Before sustained modern industrial growth gets underway, supply leading may be able to induce real innovation type investment. As the process of real growth occurs, the supply-leading impetus gradually becomes less important and the demand following financial response becomes dominant. This sequential process is also likely to occur within and among specific industries or sectors. One industry may initially be encouraged financially on a supply-leading basis and as it develops, have its financing shift to demand-following, while another industry remains in the supply-leading phase. This sequential process is also likely to occur within and among specific industries or sectors. This would be related to the timing of the sequential development of industries, particularly in cases where the timing is determined more by government policy than by private demand forces (Patrick 1989, 205).

Regardless of which process dominates, McKinnon (1986) has found that a high and rising ratio of M2 to GNP usually occurs in the more rapidly growing economies. An increase in this ratio indicates a large real flow of loanable funds. Because capital markets in many developing economies are dominated by banks the ratio of M2 to GNP usually encompasses the main domestic flow of loanable funds. In this regard it should be noted (Table 6.1) that Pakistan has lagged behind other countries in the region in expanding this aggregate.

Table 6.1
Bank-Loanable Funds in South and East Asia

Country	1960	1965	1970	1975	1980	1985	1990
(ratio of M2 to GNP)							
South Asia							
Pakistan	0.358	0.403	0.435	0.337	0.386	0.376	0.374
India	0.266	0.227	0.233	0.263	0.372	0.432	0.463
Sri Lanka	0.234	0.288	0.245	0.202	0.256	0.319	0.290
East Asia							
Thailand	0.230	0.247	0.283	0.340	0.386	0.617	0.753
Philippines	0.192	0.283	0.299	0.236	0.291	0.288	0.400
Singapore	-	-	0.651	0.612	0.664	0.698	0.959
Malaysia	0.245	0.285	0.349	0.463	0.534	0.679	0.699
Korea	0.114	0.121	0.258	0.313	0.341	0.366	0.401

Source: Computed from International Monetary Fund, *International Financial Statistics*, various issues.

THE ISSUE OF CAUSATION

Although a higher rate of financial growth may be positively correlated with successful real growth, Patrick's problem remains unresolved: What is the cause and what is the effect? Is finance a leading sector in Pakistan's economic development or has it simply followed growth in real output which is generated elsewhere. Perhaps individuals whose incomes grow quickly want financial assets simply as a kind of consumer good (i.e., an incidental outcome of the growth process. To disentangle these issues a series of causation tests were performed.

Again, following the framework developed in the Appendix, four cases are possible: (1) *Loanable funds cause economic activity* when the prediction error for economic activity decreases when the loanable funds are included in the activity equation. In addition, when economic activity is added to the loanable funds equation, the final prediction error should increase; (2) *Economic activity causes loanable funds* when the prediction error for loanable funds increases when loanable funds are added to the regression equation for economic activity, and is reduced when economic activity is added to the regression equation for loanable funds; (3) *Feedback* occurs when the final prediction error decreases when loanable funds are added to the economic activity equation, and the final prediction error decreases when economic activity is added to the loanable funds equation; and (4) *No relationship* exists when the final prediction error increases both when loanable funds are added to the economic activity equation and when economic activity is added to the deficit equation.

The data used to carry out the causation tests are from the International Monetary Fund International Financial Statistics (IMF 1995).

RESULTS

The causation analysis produced a number of interesting findings (Table 6.2):

1. With regard to the overall level of economic activity, expanded GDP Product (Table 6.2) elicits a corresponding increase in money (M1). The monetary response is fairly strong and is reflective of the growth in GDP during the two prior years.
2. The same general pattern holds for money holdings. Here, the ratio of money to GDP increases to accommodate a previous expansion in real income. This adjustment is relatively rapid, averaging about a year.
3. A fairly strong increase in the rate of growth of loanable funds also follows a general expansion in economic activity. Again the adjustment period is fairly short, averaging a year. However, in contrast to the situation with narrow money, loanable funds experience feedback effects whereby their expansion provides a further stimulus to GDP growth.
4. The process of increased financial intermediation precedes the overall growth in economic activity. However, the stimulus provided by financial intermediation is fairly weak.

In terms of Patrick's framework, therefore, it appears that financial intermediation does not passively adjust to changing economic conditions, but is a growth-initiating mechanism. The question immediately arises as to the mechanism leading from financial intermediation to growth. Is the process one of supply-led growth whereby increased financial intermediation aids investment in manufacturing? Or is it more a process of demand led growth where by increased financial intermediation facilitates increased levels of consumption?

To explore this set of alternative growth mechanisms, a similar analysis to the one undertaken for GDP was undertaken for private-sector investment. Here a distinction was made between private investment in large-scale manufacturing (Table 6.2) and private investment in smaller scale manufacturing units. Again, several interesting patterns emerged:

1. Both the expansion in money (M1) and money holdings (M1/Y) interact with private investment to form a feedback mechanism (Table 6.3). In both cases this interaction is weak in both directions—the impact of money on investment and the feedback from investment to expanded money.
2. However, expanded loanable funds (M2) provides a strong stimulus to private investment. In general this effect is stronger for increases in loanable funds over a three-year period prior to the change in private investment. In turn, expanded private investment provides an immediate but short-run (one year) stimulus to loanable funds.
3. Finally, increased financial intermediation provide a fairly strong stimulus to private investment. On average private investment is affected by increases in financial intermediation over a three-year period.
4. Similar results were obtained for private investment in small-scale manufacturing. Not surprisingly, given their relative lack of access to financial markets, the links between loanable funds/financial intermediation and private investment were somewhat weaker than that experienced by larger scale firms.

These findings strongly suggest the importance of financial intermediation in initiating the process of increased rates of private capital formation in manufacturing. However, there is always the danger that our results are simply spurious. While there is no real way to test for this possibility, it is instructive to examine similar patterns involving several macroeconomic aggregates—private consumption and government investment in manufacturing:

1. In the case of private consumption, a pattern clearly exists whereby movements in this aggregate produces changes in monetary aggregates. That is increased private consumption (presumably reflecting increased real incomes) produces increases in money, money holdings. and loanable funds. Here money is rather passive, presumably adjusting to changing needs associated with increased affluence.

Table 6.2
Pakistan: Interaction of Money (M1), Loanable Funds (M2)
and Gross Domestic Product, 1972–1991

Relationship	Direction of Causation (impact)	Optimal Lag	Relative Strength
Gross Domestic Product (GDP)			
(1) Money—M1	GDP -->M1(+)	2	m
(2) Money Holdings—M1/GDP	GDP -->M1(+)	1	w
(3) Loanable Funds—M2	Feedback(+,+)	1,1	w,m
(4) Financial Intermediation—M2/GDP	Finance -->GDP(+)	1	w
Private Investment in Large Scale Manufacturing			
(5) Money—M1	Feedback(+,+)	3,4	w,w
(6) Money Holdings—M1/GDP	Feedback(+,+)	4,2	w,w
(7) Lonable Funds—M2	Feedback(+,+)	4,1	s,w
(8) Financial Intermediation—M2/GDP	M2 -->Invest.(+)	1	m

The signs (+,-) represent the direction of impact. In the case of feedback the first term is the impact of money on GDP (or private investment in manufacturing); the second is the impact of GNP (or private investment in manufacturing) on money. Strength assessment (w) weak, (m) moderate, and (s) strong made on the basis of the improvement in r^2 and the size of the standardized regression coefficient.

2. For government investment, a distinctly contrasting pattern exists. Here increases in either money (M1) or loanable funds (M2) produce investment. However, the impact is strongly negative. That is after three years of increases in these monetary aggregates, government investment in manufacturing is severely reduced. There is no statistically significant relationship between either money holdings (M1/GDP) or financial intermediation (M2/GDP) and government investment in manufacturing.

These last two sets of findings are more or less what one might expect. Increases in private consumption are undoubtedly caused by an overall increase in real incomes. These, in turn, create increased demands for financial assets which are subsequently increased by the financial system.

Government investment in manufacturing may have a low priority (especially given the country's rather high level of defense expenditures). If this is so, austerity measures undertaken to combat inflationary pressures would be expected to reduce expenditures in areas such as public industrial capital formation.

CONCLUSIONS

In recent years, two schools of thought have emerged, namely, the financial repressionist and the financial structuralist. Both schools have provided some new insights into the causes of low savings, investment and growth in developing countries. The repressionist school led by McKinnon (1973) argues that the low (or negative) and high and variable inflation rates are the major impediments to savings, financial deepening, capital formation, and growth. The solution, therefore, lies in freeing the interest rates to find their equilibrium levels in a free market environment (Khan 1988a).

The latter school of thought led by Goldsmith (1969) attributes the low savings, investment, and growth in developing countries to the relatively less developed financial structures in terms of financial assets, institutions, and markets. Presumably a widespread network of financial institutions and a diversified array of financial instruments will have a beneficial effect on the savings-investment process and hence on growth.

Several empirical studies have found financial repression to be present in Pakistan. For example Abe and colleagues (1977) have empirically tested the McKinnon-Shaw model and found that financial repression holds domestic savings below the level that would occur under a policy of financial liberalization. The findings reported by Khan clearly point out the existence of financial repression on the one hand and lack of financial development on the other hand in Pakistan. The solution, therefore, lies in freeing the return on deposits to find their equilibrium levels and a free market environment. In particular he suggests that the authorities should strive to make the real return on deposits positive either by increasing the nominal return or by reducing inflation. Furthermore, a widespread network of financial institutions and a diversified array of financial instruments will increase savings in Pakistan (Khan 1988a, 709).

While the current study does not test directly these two approaches, its major findings do show the importance of focusing on financial reforms that eliminate financial repression. Although the growth in financial assets appears to simply adjust to the demands generated by a growing economy, their importance lies in the fact that their growth appears to be one of the most effective ways of stimulating private-sector investment in manufacturing. In this regard, the pay-off of financial reforms may be considerably higher than is usually assumed by the financial structuralist school of thought.

7

Financial Innovation in an Islamic Setting

INTRODUCTION

The financial system in Pakistan is undergoing dramatic changes. First, the introduction of Islamic modes of financing led to the creation of new financial institutions—leasing companies and *modarabas* (essentially closed end mutual funds) and instruments such as the *musharika* and *morabaha*.

With a radical program of financial sector reform initiated in the early 1990s, the government has started a process of liberalization, deregulation, and privatization. The swiftness of these changes has caught the participants in the financial markets by surprise. The definitions and roles of the past have suddenly become redundant. Many observers feel an exciting future is opening. This future will be dominated by those who are creative, pioneering, and iconoclastic (Haq 1992, 19).

This chapter focuses on the development of and problems facing two important areas of nonbank financing: *modarabas* and leasing companies.

BACKGROUND

The non-bank financial intermediaries in Pakistan (Haq 1992, 419–421) have their origins in the perception of policy makers in the 1950s, 1960s, and 1970s that the market was incapable of providing term financing for industrial projects. The private commercial banks, which had been established by families of industrialists, concentrated their activities around short-term trade and working capital financing. Long-term lending, equity investments, and important areas of the economy such as agriculture and housing were largely neglected. Furthermore, it was felt that the interlocking of finance and industrial capital would lead to the preemption of credit by established business groups, depriving emerging entrepreneurs of sources of finance. The solution was found in the form of government owned (or sponsored) financial institutions with specific charters to cater to certain market segments.

A number of institutions were set up to serve these perceived gaps in the country's financial system. Thus in the 1960s the Industrial Development Bank of Pakistan was formed to provide loans to small- and medium-sized industrial projects. The Pakistan Industrial Credit and Investment Corporation (PICIC) catered to medium- and large-sized projects. The National Investment Trust (NIT) and Investment Corporation of Pakistan (ICP) were established to mobilize small savings for investment in the equities market through investment units and mutual funds. The Agricultural Development Bank of Pakistan (ADBP) channeled credit to the agricultural sector.

In the 1970s, this list of specialized institutions was further expanded. The National Development Finance Corporation (NDFC) was set up as a statutory corporation to meet the funding needs of the public sector, which had greatly increased after the nationalization of the early 1970s. The Federal Bank for Cooperatives (FBC) was created to promote the cooperatives movement, House Building Finance Corporation (HBFC) for housing finance, and the Bankers Equity Limited (BEL) to provide financing, particularly through equity investments, to medium- and large-sized private sector projects.

The performance of the Development Finance Institutions (DFIs) in meeting the objectives set for them was mixed. There were successes, and some failures too. Notable amongst the successes were the following:

1.   An increase in private- and public- sector capital formation
2.   An expansion of credit for agricultural and rural development
3.   The promotion of new industries and entrepreneurs

In some respects, however, the DFIs failed to play the role expected of them. These included

1.   An inability to reduce dependence on the State Bank of Pakistan's (SBP's) lines of credit for agriculture, industry, and housing through the mobilization of public savings
2.   A failure to effect a fundamental transformation in the pattern and direction of industrial financing. While new industries were promoted to a certain extent, the bulk of DFI loan portfolios is concentrated in the traditional areas of textiles, sugar, and cement
3.   A poor loan recovery performance
4.   A high level of operating costs
5.   A lack of dynamism and creativity in both mobilizing and deploying loans

In a sense, therefore, the DFIs acted as passive conduits through which state credits were channeled into economic activities that were being ignored by the private sector. They were a necessary tool of state intervention. However, it was a role that could have been performed very differently had the state provided a more supportive external environment.

The failures of the DFIs can be attributed to the following impediments (Haq 1992, 421):

1. Political interference in credit and personnel policy
2. A lack of managerial autonomy, particularly in the areas of personnel recruitment, retrenchment and emoluments
3. The absence of an effective and speedy system of legal recourse against defaulting borrowers
4. An unstable and inconsistent fiscal and industrial policy framework

The NBFI sector is undergoing a major process of change, growth, and diversification. Along with the traditional DFIs, new types of institutions and instruments are emerging. The sector cannot be divided into the following distinct subsectors:

1. Modaraba funds
2. Leasing companies
3. Development finance institutions/Investment banks
4. Stock market funds

The emergence of these new institutions may be attributed to the following government initiatives:

1. Reform of the financial system toward Islamic principles of risk sharing
2. The privatization and deregulation of the financial system
3. The introduction of a market system of debt management and monetary control
4. The removal of restrictions on foreign exchange flows
5. The encouragement of foreign portfolio investments in Pakistani companies

ISLAMIC FINANCIAL INSTITUTIONS—OVERVIEW

Non-Islamic financial systems are based on the principle that capital is a factor of production and interest is a reward. In contrast, an Islamic financial system views investment as a factor of production (Khawaja 1994). Here, it is important to note that Islamic law forbids the fixed or predetermined return on financial transactions, but it does not forbid an uncertain rate of return represented by profits. For this reason, the modern concept of Islamic finance has developed on the basis of profit sharing. In the last few decades a variety of models of Islamic finance have been adopted. The general operations of these financial institutions revolve around their attractions of funds and the manner in which these funds are converted into profitable assets.

Sources of Funds

Besides its own capital and equity, the main sources of funds (Khan and Mirakhor 1990) for an Islamic financial institution involve transactions deposits and investment deposits. Transactions deposits are directly related to payments and can be regarded as equivalent to demand deposits in a conventional banking system. Although a bank would guarantee the nominal value of the deposit, it would pay no return on this type of liability. Investment deposits constitute the principal source of funds for most Islamic institutions, and they resemble more closely shares in a firm rather than time and saving deposits of the customary sort. The bank offering investment deposits would provide no guarantee on their nominal value. Nor would it pay a fixed rate of return. Depositors, instead, would be treated as if they were shareholders and, therefore, entitled to a share of the profit or losses made by the bank. The only contractional agreement between the depositor and the bank is the proportion in which profits and loses are to be distributed. The share or distribution parameter has to be agreed on in advance of the transaction between the bank and the depositor and cannot be altered during the life of the contract, except by mutual consent.

Asset Acquisition

Islamic financial institutions can acquire profit share assets via two principle modes of transactions: mudarabah and musharakah. Under the provisions of the first mode, mudarabah, surplus funds are made available to the entrepreneurs to be invested in productive enterprise in return for a predetermined share of the profits earned. Financial losses are borne exclusively by the lender. The borrower, as such, loses only the time and effort invested in the venture. The arrangement, therefore, effectively places human capital on par with financial capital.

Musharakah, on the other hand, involves two or more contributors of funds. All parties invest in varying proportions, and the profits (or losses) are shared strictly in relation to their respective capital contribution. This financing method corresponds to an equity market in which shares can be acquired by the public, banks, and even the central bank and the government. Traditionally, mudarabah has been employed in investment projects with short gestation periods and in trade and commerce whereas musharakah is used in long-term investment projects. These two modes have their historical counterparts in farming and in orchard keeping, where the harvest is shared between and among the partners based on prespecified shares.

In transactions where profit sharing is not applicable, other modes of financing can be employed, which include the following (Khan and Mirakhor 1990, 355-356).

1. *Qard al-Hasanah (beneficence loans)*. These are zero-return loans that the Quern exhorts Muslims to make available to those who need them. Financial organizations

that provide these loans are permitted to charge the borrower a service charge to cover administrative costs of handling the loan so long as the charge is not related to the amount or the period of the loan, and represents solely the cost of administering the loan.

2. *Bai' Mua'jjal (deferred payment sales).* This mode allows the sale of a product on the basis of deferred payment in installments or in a lump-sum payment. The price of the product is agreed on between the buyer and the seller at the time of the sale and cannot include any charges for deferring payments.

3. *Mai' Salam or Bai'Salaf (purchase with deferred delivery).* In this transaction the buyer pays the seller the full negotiated price of a product that the seller promises to deliver at a future date. This transaction is limited to agricultural and manufactured products whose quality and quantity can be fully specified at the time the contract is made.

4. *Ijara (leasing).* In this transaction, a person leases a particular product for a specific sum and a specific period of time. He can also negotiate for lease-purchase of the product, where each payment includes a portion that goes toward the final purchase and transfer of ownership of the product.

5. *Jo'alah (service charge).* This is a transaction in which one party undertakes to pay another a specified sum of money as a fee for rendering a specific service in accordance with the terms of the contract negotiated between the two parties. This mode facilitates consultation, fund placements, and trust activities.

This list is not exhaustive. Under Islamic law the freedom of contracts provides the parties with a flexibility that makes possible a virtually open-ended variety of forms of financial transactions and instruments. There is nothing to constrain the system from creating any contractual form so long as the contract does not include interest and both parties are fully informed of its details.

Pakistani Islamic scholars have regarded several distinctive types of finance as acceptable (Khawaja 1994):

1. Modaraba
2. Shirakah or Murabaha
3. Leasing
4. Bai'Muajjal and Mai'Salem

In addition, two other modes of financing been approved by the Islamic Ideology Council (Khawaja 1994): (1) hire purchase and (2) investment auctioning. Of these, the development of modarabas has been unique in Pakistan.

MODARABAS

Modarabas are unique to Pakistan. They were created by the Modaraba Ordinance of 1980 whose intent it was to provide a legal framework for formation and regulation of modaraba as a recognized legal entity as well as providing a framework for modaraba management though a modaraba management company (Kazmi 1994).

A modaraba is an Islamic form of limited partnership in which a managing firm agrees to invest the funds of a fairly large number of passive investors (World Bank 1994).   Shares of the management company as well as those of their modaraba funds subscribed by the private investors are traded on the stock exchange.   As long as the modarabas' activities are sanctioned by a religious board, it can engage in almost any line of business.

The first modaraba was formed in 1981. The first multipurpose moda-raba, BRR Modaraba and First Habib Modaraba, were floated in 1985.   In 1987, First Grindlays Modaraba and Modaraba Al-Mali were floated. The suc-cess of these Modarabas attracted others and by 1990 fourteen modarabas had been floated.

In part this growth was due to the relatively good profits earned by the mo-darabas. The fact that the modarabas were also managed within the injunctions of Islam made them attractive investments. Perhaps more important, section 37 of the Modarabas Ordinance   provided for tax exemption if not less than 90 percent of its profits were distributed to the holders of modaraba certificates. These factors led to a rapid expansion of modarabas with nineteen new ones floated in 1991 alone. Today there are fifty-two of these institutions operating in Pakistan (Table 7.1).

Another factor responsible for the expansion of modarabas has been the in-centives given to banks to get into this type of business. The flotation of moda-rabas allows banks to (Kazmi 1994a) (1) acquire funds at relatively low cost, (2) save income tax, (3) improve their liquidity position of banks, and (4) leverage on maximum exposure to one organization. Specifically, through their modara-bas, banks can partially extend funds from their banking operations and partly through leasing plant and machinery. This enables the banks to extend larger amounts to good clients without running up against the credit limit per party.

Modarabas account for more than 36 percent of the paid-up capital of all listed financial institutions in the country (including banks). Nearly 37 percent of the 135 listed financial institutions are modarabas. The overwhelming im-portance of modarabas and their significant contribution to the national econ-omy in the areas of leasing, stock market investments, short and long-term fi-nancing, trading and, in some cases, even manufacturing, cannot be overesti-mated.

Lines of Activity

Most of the modarabas listed on the Karachi Stock Exchange are perpetual, multipurpose, and multidimensional. Their main lines of activity include (Kazmi 1994) the following:

Finance. These provide working capital finance on profit and loss sharing basis using joint venture partnership and by supplying materials, products, and capital goods on cash and deferred mode of payment.

Table 7.1
Modarabas in Pakistan

Company	Year of Listing	Face Value	September 1994 Rates	Paid-up capital (Rs.mln)
Al- Leasing Modaraba	1992	10	9.75	50.000
Al-Noor Modaraba	1992	10	11.50	210.000
Al- Leasing	1992	10	8.25	110.000
Allied Bank Modaraba	1993	13	12.00	300.000
B. F. Modaraba	1989	10	6.60	45.696
B. R. R. Capital Modaraba	1985	10	21.00	202.818
B. R. R. Lind Modaraba	1990	10	12.00	150.000
Confidence Modaraba	1991	10	21.00	55.000
Constellation Modaraba	1991	10	6.60	64.625
Crescent Modaraba	1991	10	20.75	129.000
Custodian Modaraba	1994	10	8.50	30.000
D. G. Modaraba	1992	10	9.00	50.000
Elite Capital Modaraba	1992	10	7.75	113.400
Equity Int. Modaraba	1993	10	8.75	150.000
Equity Modaraba	1992	10	11.25	262.000
Financial Link Modaraba	1994	10	8.75	100.000
General Leasing Modaraba	1993	10	8.75	56.250
Grindlays Modaraba	1987	10	31.50	346.500
Guardian Leasing Modaraba	1994	10	10.00	100.000
Habib Bank Modaraba	1991	10	9.75	397.072
Habib Modaraba	1985	5	7.75	126.000
Do (R) AL	-	5	7.75	126.000
Hajvery Modaraba	1991	10	7.50	205.220
Ibrahim Mododaraba	1993	10	11.25	116.000
Imrooz Modaraba	1994	10	13.00	30.000
Industrial Capital	1991	10	10.00	86.250
Interfund Modaraba	1991	10	16.50	67.847
L T V Capital Modaraba	1989	5	16.25	300.000
Meharan Modaraba	1990	10	12.50	83.160

Source: *Pakistan & Gulf Economist* (September 24–30, 1994), 8.

Table 7.1 continued
Modarabas in Pakistan

Company	Year of Listing	Face Value	September 1994 Rates	Paid-up capital (Rs.mln)
Modaraba Al Mali	1987	10	14.25	142.884
Do--(R) Al	1993	10	14.00	39.690
Modaraba Al Tijarah	1991	10	17.75	66.000
National Modaraba	1989	5	4.50	52.998
Nishat Modaraba	1992	10	17.00	139.800
Pak Modaraba	1991	0	6.10	110.000
Premier Modaraba	1991	10	5.00	27.500
Professionals Modaraba	1991	10	11.30	77.674
Providence Modaraba	1991	10	6.50	63.130
Prudential Mod. 1st	1990	10	5.00	293.311
Prudential Mod. 2nd	1990	10	5.25	193.050
Prudential Mod. 3rd	1991	10	6.25	222.600
Punjab Modaraba	1993	10	17.50	270.000
Sanaullah Modaraba	1990	10	15.50	116.875
Schon Modaraba	1992	10	7.50	234.000
Tawakkal Modaraba	1990	10	6.75	258.750
Tri Star Modaraba	1990	10	11.00	96.800
Tri Star Modaraba 2nd	1993	10	13.00	110.000
Trust Modaraba	1992	10	26.50	273.000
UDL Modaraba	1991	10	21.25	188.922
Unicap Modaraba	1991	10	22.000	136.400
Unity Modaraba	1993	10	5.80	300.000

Source: *Pakistan & Gulf Economist* (September 24–30, 1994), 8.

Advisory and Investment Management Services. The modarabas often give professional analysis of noninterest bearing securities to institutional and individual investors. In addition they can provide expert financial and investment advice pertaining to Islamic modes of investment. In addition, these institutions manage investment portfolios in Halal (as approved by the Religious Board) shares and stocks, noninterest bearing securities and bonds, morabahas, musharikas, public flotation, and private placement of approved equity securities. Finally, they can act as advisers to companies in corporate or financial restructuring as well as in the preparation of resource mobilization plans.

Underwriting.   Underwriting of shares of joint stock companies.
Venture Capital.   These activities include:

1. Providing seed capital to private companies with exceptional potential for growth and capital restructuring with the ultimate aim of floating shares and securities of the company to the general public
2. Co-sponsoring the companies being floated
3. Providing funds through musharika and morabaha arrangements
4. Acting as a financial intermediary, raising venture capital and equity capital for existing and new companies.
5. Rehabilitating potentially viable, but sick or near sick, companies

Leasing.   Subject to the approval of the Registrar of Modaraba, they engage in the business of leasing for which the funds are generated through certificate flotation or musharika arrangement and other lawful resources.

Investment.   They invest in equity and noninterest bearing securities listed and traded at the various stock exchanges.

Resource Mobilization.   They mobilize substantial resources through musharika, morabaha, modaraba and other permissible Islamic modes.

In recent years modarabas have obtained around 70 percent of their revenues from leases, 16 percent from trading and other sources, 9 percent from Morabaha and Musharika, with income from equity investments comprising the rest.   On the asset side, around 51 percent has consisted of assets leased out; morabaha and musharika finance accounting for 18 percent investment in equity securities 8 percent, with cash and other assets comprising the remainder (Kazmi 1994).

LEASING

Leasing (Table 7.2) is a rapidly growing business in Pakistan, and the future for companies in this line of business looks very bright.   It provides users with capital equipment without initially owing it.   Leasing is basically a term loan or industrial credit that is structured according to the cash flow and taxation position of the borrower.   Leasing offers a range of options to an investor or equipment user and has been recognized as one of the acceptable modes of financing under the non-interest based/Islamic system of financing.

Leasing has spread gradually to a number of developing countries, following initiatives by the International Finance Corporation (IFC), the private-sector arm of the World Bank, and several major banking and leasing groups. The IFC has been instrumental in establishing leasing companies in developing countries such as Jordan, Peru, Sri Lanka, and Thailand. The IFC participated in the formation of the National Development Leasing Corporation (NDLC) in Pakistan. We also find participation in equity and transfer of knowledge in Orix Leasing Pakistan Limited and Atlas-Bot Leasing Limited. Asian Development Bank has

Table 7.2

Pakistan: Major Leasing Firms and their Investments

(Rs in million)

Company	Head Office	Branches	Lease Raised Finance	Investment
Atlas Bot Lease Co. Ltd.	Karachi	Lahore	20.000	377.540
Asian Leasing Corp. Ltd.	Lahore	Lahore	123.530	384.250
National Asset Leasing	Karachi	Karachi	21.808	72.273
National Development Leasing	Karachi Islamabad	Lahore	549.211	1197.123
Orix Leasing Pakistan Ltd.	Karachi Peshawar Sialkot Faisalabad	Lahore	178.655	817.572
Pakistan Industrial Commercial Leasing Ltd.	Karachi Lahore Islamabad Multan	Faisalabad	86.000	154.371
Pakistan Industrial Leasing Corp. Ltd.	Lahore Faisalabad Islamabad	Karachi	376.397	348.570
TOTAL			1357.601	3351.699

Statement showing fund mobilization and Investment In Lease financed by Leasing Companies for the year 1991. Source: Javeed M. Pannni, "Leasing in Pakistan, Past, Present and Future: Industry Overview" *Economic Review* 24, No. 3 (March 1993), 27.

provided a credit line of US $5 million to Pakistan Industrial and Commercial Leasing Limited. for leasing operations.

In recent years leasing has become the most popular form of financing the capital assets in Pakistan (Jabir 1990). Leasing and modaraba companies are considered to be one of the most secure forms of investment. In large part this stems from the fact that they have the capacity to absorb any amount of selling and fractional price variations. As noted above, these companies have come into existence with the introduction of Islamic banking system in the country.

Advantages

One of the major attractions is the element of tax write-offs offered by leasing. This explains its popularity in high-tax countries. But this is certainly not the only benefit that accrues from the instrument. With the growth of the projects in size and sophistication, and with the modernization of economic activities in Pakistan, it is felt that leasing rather than traditional process can easily meet the needs for plants, equipment, and machinery (Jabir 1990).

In a lease financing operation the end user or borrower, called "the lessee," does not purchase the required equipment at the outset but has the right of using it for a certain period for which payments of rentals are made to "the lessor," who remains the owner of the said equipment for the lease period. At the end of the lease period an option is provided to the lessee to purchase the equipment at its financial residual value.

In the industrialized countries, a significant volume of capital assets have been leased, thereby releasing funds that would have remained tied in the ownership of these capital assets for growth, as well as, for working capital needs. Certain advantages of leasing arrangements to the end user "the lessee" are given as follows (Economic Review 1994):

1. Leasing provides funds for 100 percent of the equipment, cost including associated costs such as import duties, and surcharges, and so forth.
2. It improves the return on equity through increased use of leverage.
3. It increases turnover/sales without committing the resources of an enterprise.
4. Leasing rentals represent a periodic expense, which may be set according to the cash flow generation by the leased equipment over the period of a leasing arrangement.
5. Leasing preserves borrowing capacity for other equipment or activities and has a positive effect on the cash flow, as the principle of leasing is "pay-as-you-earn."
6. Generally, leasing contracts provide similar financing terms as normal bank loans while the cash cost is lower.
7. A major advantage for cash flow and capital budgeting purposes is that lessee rentals may be fixed at the inception of the contract and, therefore, do not change during the lease period.
8. Leasing arrangements may be flexible. Rental payments are generally modulated according to the revenue expectations of the lessee.
9. Through leasing their assets, companies (as lessees) are permitted to charge monthly lease rentals as an allowable expense for the purposes of computing taxable profit.

For profitable companies, paying corporate tax at rates of 40 percent to 55 percent the benefit through tax relief may be considerable.

10. Companies may be eligible for tax credit in respect of plant and machinery installed under a lease arrangement approved by the Central Board of Revenue for extension programs. The amount of tax credit shall be computed on the basis of the amount expended by the lessor for the purchase of such plant and machinery.

Problems

The promoters of many leasing companies complain of the grievous lack of government support by way of incentives and concessions to facilitate mobilization of public funds. Consequently, these companies have to depend heavily on borrowing from banks and DFIs or rely on their own capital funds. Those companies that are joint ventures between large businesses and financial institutions have a definite edge over the independent leasing companies that have no bank affiliations (Jabir 1990). It has, therefore, been suggested that these companies should be allowed to raise funds by direct financing such as through term deposits and public and private placement of bonds: The modaraba companies may be allowed to issue musharika certificates to be redeemed on maturity with profit. This will enable the leasing companies and modarabas to mop up untapped savings and put them into investment channels to the benefit of the national economy.

The need for effective and efficient monitoring of these organizations by the Government to ensure proper utilization of funds can hardly be overemphasized (Jabir 1990). In this connection, the experts suggest that, like India, here also the leasing companies should be declared nonbank financial institutions and be allowed to accept term deposits up to ten times of their own funds. This is even more necessary because mobilization of funds through issuance of equity capital and through flotation of bonds and debentures is a cumbersome process and an expensive procedure.

However, it is disturbing to note that the basic purpose of some of the recently established modarabas is trading. This has given rise to the fear that these modarabas will be mainly be used to reduce the tax liability of the overall group by transferring profits from tax-paying companies of the group of the non-tax-paying modaraba (Jabir 1990). There is an urgent need to guard against such tendencies so that the government may not be deprived of its revenues. Some experts maintain that the fear is unfounded because modarabas are exempt from paying tax only if a minimum of 90 percent of the profit is distributed to the certificate holders. If a company distributes so much profit, it will impair its efforts to grow. It has been suggested that to check abuses, the government should limit the ownership of the equity by the managers to 25 percent.

The problems faced by the leasing companies are also many and varied. They merit immediate government attention if the companies are to attain a pattern of steady, profitable expansion. Today, modarabas are prevented from procuring finance on the basis of a markup. Hence, it is not possible for these companies to raise funds from the general public through issuance of term finance certificates. Modarabas are also disallowed to acquire foreign currency on the basis of interest. This constitutes a serious hurdle for the modarabas and has put them at a disadvantage as compared to the leasing companies that are obtaining foreign currency on interest basis.

At present, no lessor can import equipment for leasing on its account. This limits their ability to provide leases for imported equipment. In case a lessor has a lessee available to whom the equipment can be leased, he should be allowed to import it on his own account. Since industrial importers are importing machinery at concessional custom rate, the lessors should also be provided this facility.

COMPANIES

First Al-Noor Modaraba

First Al-Noor Modaraba (Economic Review 1993) managed by Al-Noor Modaraba Management (Pvt.) Limited was floated on 19 October 1992. The company's objective was to engage in domestic and international trading activities as a trading house under prevalent mercantile practices that are not in violation of the injunctions of Islam. The Modaraba is specifically trading in the following commodities and products:

1. Agriculture and food products
2. Chemical and petrochemical products
3. Construction materials and capital goods
4. Jute and jute products
5. Leather and leather products
6. Textile products and fiber

Capital Structure. The Authorized Capital of the company is Rs 400.00 million divided into ordinary shares of Rs 10 each, against which the paid-up capital stood at Rs 200 million. The company has made investments in various industrial sectors including banking and investment, construction, fertilizer, fiber board, insurance, sugar, and trading. The company belongs to well-known Al-Noor Industrial Group.

Resource Mobilization. The company mobilizes additional resources without the element of Riba using the modes of musharika, morabaha, modaraba (and all other permissible Islamic modes approved by the Religious Board).

Concepts of Trading Transaction. The company abides by the following trading concepts:

1. Modaraba does not enter into any transaction, business, sale or purchase dealing that violates the injunctions of Islam. In all its dealings and transactions the Modaraba observes the principles of Sharia.

2. Modaraba only transact sale of the products and commodities that it owns as principal or when acting as agent, the product/commodity is owned by its principal.
3. The products/commodities sold or purchased are in the physical or constructive possession of the seller who also bears the risk corresponding to the possession.
4. The sale price on credit is disclosed before an offer of sale.
5. The contract of sale is not contingent.
6. The delivery of goods or the payment of price is also not contingent on an event that may or may not occur in future.

LTV Modaraba

From a position of near bankruptcy in November 1992 (at the time of change in management), LTV has become one of today's leaders in the financial services sector. In August 1994, before the announcement of the results for the year ended June 30, 1994, LTV had a paid-up capital of Rs 200 million. This amounted to about 2.7 percent of the modaraba sector paid-up capital and about 8.5 per cent of the sector's market capitalization. It was not only the most traded modaraba share but it also earned the distinction of being one of the highest traded shares on the Karachi Stock Exchange.

In 1994 the company produced a return on capital to shareholders of 66.6 percent and a dividend of 50 percent. This was a record for the Modaraba sector. As part of its strategic investment policy, LTV has purchased a controlling equity investment of Rs 25.5 million in Interfund Housing Finance Limited (present paid-up capital being Rs 60.0 million). The housing finance company is a joint venture with the UDL Group, Bank of Khyber, First Interfund Modaraba, and Inter Asia Leasing Company Limited.

In the continuing quest for solving the resource mobilization problem for the modaraba sector, the management of LTV believes that it has achieved a major breakthrough in the proposed LTV redeemable certificate. The proposed instrument is an interest-free bond with warrants attached to and will be offered to the present shareholders of LTV. It meets the approval of the Corporate Law Authority and is being submitted to the Religious Board for the final approval. Not only will the instrument provide LTV with zero-interest financing, it will dramatically increase the earnings of the modaraba, which will be paid out to the redeemable certificate holders (the present shareholders of the modaraba), after they have subscribed for the LTV certificate through the warrants attached to the redeemable certificate.

In view of the excellent results for the year ended June 30, 1994, and taking into account that the certificate holders of LTV had not received any dividends for the past two years, the board of directors decided to announce a dividend of 97.4 percent of the net profit (after adjusting the accumulated losses from the previous years). As the modaraba has an ambitious business expansion plan, the dividend was in the form of a 50 percent bonus (which the modaraba will capitalize for maximum returns, to certificate holders in future years). To further meet the modaraba's growing capital requirements, the board of directors also recommended a 50 percent Right Issue at par.

In arriving at the net profit figure of Rs 133,172,626, the board of directors decided to charge only Rs 3.5 million as its management fee. If the maximum allowable rate of 10 percent had been charged, the fee would have amounted to Rs 12,424,784. In addition, the board also appropriated one million rupees for setting up a charitable technical school (ER 1994a).

In sum, the management of LTV Modaraba strongly believes that Pakistan today offers unique opportunities for entrepreneurs. The success story of LTV itself is one of the most prominent examples of effective use of entrepreneurial skills. Based on its optimism for Pakistan's future growth, LTV Modaraba has decided to set up a Strategic Investment department. The function of this department will be to identify viable projects and local entrepreneurs and to invest in projects, including venture capital projects that encourage technology transfer and international joint ventures. During 1993–94, the first project that was identified was Spell-Fujiya Limited, operating in Hattar. The Modaraba has also decided to take majority holding in a company (LTV Power Generation Limited) which will be setting up a 108 megawatt power plant in Pakistan. The power project will provide high return to the modaraba in the form of earnings and capital gains, and will also help the modaraba develop a solid asset base. The estimated equity investment of LTV will be Rs 200 million.

First Interfund

First Interfund Modaraba (FIM) is a multipurpose modaraba (P&GE 1994) listed on all three stock exchanges of Pakistan. It is a member of the Interfund Group which includes Long Term Venture Capital Modaraba, Inter Asia Leasing Company Limited, and Interfund Housing Finance Limited.

FIM was launched in May 1991 by a group of professionals dedicated to their mission of positive contribution to the economy. Initially it had a paid-up capital of Rs 35 million which was increased to Rs 60 million in 1993.

The reason for this successful track record is development of innovative services supported by extensive research. The company offers the following services:

1. Stock market investment advisory services
2. Client fund management
3. Corporate research
4. Stock market brokerage and placement of stocks, underwriting of public issue of shares and development and placement of corporate bonds

The company feels that the capital market in Pakistan is mainly confined to shares, whereas the secondary market for banks' certificates, treasury bills, and other instruments is still in a very rudimentary state. Even in the stock exchanges, major buying and selling decisions are made by the brokers who mostly depend on their hunch rather than on a detailed analysis of a company. The company feels that to gain advantage in today's market, it will have to increasingly rely on its leadership in security analysis and advisory services.

Asian Leasing Corporation

Asian Leasing Corporation Limited (ALC) is a Public Limited Company (ER 1994) formed under the Companies Ordinance 1984 with seed capital on Rs 50 million. It is a joint venture of the National Development Finance Corporation with private-sector sponsors set up to promote the concept of lease financing in Pakistan. It commenced operations in 1987.

ALC is presently providing lease financing to a wide range of industrial and commercial enterprises under full dividend financial leasing arrangements. It is geared to expeditiously service the capital investment financing needs of enterprises. ALC's main objective is to boost the national economy through provision of a wide range of sophisticated and specialized financial services to a variety of industrial and commercial enterprises for capital asset leasing.

POTENTIAL PROBLEMS

The replacement of an interest-based banking system by an alternative system that relies primarily on profit-sharing arrangements raises a number of fundamental theoretical and practical questions (Khan and Mirakhor 1990):

1.   How will an Islamic banking system function?
2.   What would be the effect of adopting such a system on the economy and, in particular, on macroeconomic variables like savings and investment?
3.   What role if any would monetary policy play in the Islamic system?

Macroeconomic Stability

Research on these types of questions is still in its very early stages (Naqvi 1994). Nevertheless, in recent years there have been a number of studies (Khan and Mirakhor 1987; Zaidi 1987; Sattar 1989; Zanganeh 1989; Anwar 1992; Zuberi 1992; Chapra 1993; Siddiqi 1994) that have attempted to conceptualize the basic ideas underlying Islamic banking as well as the likely consequences that would follow from the institution of this system. Taking the view that the reliance on profit-sharing arrangements makes the Islamic system akin to an equity-based system, relatively straightforward theoretical modes have been developed analyzing the workings of the system. In these models, depositors are treated as shareholders (as in a mutual fund or investment trust) and the banks provide no guarantee on the rate of return or the nominal volume of shares. Symmetrically, banks themselves become partners with the borrowers and accordingly share in the returns obtained from the borrowed funds.

An interesting result that emerges from such models is that the Islamic system may be better suited to adjust to shocks that can lead to banking crises than an interest-based banking system. In an equity-based system, shocks to the asset positions of banks are immediately absorbed by changes in the nominal value of shares (deposits) held by the public in banks. Therefore, the real values of assets and liabilities would be equal at all points in time. In the conventional banking system, since the nominal values of deposits are guaranteed by the bank, an adverse shock to assets of the bank can create a divergence between real assets and real liabilities—leading possibly to negative net worth for the bank—and it is not clear how the disequilibrium would be corrected and how long the process of adjustment would take.

The elimination of a risk-free asset with a positive predetermined return is expected to have significant consequences for savings, investment, financial development, and so forth, as well as for the conduct of monetary policy. For example, in the area of investment the adoption of a profit-sharing arrangement between the lender, that is the bank, and an investor may raise monitoring costs and discourage investment. To avoid this adverse effect and moral hazard issues that arise when the lender and investor have different information of the profits from this investment requires the implementation of a legal and institutional framework that facilitates appropriate contracts. The form of these contracts, and the mechanism for enforcing them, still need to be spelled out. Insofar as monetary policy is concerned, the central bank would lose the ability to direct set financial rates of return in an Islamic banking system. However, theoretical work has shown that indirect methods through control of credit extended by banks, reserve requirement changes and varying of profit sharing ratios can achieve results for monetary policy similar to those in a conventional interest-based economy.

Financial Viability

Although Islamic finance has been accepted as an alternative, independent system of banking free from Riba, it is still passing through a host of difficulties and impediments (Lawai 1994).

Financial Frauds in the Guise of Islamic Banking. During the last two decades, there have been cases of financial frauds perpetrated on the small savers under the guise of lucrative and regular financial profits using the name of Islamic techniques of financing. In Pakistan seventy and in Egypt fifty financial companies claiming Islamic business misappropriated public money and fled.

Doubts about Instruments Used in Islamic Banking. Certain instruments used by Islamic bankers are still under criticism of some Islamic jurists. In particular, doubts have been particularly raised regarding sale and purchase of currencies and murahaba and financial leases. The Federal Sharia Court of Pakistan has given a judgment that the current form of markup financing in the shape of murahaba is not in accordance with the Islamic injunctions.

Inadequate Economic, Financial and Legal Infrastructure. In most countries where Islamic banking has emerged, common areas of concern are known to exist, namely, that their economic policies are lopsided, volatile, and without a uniform regulatory framework. In addition, fiscal and financial disciplines are lacking, while their legal frameworks and taxation structures are generally ineffective and not conducive to Islamic banking.

DIFFICULTIES SPECIFIC TO PAKISTAN

These problems have to one extent or another affected the growth and development of modarabas in Pakistan. The result has been that (Kazmi 1994a):

1.   While more than fifty Modarabas have been listed on the Karachi Stock Exchange, most of them are quoted below par.
2.   While most modarabas declare stock dividends, local banks are often reluctant to extend funds to them on a musharika basis.

One explanation for these patterns is that the Modarabas are overregulated, while another focuses on the changing tax liabilities and differential controls and access to credit faced by the modarabas.

Regulation

Modaraba companies are regulated by six bodies:

1.   Registrar Modarabas
2.   Controller of Capital Issues
3.   Corporate Law Authority
4.   Monopoly Control Authority
5.   Stock Exchange
6.   The State Bank of Pakistan

In part, the large number of regulators reflects the government's concern over the increasing number of financial scandals. The scope of these regulations covers the capital structure of the modarabas, creation of reserves, and per party exposure. Some of the more salient features of these rules are (Economic Review 1995) as follows:

1.   Modarabas will maintain, both for funded and nonfunded financing in each case for the first two years of operation, a ratio of equity to liabilities not less than one to seven and thereafter the ratio may be increased for each to one to ten.
2.   Not less than 20 percent of the after-tax profit of modarabas shall be credited to a reserve fund till such time as the reserve fund equals the amount of paid-up capital of the modaraba. Thereafter, a sum of not less than 5 percent of the after-tax profit will be credited to a reserve fund.
3.   Not less than 15 percent of the modarabas' liabilities excluding paid-up capital, borrowings from financial institutions, and the lease key money will be invested in NIT units or any other investment permitted by the Religious Board.

4. Total exposure of the modaraba to a single borrower will not exceed 20 percent of the equity. In the case of listed companies, total exposure will not exceed 20 percent of the total assets of the modaraba.
5. While granting a credit facility, every modaraba will ensure that the total facilities availed by the borrower do not exceed ten times the capital and reserves (free of losses) of the borrower.
6. Every modaraba will have at least 70 percent of its assets in its principal line of business.

With regard to regulation, it is clear that certain controls are unnecessary (Kazmi 1994a):

1. Until late 1994, modarabas were not allowed to mobilize resources through offering deposits. As such, the regulatory role of the Central Bank of modarabas was unjustified.
2. State Bank monitoring is excessive. State Bank procedures require the (often understaffed) Modarabas to file over 150 returns annually.
3. Changes in regulations occur frequently and are unpredictable. The result has been to undermine the confidence of modaraba certificate holders and the general public.

Taxation Problems

Another problem faced by the modarabas is their changing tax status (Husain 1994). In the 1992 budget, the government proposed initiating a 25 percent tax on the income of the modarabas (after their first three years of tax exemption). This action created considerable uncertainty, as the modarabas were assumed to be permanently tax-free. In addition, the tax removed the obligation of payment of a 90 percent dividend to modaraba certificate holders, thus creating uncertainty over future dividends. The change in taxation not only applied tax on income but to a number of other taxes as well, including the Turn Over Tax of half a percentage and Withholding Tax of 2.5 percent.

After considerable bargaining between the Modaraba Association of Pakistan and the Ministry of Finance, the Turn over Tax was withdrawn from the modaraba sector. The Withholding Tax of 2.5 percent on transactions of the modarabas was reduced to 1 percent. Further concessions were allowed in the budget of 1993 with two years of lower taxation of 12.5 percent, after the three-year exemption, and thereafter 25 percent tax.

However, the tax problems of the modarabas have not been completely resolved. The application of Capital Value Tax on the purchase of commodities by modarabas (which were tax exempt and were therefore, unable to show an assessment of tax for the Assessment Year 1993) has badly hurt the modarabas doing leasing business. They have to pay a 5 percent Capital Value Tax on the purchase of any vehicle or machinery for leasing and are, therefore, losing business to leasing companies unaffected by this tax. The Withholding Tax of 2 percent on imports of goods and 2.5 percent on sale is also adversely affecting the trading of the modarabas.

Regulatory Discrimination

The government has imposed a condition whereby modarabas are required to retain 20 percent of their income as reserve. This directly reduces that amount disbursable to certificate holders. Numerous other regulations exist:

1. Although the modarabas can issue bonus certificates against this reserve, consistent issue of bonus shares will eventually reduce the income per certificate that they can offer.
2. Until quite recently (ER 1995), modarabas were not allowed to raise money by issuing Certificates of Investment (COIs). Instead, they were forced to increase availability of funds through issue of Right Shares. This was a very dangerous practice. On the one hand, it reduced earnings per share, and on the other, it was a direct constraint on expanding the business. Although investment banks could have a liability versus an equity ratio of ten to one, modarabas could not do so. This put them in a disadvantageous position.
3. Similarly, while leasing companies have been allowed to raise money through issues (COIs), modarabas, until very recently, were not allowed to issue COIs on musharika basis. This put the modarabas doing leasing business in a disadvantageous position—finance constraints have restricted the growth of modarabas.

Availability of Finance

As noted, the modaraba sector in general has been facing liquidity problems and operating in an environment that essentially restricted their resource mobilization capacity. This has kept the modaraba certificates grossly underpriced in spite the presence of quite a few well-managed modaraba companies (ER 1995).

1. Many companies are in the leasing business. The average lease is spread over three to five years. For their business to grow, modarabas need additional funds each year since the rentals received are not sufficient to maintain the same volume of fresh leasing every year.
2. Not so much a problem for the larger modarabas as they have started receiving funds from international agencies like IFC and others; however, a large portion of these funds is in the form of equity, not in the form of a more flexible line of credit.

Another reason for limited availability of funds with the commercial banks is the pressure on them to buy treasury bills offered by the government to meet its borrowing. In Pakistan, because of unsound planning and indiscriminate spending, the government has become the biggest borrower. It is obvious that once such large amounts are committed in these bills, the remaining amounts are not sufficient to meet the requirement of the private sector for projects that play an important part in increasing GDP and the creation of employment (ER 1995).

In addition, the government offers such excellent returns on their securities that people who want a safe, stable guaranteed return and securities of investment prefer to invest in these securities. For example, the Defense Saving Certificates alone offer a return of nearly 30 percent profit per annum. It is surprising that only the government of Pakistan offers such fantastic returns on its securities, whereas around the globe government securities carry a low return, as these are considered the most secured investment. Perhaps the only reason is that the government of Pakistan is the biggest domestic borrower, and to attract such huge amounts it has to offer high returns.

Again, it should be noted that many of these problems will be mitigated by recently allowed musharika certificates. This long-awaited decision will help the modarabas in resource mobilization, a crisis prevailing since the inception of this Islamic mode of financing in 1985.

The Corporate Authority has also agreed in principle to allow modarabas to introduce yet another financial instrument, redeemable certificates, to strengthen the financial condition of the institutions. A specific number of these certificates will be convertible to modaraba certificates at a predetermined price every year and will be transacted at the stock exchanges.

ASSESSMENT AND FUTURE PROSPECTS

Modarabas have come to fill an important niche in the country's evolving capital markets. While commercial banks provide short-term finances and non-bank financial intermediaries are involved in project financing, the Modarabas occupy an important slot for providing short- and medium-term finance (ER 1995).

The attractiveness of modarabas lies in their versatility. They can engage in leasing and contribute to capital formation directly. They can provide short-term funds for seasonal inventory and trade and thus support the marketing of commodities and exportable surpluses. Or, they can invest in the capital market and contribute to its development. Finally, modarabas can be established for the specific purpose of taking over and rehabilitating sick industries, or those being privatized. Venture capital modarabas could be the financing solution to the funding problems of many small enterprises with the potential for growth (Haq 1992).

Yet it is clear that modarabas have yet to reach their true potential in the financial intermediation market. In the more developed financial systems of the West and Southeast Asia, mutual funds are playing a far greater role in the mobilization and investment of funds for economic development than in Pakistan. On the other hand the modarabas are facing a number of serious problems:

1. In recent years, to many modarabas have been floated in too short a time. The result has been excessive competition and falling rates of profit.
2. They are controlled and regulated by too many agencies and face too many arbitrary restrictions.
3. Their basic problem is financial. Modarabas have to obtain Sharia-based finance, that is musharika based finance from institutions or morahaba-based. Normally

commercial banks are not inclined to finance the modarabas because they operate on more or less a markup basis that is interest.

4.   The same applies to international agencies like the World Bank, IFC, and the Islamic Development Bank that would normally finance and allocate lines of credit. Recently, however, these organizations are indicating a willingness to consider taking shares in the modarabas. If this trend continues, a valuable source of finance will become available to the modarabas (Zafarunnin 1995).

If we assume that changes in government policy toward the modarabas will enable them to better compete for resources and that willingness of international agencies to lend to the modarabas will increase, several developments are likely during the remainder of the 1990s (Kazmi 1994a):

1.   With increased competition, there is likely to be a series of mergers involving the smaller modarabas.
2.   With the passage of time, the international agencies will understand the working of modarabas and also develop faith in this Islamic mode of financing and will participate more readily.
3.   Allowing of COIs on the musharika basis will provide a major stimulus to the modarabas by enabling them to raise adequate funds to expand their operations.

8

Transport Policies

INTRODUCTION

In 1991 a major assessment of Pakistan's transport system concluded that the "transportation system in Pakistan is in a mess and has failed to keep pace with the demands placed upon it. Railways' performance has continuously declined and the road transportation has increased without the requisite development of highway infrastructure. Government has also entered most of the transportation fields and created inefficient and highly unprofitable organizations, like NLC, PNSC, PRTB and STC" (Amin 1991).

One striking transport pattern has been the decline of the country's rail system, with a major shift away from rail and toward road transport taking place during the last decade. The purpose of this chapter is to examine the factors contributing to the expansion of road-related transport services. Here, we are interested in determining the following: How much progress in improving road transport has been made in recent years? Is the private sector playing a larger role in providing highway transport services? Is the road transport system responding to the country's needs? Which areas will require immediate government attention to assure that highway transport bottlenecks do not suppress the country's future economic expansion? Regarding the systems present difficulties, which areas of policy reform appear essential?

HIGHWAY INFRASTRUCTURE AND VEHICLE EXPANSION

As in most countries, Pakistan's highway system has several common characteristics: strong links to economic development, high fixed costs and considerable lumpiness in investments, long economic life and large operations and maintenance costs, high level of externalities, important network effects, and interactions with other elements of infrastructure, strong traditional public-sector involvement and difficulties in recovering costs from users (Faiz 1992, 192).

Infrastructure

A look at a map of Pakistan shows that most of the country's road communications run from north to south. Of the nation's roads, the National Highway (N-5), which runs from Peshawar in the northwest via Rawalpindi, Lahore, Rohri, and Hyderbad to Karachi on the eastern part of the southern coast, is by far the most important.

The importance of the N-5 has been further elevated in recent years by the lack of investment in the country's rail network and the general increase in road-bound traffic. In 1988, the Nawaz Sharif government decided to place road building and telecommunications at the top of their priority list. A large part of this development is being undertaken with funds provided by international agencies such as the World Bank and the Asian Development Bank, as well as by contractors engaging in build-operate-transfer (BOT) projects. The project, carried out simultaneously along the whole 1,765 kilometer of the link, has been divided into roughly sixteen equal sections. The sheer volume of work involved has made it one of the largest road-building projects in the world (CP 1995).

The road system itself (Table 8.1) of some 188,000 kilometers translates into a spatial density of 23 kilometers per 100 square kilometers. This is low by South Asian standards but is similar to other low- and middle-income countries. Several patterns stand out (Table 8.2):

1. For the period as a whole (1955–56 to 1992–93) the country's roads expanded in length at an average rate of increase of 3.0 percent per annum.
2. However, growth of the system has accelerated with time from an average annual rate of increase in 1955–56 to 1965–66 of 1.7 percent to 1.9 percent during 1966–67 to 1976–77 to 5.2 percent for the 1977–78 to 1987–88 period and finally 5.6 percent for the 1988–89 to 1992–93 period.
3. Paved, high type, roads have grown much more rapidly than low, unpaved roads. Over the entire period examined, 1955–56 to 1992–93, paved roads expanded at an average annual rate of 5.1 percent versus 1.8 percent for unpaved roads. Consequently, the ratio of high to low type roads increased (Table 8.1) from 0.318 in 1955–56 to 1.034 in 1992–93.
4. Despite their apparent decline in importance unpaved roads have increased relatively rapidly in recent years, averaging 1.1 percent per annum during the 1955–56 to 1965–66 period. From this rate the growth in unpaved roads declined to 1.0 percent during the 1966–67 to 1976–77 period, only to increase to 3.5 and 4.7 during the 1977–78 to 1987–88 and 1988–89 to 1992–93 periods, respectively.

By international standards (Table 8.3) Pakistan's roads expanded at rates considerably below the developing country norm (3.92 versus 7.41 and 4.38 versus 8.11) during the 1960s and 1970s. During the 1980s the country's paved

Table 8.1
Expansion of the Transport Sector

Year	Total Roads	High Type	Low Type	Ratio	Road Vehic
1955–56	62,244	15,048	47,196	0.318	75
1956–57	62,667	15,442	47,225	0.327	78
1957–58	62,805	15,737	47,068	0.334	86
1958–59	62,242	16,216	46,026	0.352	93
1959–60	63,493	16,489	47,004	0.351	102
1960–61	66,236	16,860	49,376	0.341	117
1961–62	68,082	17,462	50,620	0.345	137
1962–63	69,028	18,340	50,688	0.362	154
1963–64	70,631	18,933	51,698	0.366	177
1964–65	71,239	20,220	51,019	0.396	201
1965–66	73,788	20,983	52,805	0.397	236
1966–67	70,007	22,063	47,944	0.460	233
1967–68	72,463	23,095	49,368	0.468	248
1968–69	71,428	23,799	47,629	0.500	282
1969–70	72,153	24,253	47,900	0.506	302
1970–71	73,006	24,776	48,230	0.513	364
1971–72	74,187	25,418	48,769	0.521	403
1972–73	76,029	28,927	50,102	0.577	426
1973–74	76,660	26,641	50,019	0.533	458
1974–75	78,630	28,222	50,408	0.560	511
1975–76	80,623	29,603	51,020	0.580	585
1976–77	84,589	31,769	52,820	0.601	675
1977–78	85,757	33,159	52,598	0.630	743
1978–79	87,715	34,804	52,911	0.657	876
1979–80	94,173	35,890	58,283	0.616	1,016
1980–81	93,960	38,035	55,925	0.680	1,110
1981–82	96,859	40,380	56,479	0.715	1,190

Source: *Economic Survey, 1993–94* (Islamabad: Government of Pakistan, 1994), p.85.
Note: Roads are in kilometers; vehicles are in thousands.

Table 8.1 continued
Expansion of the Transport Sector

Year	Total Roads	High Type	Low Type	Ratio	Road Vehic
1982–83	99,793	42,773	57,020	0.750	1,330
1983–84	111,916	48,325	63,591	0.760	1,484
1984–85	118,471	52,120	66,351	0.786	1,659
1985–86	126,243	56,318	69,925	0.805	1,841
1986–87	133,953	61,464	72,489	0.848	2,017
1987–88	142,941	68,880	74,061	0.930	2,201
1988–89	151,449	74,335	77,094	0.964	2,370
1989–90	162,345	81,891	80,364	1.019	2,538
1990–91	170,823	86,839	83,984	1.034	2,713
1991–92	179,364	91,181	88,183	1.034	2,924
1992–93	188,332	95,740	92,592	1.034	3,150

Source: *Economic Survey, 1993-94* (Islamabad: Government of Pakistan, 1994), p.85.
Note: Roads are in kilometers; vehicles are in thousands.

road system expanded at an average annual rate considerably above (8.61 versus 2.99 percent) that of other low income countries.

Vehicle Fleet

As noted above, road vehicles have expanded much more rapidly than the country's highway infrastructure:

1. In contrast to the expansion in highway infrastructure, the numbers of road vehicles increased at an average annual rate of 10.6 percent per annum over the 1955–56 to 1992–93 period (Table 8.2).
2. Again, in contrast to the growth of the road network, the expansion in highway vehicles (Table 8.2) has remained relatively high during each period (around 11–12 percent), only to decline somewhat (7.4 percent) during the most recent (1988–89 to 1992–93) period.
3. Among registered vehicles (Table 8.4), the number of motor cars grew at around 8.5 percent per annum, while taxis expanded at 9.2 percent.
4. Interestingly, both buses and trucks increased as a slower pace with buses increasing at 8.1 percent during the 1954–71 period and 6.3 percent during the 1972–93 interval. The corresponding rates for trucks were 7.6 and 4.3 percent.
5. Similar patterns characterize the numbers of vehicles actually on the country's roads (Table 8.5).

Table 8.2
Growth of the Transport Sector

Year	Total Roads	High Type	Low Type	Ratio	Road Vehic
1955–56/ 1965–66	1.7	3.4	1.1	2.2	12.1
1966–67/ 1976–77	1.9	3.7	1.0	2.7	11.2
1977–78/ 1987–88	5.2	7.6	3.5	4.0	11.5
1988–89/ 1992–93	5.6	6.5	4.7	1.8	7.4
1955–56/ 1973–74	1.2	3.2	0.3	2.9	10.6
1974–75/ 1992–93	5.0	6.1	3.4	3.5	10.6
1955–56/ 1992–93	3.0	5.1	1.8	3.2	10.6

Source: Based on Table 8.1.

Table 8. 3
Paved Road Expansion in the Developing World, 1960–90

COUNTRY	Growth in Paved Roads		
	1960–70	1970–80	1980–90
Sample Country Mean	7.41	8.11	2.99
Pakistan	3.92	4.38	8.61
Mozambique	.	6.02	2.52
Ethiopia	.	19.32	1.55
Tanzania	.	.19	.38
Sierra Leone	9.94	1.51	2.32
Nepal	8.70	4.01	3.21
Uganda	6.34	5.73	-4.60
Burundi	.	16.39	10.73
Malawi	4.46	9.77	1.99
Bangladesh	.	1.72	4.45
Chad	.	-22.18	3.42
Madagascar	.	11.29	.37
Rwanda	6.14	17.91	5.92
Niger	.	18.58	4.12
Upper Volta	.	.58	6.67
India	2.47	6.75	1.99
Kenya	.	8.02	2.19
Mali	.	1.18	12.75
Nigeria	.	7.03	.33
Nicaragua	7.13	2.70	.
Togo	.	11.11	2.16
Benin	.	.	1.51
CAR	.	20.60	1.72
Ghana	.	5.71	.25
Guinea	.	21.66	1.98
Mauritania	.	61.94	.73
Zimbabwe	:	3.36	.90
Lesotho	.	.	2.40
Honduras	22.60	7.48	3.29

Source: Computed from data in: *World Development Report 1994* (New York: Oxford University Press, 1994).

Table 8.3 continued
Paved Road Expansion in the Developing World, 1960–90

COUNTRY	Growth in Paved Roads		
	1960–70	1970–80	1980–90
Egypt	.	2.32	1.44
Indonesia	6.74	10.37	7.50
Somalia	.	17.89	3.03
Sudan	.	24.52	1.40
Yemen	.	10.05	5.44
Zambia	.	6.84	1.06
Ivory Coast	4.26	9.29	3.27
Bolivia	5.23	3.92	2.43
Philippines	9.34	5.94	-2.15
Senegal	.	5.09	1.50
Cameroon	.	10.36	3.71
Papua New Guinea	.	14.65	.
Peru	1.92	2.64	1.76
Guatemala	6.20	2.02	2.03
Congo	.	4.03	5.79
Morocco	1.79	1.88	1.40
Dominican Republic	1.97	10.59	.
Ecuador	15.00	3.96	3.95
Jordan	4.98	5.02	3.70
El Salvador	2.07	2.77	.91
Colombia	7.15	7.20	-1.47
Jamaica	.03	.	.
Paraguay	12.38	6.40	7.05
Tunisia	2.90	3.03	3.61
Algeria	.	1.68	1.28
Thailand	13.42	9.35	5.39
Costa Rica	.	5.64	8.73
Turkey	.	6.50	2.48
Iran	16.32	12.41	.
Panama	9.78	3.35	1.04
Chile	11.03	2.86	1.12
Syria	10.60	4.85	6.37

Source: Computed from data in: *World Development Report 1994* (New York: Oxford University Press, 1994).

Table 8.4
Expansion of the Registered Vehicle Fleet

(average annual rates of growth)

Years	Motor Cars	Cabs Taxis	Buses	Trucks	Motor Cycle 2 Wheels	Motor Cycle 3 Wheels	Other	Total
1954 - 1964	9.5	13.0	7.3	8.2	16.6	25.8	27.3	11.4
1965 1975	6.7	8.2	10.1	6.3	13.3	6.5	18.2	9.5
1976- 1986	8.6	3.3	6.2	2.7	14.0	4.9	19.6	11.6
1987- 1993	7.3	13.4	3.5	3.6	6.3	2.7	4.6	6.1
1954- 1971	9.0	11.6	8.1	7.6	16.1	17.9	22.7	11.0
1972 1993	8.5	7.5	6.3	4.3	12.3	4.9	16.4	10.3
1954 1993	8.5	9.2	7.2	5.7	13.9	10.4	19.0	10.5

Source: Computed from: GOP, *Economic Survey 1993–94* (Islamabad: Government of Pakistan, 1994), 88.

Table 8.5
Motor Vehicles on Road in Pakistan

Year	Motor Cycle Scooter	Motor Car	Jeep	Station Wagon	Tractor	Bus
1967	41,777	42,264	6,359	4,318	1,872	7,974
1970	64,065	57,234	8,613	5,846	3,844	9,592
1971	73,946	59,200	8,908	6,047	5,495	10,312
1972	82,131	63,857	9,609	6,524	7,619	11,594
1973	95,359	66,975	10,078	6,844	9,020	13,482
1974	99,070	55,934	8,257	5,612	9,324	14,377
1975	112,975	62,172	9,978	5,964	12,638	15,372
1976	135,105	70,061	11,608	6,777	21,589	18,080
1977	166,765	81,565	13,427	7,764	29,955	18,900
1978	206,431	95,632	15,669	9,034	38,204	20,151
1979	241,944	109,382	17,834	11,171	45,558	21,822
1980	287,622	148,334	16,875	15,413	68,187	25,275
1981	326,420	154,241	16,680	15,839	79,407	26,881
1982	376,071	182,863	14,108	21,736	88,199	25,620
1983	424,215	201,994	15,399	25,671	106,479	27,361
1984	517,448	230,765	17,196	32,501	135,712	30,955
1985	581,255	268,934	19,755	39,129	157,043	32,947
1986	657,569	297,958	20,730	46,536	181,102	34,637
1987	700,004	323,062	23,139	52,083	198,891	36,117
1988	751,970	350,217	25,939	59,236	217,646	38,641
1989	818,398	395,672	28,226	64,172	242,493	40,814
1990	896,179	427,726	30,840	69,290	258,169	43,275
1991	964,408	452,953	33,430	74,984	269,516	45,637
1992	1,060,555	500,606	36,559	85,649	301,557	48,521
1993	1,166,491	554,907	40,009	98,053	337,445	51,651
Rates of Growth						
1967–1977	14.8	6.8	7.8	6.0	32.0	9.0
1978–1988	13.8	13.9	5.2	20.7	19.0	6.7
1988–1993	9.2	9.6	9.1	10.6	9.2	6.0
1967–1993	13.7	10.4	7.3	12.8	22.1	7.5

Source: GOP, *Economic Survey 1993–94* (Islamabad: Government of Pakistan, 1994), 89.

Table 8.5 continued
Motor Vehicles on Road in Pakistan

Year	Motor Cab Taxi	Motor Cab Rikshaw	Delivery Van	Truck	Other	Total Vehicles
1967	5,690	10,707	1,070	19,616	1,046	142,693
1970	6,264	11,747	1,163	21,331	2,152	191,851
1971	6,871	12,891	1,240	22,741	3,079	210,730
1972	7,744	14,535	1,297	23,773	4,265	232,948
1973	8,544	16,045	1,163	21,323	5,049	253,882
1974	7,777	14,557	1,054	18,920	4,072	238,954
1975	8,564	16,195	1,433	21,087	4,227	270,605
1976	10,995	18,619	1,769	23,794	5,466	323,863
1977	11,696	19,968	2,635	25,745	6,738	385,158
1978	12,587	22,857	3,704	28,486	8,261	461,016
1979	14,115	26,403	5,299	31,220	9,845	534,593
1980	16,854	31,950	8,503	34,193	28,853	682,059
1981	17,720	33,707	9,956	36,842	38,005	755,698
1982	15,524	34,551	11,941	40,058	31,933	842,604
1983	16,661	36,228	13,259	42,761	33,874	943,902
1984	19,023	37,211	30,439	49,165	37,791	1,138,206
1985	21,177	37,723	35,106	54,428	40,537	1,288,034
1986	22,228	38,384	38,294	60,354	43,023	1,440,815
1987	23,446	38,818	41,661	66,120	44,974	1,548,315
1988	24,870	39,366	46,161	71,660	48,096	1,673,802
1989	28,382	40,206	52,892	78,413	49,836	1,839,504
1990	30,873	41,282	57,563	82,678	51,516	1,989,391
1991	33,492	42,310	60,944	86,872	52,256	2,116,802
1992	36,199	43,181	74,253	96,928	55,638	2,339,646
1993	39,131	44,071	91,015	109,357	59,541	2,591,671
Rates of Growth						
1967-1977	7.5	6.4	9.4	2.8	20.5	10.4
1978-1988	7.0	5.6	28.7	9.7	19.3	13.8
1988-1993	9.5	2.3	14.5	8.8	4.4	9.1
1967-1993	7.7	5.6	18.6	6.8	16.8	11.8

Source: GOP, *Economic Survey 1993–94* (Islamabad: Government of Pakistan, 1994), 89.

International Comparisons

As for population served, a service ratio of 1.2 kilometers per 1,000 population is about half that of India and Kenya, but is of the same magnitude as Indonesia, Republic of Korea, and Thailand. Over half the road network is paved, a proportion similar to other South Asian countries, but significantly below middle- and high-income Asian countries. A broad indicator of the economic burden of road provision and maintenance is the ratio of the length of a country's road network to its gross national product. As expected, this ratio is significantly higher for low-income countries, although the ratio for Pakistan is only half of India's (Table 8.6).

What sets Pakistan's road network apart is its poor condition. Considering the main paved roads, four out of every five kilometers are considered in fair to poor condition. The unpaved roads are in worse shape with only one kilometer out of twenty rated in good condition (Table 8.7). If road conditions are compared with motorization levels and road accidents (Table 8.8), it would be no exaggeration to state that as to condition and performance, Pakistan has one of the poorest road systems in the world. The road infrastructure consists of aging and obsolete roads that have neither the geometric capacity nor the structural strength to carry the increasing traffic and vehicle loads. Poor quality of construction and outmoded maintenance methods have not helped the situation.

A program of road improvement and modernization is urgently needed. It has been estimated (Faiz 1992, 193) that just to bring the condition of the road system at par with Kenya and Indonesia (with no expansion of the road system and keeping the percentage of paved roads at its present level) would require an expenditure of $300 to $400 million. Upgrading the road system to the quality and conditions observed in middle-level countries such as Malaysia and Thailand would require an expenditure of more than $3.5 billion.

FREIGHT TRANSPORTATION

Most authorities on the Pakistani transportation system (Beg 1995) concede that the country's planners should have opted for the minimum use of financial and energy resources in designing the country's transport problems. It follows that the country should not have promoted the road transportation system. Railways have proved the most economical mode for mass transportation of passenger, goods, and raw materials and should have received a far greater share of capital resources (Beg 1995). However, here also the road transportation lobby prevailed in the same manner as General Motors did in the United States (Beg 1995a).

Table 8.6
Road Network: Length and Density, Mid-1980s

Countries	Area	Length	Percent Paved	Density in kilometer per		
				100 sq. kms.	1,000 Population	$1 million GDP
Low Income						
Pakistan	796	122.8	44	15.4	1.2	3.30
Bangladesh	144	34.5	41	24.0	0.3	1.86
Nepal	141	7.3	35	5.2	0.4	2.24
India	3,288	1,772.0	47	53.9	2.2	6.39
Sri Lanka	66	77.7	36	117.8	4.7	11.15
China	9,561	982.0	18	10.3	0.9	2.73
Indonesia	1,905	219.0	62	11.5	1.3	2.85
Nigeria	924	108.0	20	11.7	1.0	3.38
Kenya	580	53.8	12	9.3	2.4	6.49
Middle and high income						
Thailand	513	167.4	21	32.6	3.1	3.07
Malaysia	330	42.3	66	12.8	2.5	1.29
Korea	99	55.8	61	56.3	1.3	0.37
Japan	378	1104.3	67	292.1	9.0	0.43

Source: C. Harral and A. Faiz, "Road Deterioration in Developing Countries: Causes and Remedies," *A World Bank Policy Study* (Washington, D.C.: The World Bank, 1988).

Notes: Area = thousand square kms.; Length = thousand kms.

Table 8.7
Road Network: Condition, Mid-1980s

Countries	Condition of Main Network (percentage)					
	Paved			Unpaved		
	Good	Fair	Poor	Good	Fair	Poor
Low Income						
Pakistan	18.0	50.0	32.0	5.0	25.0	70.0
Bangladesh	15.0	40.0	45.0	10.0	40.0	50.0
Nepal	40.0	35.0	25.0	15.0	45.0	40.0
India	20.0	45.0	35.0	20.0	40.0	40.0
Sri Lanka	10.0	40.0	50.0	NA	NA	NA
China	10.0	70.0	20.0	50.0	25.0	25.0
Indonesia	30.0	30.0	40.0	22.0	47.0	31.0
Nigeria	62.0	15.0	23.0	0.0	10.0	90.0
Kenya	32.0	52.0	16.0	66.0	17.0	17.0
Middle and High Income						
Thailand	50.0	30.0	20.0	45.0	30.0	25.0
Malaysia	52.0	36.0	12.0	NA	NA	NA
Korea	70.0	25.0	5.0	60.0	20.0	20.0
Japan	90.0	10.0	0.0	NA	NA	NA

Source: C. Harral and A. Faiz, "Road Deterioration in Developing Countries: Causes and Remedies," *A World Bank Policy Study* (Washington, D.C.: The World Bank, 1988).

Table 8.8
Motorization and Road Accidents, 1988

Countries	Motor Vehicles (000)			Vehicles per Population (000)		Road Acidents	
	Cars	Trucks/ Buses	2 & 3 Wheelers	Cars	All Vehicles	Number	Fatalities
Low-Income							
Pakistan	504	151	636	4.7	12.1	11,819	5,281
Bangladesh	60	58	201	0.5	2.9	3,510	1,431
Nepal	12	7	14	0.7	1.9	NA	NA
India	1,730	1,599	7,658	2.1	13.5	NA	NA
Sri Lanka	150	130	226	9.0	30.5	33,028	NA
China	900	3,425	3,023	0.8	6.8	NA	NA
Indonesia	965	1,041	5,898	5.5	45.2	38,027	9,714
Nigeria	773	606	371	7.0	15.9	25,792	9,077
Kenya	128	143	22	5.7	13.1	9,783	1,889
Middle and High Income							
Thailand	816	1,407	2,770	15.0	91.6	35,289	2,015
Malaysia	1,333	374	2,461	78.9	246.6	73,250	3,335
Korea	1,118	917	1,067	26.6	73.9	225,062	11,563
Japan							

Source: Asif Faiz, "Financing Infrastructure Development," in Anjum Nasim ed., *Financing Pakistan's Development in the 1990s* (Karachi: Oxford University Press, 1992), 195.

Shift from Rail to Road

Modal split (distribution of the load between rail and road) plays a vital role in optimal utilization of transportation resources and reduction in overall transportation cost. According to one major study (Ali 1994) the economic breakdown even distance has been calculated at 489 kilometer. This implies that rail is economically preferable for transporting goods more than 489 kilometer and road transport is economically desirable for shorter distances. Based on this study, the modal split between road and railways in goods transport in year 2005–6 is forecast to be (Table 8.9):

Table 8.9
Pakistan: Projected Composition
of Freight by Mode of Transport, 2005–06

Commodity	% Railway	% Road	Total
Wheat	38.3	61.7	100.0
Rice	44.7	55.3	100.0
Cotton	45.9	54.1	100.0
Edible Oil	49.0	51.0	100.0
Sugar	38.4	61 .6	100.0
Cement	36.6	63.4	100.0
Fertilizer	27.1	72.9	100.0
Iron & Steel	51.6	48.4	100.0
Mining Product	6.9	93.1	100.0
Coal & Coke	54.9	45.1	100.0
Petroleum	59.1	40.9	100.0
Firewood	19.8	80.2	100.0
Sugar Cane	0.0	100.0	100.0
Fruits & Vegetable	0.0	100.0	100.0
Livestock	0.0	100.0	100.0
Rock Phosphate	100.0	0.0	100.0
Others	31.0	69.0	100.0
Total	34.3	65.7	100.0

Source: Beg 1994

NATIONAL LOGISTIC CELL

In addition several crises have played a major role in shifting the composition of freight transport from rail to roads. For example, the National Logistic Cell (NLC) was created in 1978 to meet the crises of rapid transportation of wheat and fertilizers to meet the challenges posed by the famine that year. The army first used its own resources to launch the scheme and transport massive quantities of wheat and fertilizers, namely, 2.0 million tons each. Its initial choice of Mercedes Trailers has carried onto the present. Presently it has 1,573 dry cargo carriers, more than 30 percent of which are still Mercedes vehicles, besides 371 liquid carriers. In 1992–93 they carried 1.176 million tons of dry cargo and liquid cargo at the rate of 36,838 barrels per day (Beg 1995).

The NLC has a share of only 10 percent in total freight haulage, but it is the one coordinating the mass movement of fright. NLC has more than 1500 dry cargo vehicles with a total lift capacity of 48,175 tons. Of these, over 700 are forty-foot flat-bed semi-trailers, fitted with twist locks, including midposition locks, for the safe carriage of 20/40-foot containers. The rest of the NLC fleet is also convertible for container carriage. Thus NLC can lift at one time up to 3000 containers, if needed. With this enormous potential, NLC can guarantee transportation services to the shipping lines, with joint fore planning and mutual coordination between the two (Ali 1994).

Staging Sections. NLC has a chain of staging sections suitably located all along the National Highway/Grand Trunk Road. These provide full security, monitoring, repair, and recovery to the vehicles moving in their respective areas of responsibilities. These staging sections have good communications and clients can be advised of any problems concerning their consignments (Ali 1994).

Dry Port Detachments. NLC has a small detachment on every port that besides providing transport to the business community resolves all issues related to movement of goods by road (Ali 1994).

Sialkot Dry Port Trust. This organization has about five forty-foot semi-trailers of their own with another 90 registered from the local market (Ali 1994).

Faisalabad Dry Port Trust. This recently established dry port does not possess any load carrier. Its transportation needs are being met by NLC (Ali 1994).

Problems With the Existing System

The wastage of energy during the last twenty-four years by encouraging road transport at the expense of railways and setting up the NLC has received wide publicity. The NLC did yeoman service in 1977–78 when both the railways and Karachi Port failed miserably in clearance of imports, but it should have been wound up when the crisis was over (Kalam 1991).

Energy Wastage. It is hardly necessary to elaborate that a 3000 horsepower (HP) Locomotive costing Rs 30 million can move 2000 tons of freight on rails, while a 300 HP truck costing Rs 3 million can move only 20 tons on the road, that is a ten to one cost-effectiveness ratio. Yet successive governments have brushed aside this simple arithmetic because their planning has been based not on improvement of technology but on accommodation of vested interests. The consequent wastage of energy in the form of oil has naturally restricted its availability for power generation that in turn could have been made available for industrial development (Kalam 1991).

Revenue Loss. The same NLC that depends for its efficiency on exemption from payment of all import duties and government taxes—to say nothing of freedom from police extortion—but is nevertheless wasteful of energy has also ruined the country's road network that was never intended to carry such heavy axle loads; there would, in fact, have been no need at all for such heavy road vehicles if the railways had continued to carry all heavy freight (Kalam 1991).

Deterioration of Highway Infrastructure. The NLC has also forced competing private road haulers to switch to higher axle-load vehicles thus inducing further stresses on the already-collapsing road network and reducing the number of light trucks that would be the most economical for light industries in rural areas. The Production Ministry and the NLC being under single control from 1977 to 1984 resulted in the unwise decision to abandon production of the Bedford truck, components of which—even cylinder heads and blocks—were being extensively manufactured then and set back indigenous Diesel engine manufacture by at least twenty years (Kalam 1991).

The massive loads carried by the trucks were beyond the load-bearing capacity of the roads and the latter have had to succumb to their weight. Complicating this is the financial position of the government. Recent austerity measures have drastically reduced the amount of funding available for highway maintenance and repair. Similar is the case with the upgrading of the roads, and this is why the roads once degraded by the slightest drizzle are seldom repaired in time. The roads are thus left in their dilapidated condition for a long time. This applies equally to the National Highway-5 or the Karakorum Highway (Beg 1995).

In fairness however, oversized trucks are not the sole factor responsible for the country's substandard road system. Poor construction has also played a major role. The roads are poorly lighted. The absence of road signs, protective railings, and the failure of traffic police to check speeding, often results in fatal accidents. It is a common observation that while the number of vehicles using the highways has increased manifold, there has been no corresponding expansion in the number of lanes (Kazmi 1994b).

The apparent reason for such badly built roads is that the contractors use sub-standard material. No efforts are made to estimate traffic flow and load-bearing capacity, and the proper mix is not used. Water-logging is a major source of road damage. Since most of the time water courses are alongside the roads, constant seepage and overflow accelerate the erosion process. As no proper soil sampling is done at the time of road building, the roads are often completely washed away even during mild monsoons. Also because fields are often higher than the roads they border, water often simply stagnates on the road, speeding up the deterioration process (Kazmi 1994b).

Another problem is the absence of by-passes. As a result, the traffic often has to pass through the smaller towns. Here, bazaars have developed alongside the roads, resulting in the elimination of any possibility of road expansion. During peak hours or breakdown of a vehicle there are frequent and prolonged traffic jams (Kazmi 1994b).

A very serious situation demanding attention is the presence of narrow, old, and weak bridges on these expressways. If these bridges collapse, many cities can lose their road links with the rest of the country. At the time these bridges were built, traffic was relatively sparse. However, first with the establishment of the NLC fleet and later with long chassis loading trucks becoming common, these bridges are being destroyed since they were not designed to handle such heavy vehicles (Kazmi 1994b).

Construction of bridges is one area that has been responsible for delay in construction of expressways or even expansion of existing budges. Since the contractors are forced to build conventional bridges, because of limited availability of financial resources and technology, it takes years to build a bridge. While hanging bridges have become a common feature globally, Pakistan has not been able to use this technology (Kazmi 1994b).

One reason the Pakistani government should give immediate attention to road construction is that with the creation of the new Russian Confederation, the volume of transit trade will likely increase dramatically (Kazmi 1994b). In a related way, increased trade with the Economic Cooperation Organization (ECO) should also contribute to freight traffic (Beg 1994a).

Non-Economic Modes of Transport. In addition, in those few transport sectors where road traffic should be encouraged, for example between Rawalpindi and Gilgit, the Transport and Communications section of the Planning Commission has been encouraging of all things air travel that is generously subsidized but adds unnecessarily to Pakistan International Airlines (PIA) expenditure. Except in emergencies there is no need for air travel on this route; tourists can well afford to pay very much higher fares. If air traffic were not subsidized, the infrastructure in this area would develop because of vastly increased road traffic and this, in turn, would encourage more rapid small-scale industrial development.

One difficulty faced by the freight haulage is that the bulk carriers are assured of their services from Karachi but not from the northern areas. Trade and traffic to the area must be diversified, and other markets such as those in the Central Asian countries should be explored. The Karakorum Highway (KKH) built for political reasons and sought by China as an alternative to the earlier Silk Route should now be utilized in full. The recent agreements among the authorities from China, Kazakhstan, Kyrgystan, and Pakistan has made this route an important linkage between the four countries and are a step in this direction.

Transport Reform—Freight

Because of these problems, many Pakistani analysts (Amin 1991) are quite critical of the public sector's role in freight transport, arguing that the government should leave it entirely to the private sector and dispose of the present government-owned companies. Here the main argument is that the NLC deprives the government of import duties, income tax, registration, and tolls and should be privatized as it is providing an unfair competition to the transporters. Road transport should be entirely in the private sector (Amin 1991).

The present highway network requires an infusion of resources that unfortunately are beyond the government's means at the present time. The principle of investment in infrastructure is that the user who benefits from it should pay for it. Fuel consumed by the road users should be taxed, and its revenue utilized for development of roads. Also the roads are damaged by heavy trucks that should be taxed according to their capacity to damage the road. In case of the United States there is a Federal Highways Trust Fund financed by a fuel levy and tax on heavy vehicles and tires. Pakistan had a similar tax that was unfortunately discontinued in 1973 (Amin 1991).

To implement the development of national highways, a National Highways Authority is being created. This authority should be completely autonomous and should be allowed to generate its own resources by floating bonds and taking loans for the construction of toll roads. In addition, the National Highways Authority should be provided funds based on fuel consumed on highways as roads are currently being used without any fee. A fuel tax comparable to that found in other countries with a similar level of income would no doubt go a long way in providing adequate funds for road maintenance and expansion.

ASSESSMENT

Although Pakistan's basic transport network is in place and the road transport industry is competitive, transport costs are high. Clearly, there is need for rehabilitating highway infrastructure, for improvement in operational efficiency and for the adoption of new transport technology. The poor state of the overall transportation system results in part from the cumulative effects of inadequate past maintenance and upgrading. This, together with the expectation that transport demand will more than double by 2005, presents transport policy makers with the challenge of how best to ensure that, within the limited amount of resources available, the capacity and quality of Pakistan's transport system is expanded to meet the growing needs of Pakistan's economy (IBRD 1992, 47–48).

Most of Pakistan's trade logistics system (storage, handling, freight forwarding, transport and assorted information, and financial activities) is the responsibility of the private sector. Those regulations and public-sector practices that constrain growth and development of the private sector, therefore, need to be eliminated. Following World Bank recommendations, these include (IBRD 1992, 48) the following:

1. Modifying automotive industry policies to permit truck and bus operators to have access to a wide range of modern vehicles.
2. Loosening the regulation of bus fares to permit quick and adequate adjustment to cost increases. Inadequate fare increases have been the primary cause of inadequate growth of bus operations in urban and intercity services.
3. Curtailing the government's cost plus practices of paying for the costs of storage, handling, and transport of strategic commodities such as foodgrains, fertilizers, and

petroleum products. Such practices have been a disincentive for encouraging logistical efficiency or investment in modern systems.

4. Simplifying trade facilitation procedures, which have impeded Pakistan's international trade.

Public-sector involvement in transport goes beyond the provision of highway, port and aviation infrastructure and includes railways, airline, bus, and shipping operations. Greater autonomy and accountability is needed in most areas to improve institutional and financial performance. Loss-making government bus and shipping operations should be curtailed since equivalent services are being provided by other operators at no burden to the government's budget. Private-sector participation needs to be encouraged in railway, port, and aviation development both to reduce the requirement for public-sector funds and to introduce innovative approaches into these activities. The scope for participation is more limited in the highway sector (IBRD 1992, 48).

Professionally capable institutions are needed to manage Pakistan's rapidly growing highway program and to carry out modern cost-effective maintenance planning, supervision, and execution methods. Moreover, rapidly growing traffic levels have made existing efforts to rehabilitate and utilize existing roads insufficient to improve the quality of intercity roads on Pakistan's major transport corridor linking Karachi, Lahore, Rawalpindi, and Peshawar. Ribbon development and uncontrolled access greatly reduce the capacity of existing roads (IBRD 1992, 48).

A phased program to modernize the intercity highway network needs careful consideration. The government is proposing a Rs 66 billion program for this purpose. Financing and cost recovery will, however, be critical constraints to such a program that also would call into serious question Pakistan's overall developmental priorities and macroeconomic framework. Proper construction and maintenance will require greatly increased capability of highway institutions, and also a major upgrading of contractors, who have to date had great difficulty in performing adequately on existing roads.

Tolls revenues can provide a partial source of financing for modern intercity roads, but totally privately funded BOT schemes are unlikely to prove viable except in a few cases of urban expressways. Budgetary requirements for road programs will inevitably increase, and the federal and provincial governments will need to take full advantage of the scope for raising additional resources from major increases in diesel fuel taxes and annual license fees on vehicles (IBRD 1992, 48–49).

Part III

POLICY ISSUES

9

Policy Options to 2000

INTRODUCTION

Toward the end of 1988, Pakistan's deteriorating resource situation caused a financial crisis, many remnants of which still exist today. In 1988 the government's budget deficit reached 8.5 percent of the gross domestic product (GDP), inflation accelerated, the current account deficit doubled to 4.3 percent of Gross National Product (GNP), the external debt service ratio reached 28 percent of export earnings, and foreign exchange reserves fell by half to $438 million, equal to less than three weeks of imports (IBRD 1991, ii).

These developments have eroded the ability of the government to affect the country's development process. In fact, the encouragement of private-sector activity, particularly investment, is the only viable option open to the authorities. It follows that for policy purposes the most important issue involves restructuring government expenditures and their financing in a manner that would provide the maximum inducement to private-sector capital formation, especially in manufacturing. Operationally, this means finding an optimal balance between the government's three most important budgetary items: defense, public consumption, and infrastructural development. What is more important, because there is abundant evidence (Kemal 1989); (Burney and Yasmeen 1989); (Khan and Iqbal 1991) that the government's deficits have crowded out a certain amount of private investment, the authorities must achieve this balance within the context of a reduced level of expenditures and/or tax increases.

Defense expenditures are an obvious candidate for expenditure reductions. As noted in the next section, the country's defense burden is one of the heaviest in the world. At round 7 percent of the GNP, it is more than twice that of India. Moreover, during most of the 1980s worldwide defense expenditures contracted while Pakistan's expanded. This trend occurred even after the hostilities in Afghanistan had subsided.

While the defense expenditure to GNP ratio has remained about the same, debt servicing has overtaken this category as the single largest item of government spending. In 1971 this item was 3 percent of GNP; by 1993–94 it had risen to 8.2 percent. During fiscal 1994–95, debt servicing will account for 8.2 percent or 35 percent of total budget spending (Blum 1994, 2), compared with 26.4 percent for defense (Rashid 1994). Apparently, the government recognizes the burden that defense expenditures have placed on the economy. For the 1994–95 budget, defense expenditure will increase only 8.6 percent whereas in the previous year India increased defense expenditures by 20 percent (Bokhari 1994).

Against this background, the purpose of this chapter is to examine Pakistan's macroeconomic economic prospects for the remainder of the 1990s. In particular (and assuming it politically possible), we are interested in examining the scope for stimulating economic growth and expansion through restrained allocations to the military (Ahmed 1994). What impacts have defense expenditures had on the economy? Are these impacts largely direct or have they operated primarily through their effect on the budgetary deficits? In this regard, defense expenditures are a logical area for budgetary cuts: current expenditures account for the major part of government budgetary allocations, averaging 65–75 percent during most of the 1980s and into the 1990s. Since the late 1980s, defense expenditures together with debt servicing have accounted for around 80 percent of current expenditures.

PREVIOUS STUDIES ON DEFENSE SPENDING

Intuitively, one might imagine that increased defense expenditures over time would be detrimental to an economy. The classical argument is that soldiers and armaments do not create goods and services that can be consumed by others: thus, military spending necessarily subtracts from a nation's total resources. Following this line of argument, reductions in arms expenditures should provide a sizable peace dividend that could be used for development purposes (Bayoumi, Hewitt et al. 1993).

The issue is not so clear-cut, however. There is another side to the debate, offered by those who emphasize the economic benefits of defense expenditures. Advocates of "Military Keynesianism" (Treddenick 1985) stress the advantages of using domestic defense expenditures as a mechanism for stimulating the economy, and thus increasing the overall rate of economic growth. Unfortunately there is ample empirical evidence to support each assertion (Harris 1988a; Chan 1986; Looney 1994d).

A balanced position on the defense versus growth controversy is that while economic benefits should result from reductions in military spending, there is nonetheless uncertainty as to the likely size and distribution of these benefits over time. Reductions in government spending on the military will have significant macroeconomic effects, particularly upon interest rates, exchange rates, and trade patterns, all of which will influence the size and distribution of gains from cuts in military expenditures. Furthermore, there is considerable concern, often expressed in the popular press regarding short-term increases in unemployment and a lowering of economic growth that might result from the deflationary effects of decreasing military expenditures.

With this context in mind several studies have examined the manner in which Pakistani defense expenditures have interacted with various macroeconomic aggregates. These studies can be broken into four types: (1) "Causation Analysis" where an attempt is made to assess whether defense expenditures initiate economic change or, in contrast, are affected by changes in the macroeconomy, for example, do increases in defense expenditure cause a follow-on change in the economy, or instead, do economic changes result in movements in defense funding? (2) "Linkage Identification" where the strengths of the identified causal patterns are estimated, that is, how much does a rupee of defense expenditures alter the GDP over time? (3) "Budgetary Priority Analysis" where expenditure priorities and budgetary tradeoffs are identified, and (4) "Modeling" where, drawing on 1, 2, and 3, defense expenditures are examined in the context of alternative fiscal packages, for example, how does varying the existing size of the budgetary deficit affect the manner in which defense expenditures affect the macroeconomy? The present study falls in this category.

Causation and Linkages

The main finding (Looney 1991) from analysis of the causal links between defense and the economy is that the impact of defense expenditures on the GDP has shifted over time. In an earlier period (1958–73), defense expenditures had a negative impact on economic growth. While in the latter period (1973 to the present) this impact has shifted to a positive one. Specifically,

1. The earlier negative impact appears to have been directly associated with the speed of increase in defense expenditures. During periods of rapid mobilization (the arms race with India), defense expenditures had a negative impact on the economy. That is, increased defense expenditures during this period dampened the growth in the GDP.
2. After 1973 (and at a time when Pakistani defense expenditures were not modified by developments in India), increased growth in the economy provided additional resources for defense. In turn, defense expenditures stimulated further growth.
3. In contrast there were no strong linkages from nondefense expenditures to economic growth.

Another pattern of significance (Looney 1991, 52–53) involves the relationship between defense and non-defense expenditures. There has been a tendency over time for defense expenditures to lead in the timing of government allocations. That is, when defense expenditures change, a corresponding adjustment (again with a lag of several years) occurs in allocations to non-defense activities.

As noted above, a recurring theme in the Pakistani literature is that of government deficits and or expenditures "crowding out" private investment. This phenomenon has been confirmed by several recent studies (Khan and Iqbal 1991; Khan 1988; Burney and Yasmeen 1989; Haque and Montiel 1992) that found evidence that government activities have preempted funds that would otherwise have flowed into private capital formation. These patterns have also been the subject of causality analysis (Looney 1994c). Here attention has focused on the direction of impact between the different broad types of public expenditures (defense, consumption, and general government investment) and potential sources of funding (deficits, domestic borrowing, and foreign borrowing). Do expenditures create subsequent deficits and borrowing requirements or, instead, does lax fiscal policy and easy credit encourage expanded expenditures? The main patterns found suggest the following:

1. Of the three types of government expenditures, those allocated to defense appear to have the most complex budgetary linkages. In one sense the military faces a hard budgetary constraint in the sense that increases in past deficits tend to suppress the expansion in allocations to the military. On the other hand, increased defense expenditures do force an expansion in future deficits.

2. This general framework carried over to the borrowing patterns associated with military expenditures. For most measures of domestic borrowing, higher growth rates in funding from the domestic markets tend to suppress the expansion in future military expenditures. These suppressing effects are most important in cases where the rate of borrowing (domestic or foreign) expands over its anticipated (or longer term) growth rate. Still, feedback effects are present whereby military expenditures are, in turn, generally funded in part through both domestic and foreign borrowing.

3. Since a large portion of public consumption consists of allocations to the military, the budgetary patterns of this expenditure category are in some ways similar to that characterizing defense, particularly consumption's relationship to the fiscal deficit.

4. Several important differences do occur however. The major difference between defense expenditures and public consumption is associated with the manner in which each is funded. Increased growth in public consumption definitely contributes to expanded domestic borrowing requirements over time. In addition, the expansion in public consumption was more constrained than defense during periods of expanded foreign borrowing.

5. Of the three types of government expenditures examined, general government investment has the strongest impact on the public-sector deficit.

6. For all four measures of the deficit, increases in general public investment tend to result in expanded fiscal imbalance. While expanded deficits (actual and deviations from the exponential trend) facilitate a future expansion in public investment, this effect is weak compared with the impact of investment on the deficit.

7. A clear link also exists between expanded public-sector investment and increased future domestic borrowing requirements. Interestingly enough links exist between the growth in public investment and the country's pattern of external pubic borrowing.

While these findings do not provide a definitive proof of the existence of the crowding out mechanism in Pakistan, they are quite consistent with what one might find if the phenomena were present. Public investment and infra-structural development appear to have the least stimulating (and sometimes negative) affect on private sector investment. This is ironic given that a major purpose of these allocations is to provide a stimulus to follow on private invest-ment. Clearly, this effect stems from the large demands placed on the domestic capital market by this type of expenditure.

At the other extreme is defense. Again a somewhat ironic pattern exists by which expanded military expenditures provide a generally strong stimulus to private investment in large-scale private manufacturing. While the analyses does not let us identify the cause of this stimulus (general Keynesian demand expansion and/or direct linkages to the country's military procurement pro-gram), the fact remains that the government has shown restraint in funding de-fense expenditures once domestic borrowing begins to accelerate.

General public consumption falls somewhere between defense and investment in affecting the private-sector's willingness (or ability) to commit capital to manufacturing. While the government does fund increased consump-tion through expanded domestic borrowing, the magnitudes involved are not nearly as great as with investment. Thus, government consumption is still able to provide a net positive stimulus to small-scale private investors (who pre-sumably are not as reliant on the domestic capital markets as are their larger scale counterparts).

Budgetary Patterns

While the development of a sophisticated model for analyzing budgetary priorities is beyond the scope of this book, several striking patterns characterize Pakistani budgetary allocations (Looney 1993; Frederiksen and Looney 1994):

1. A clear pattern exists whereby long-run defense expenditures impact negatively on development. Since development does not reduce defense over time, defense has a higher priority than development.
2. Defense has a positive short-run affect on interest payments with increased shares of the budget allocated to interest payments. In contrast interest payments are neutral (in both the short and long run) with regard to the share of the budget allocated to defense. Again, this is a clear-cut case of defense having the higher priority.
3. Priorities between development expenditures and interest payments are much more difficult to deduce: development expenditures reduce (in both the short and long run) the budgetary share going to interest payments. In turn, increased interest pay-ments reduce (again in both the short and long run) the shares of the budget going to the capital account.
4. Complicating identification of the development/interest priorities is the fact that in both cases the expected and unexpected deficit terms are negative. Both variables are reduced with increases in the deficits. Furthermore, these patterns occur in both the short and longer run. However, since the deficit terms are stronger in the case of

development (with a higher level of statistical significance), it appears that interest payments have a slightly higher priority than that afforded development.

Although the budgetary shares of the other main items of the budget were not directly tested against each other, it is probably safe to conclude that subsidies are next in priority. While their allocations suffer with increases in defense expenditures, they are immune from cuts resulting from expanded interest payments or development allocations. In addition, the government appears willing to run higher deficits to fund these programs. Administration has the next highest priority. This category appears immune to cuts stemming from increases in defense, interest, or development. In addition, these allocations do not seem to face cuts during periods of increased deficits.

In conclusion, one may quibble over the importance of administration, social security/welfare, and other expenditures. However, the general picture of Pakistan's budgetary priorities is clear. Defense expenditures have by far the highest priority. While the government may cut these programs when deficits expand more than anticipated, the government is inclined to cut other programs (Frederiksen and Looney 1994) rather than reduce the budgetary share going to the military.

Modeling

In an earlier study (Looney 1994) focused on determining the rough magnitudes of the impact of defense (and nondefense) expenditures on the major economic aggregates. It was found that there was a generally positive link between defense and the economy. On the other hand, nondefense expenditures had a negative impact on economic growth. Given this, it was found the actual impacts of defense and non defense expenditures can change fairly dramatically as the economic context (i.e., the fiscal deficit) in which these expenditures occur varies.

DEFENSE AND THE MACROECONOMY

Drawing on a thirty-three equation (Table 9.1) policy model, our main concern was identifying the main linkages between defense expenditures and economic activity. These links are assumed to be both direct (as with Keynesian demand creation) and indirect (through possible deficit-induced crowding out of private activity and/or diversion of private savings to the public sector). Concerning the more important individual equations:

1. *Gross Domestic Product* is affected mainly by expansion in the private and public stocks of capital, employment, and military expenditures. Here it should be noted that the links between GDP and nondefense expenditures were not statistically significant.

Table 9.1
Pakistan: Defense and the Macroeconomy, Simulation Model, 1973–91

(constant 1985 prices)

Structural Equations

(1)   Gross Domestic Product (GDP)
GDP = -53.4 +1.70 K + 1.59 GK + 6.38 EMP-1 + 3.21 MILX
        (-1.55) (9.42)*** (2.81)**   (5.25)***   (2.75)**
    r2(adj) = 0.998; SE = 5.94; DW = 1.96; F = 2280.7***

(2)   Employment (EMP)
EMP = 3.05 + 0.42 EMP-1 + 0. 12 POP + 0.04 IGT-1
        (2.93)** (2.13)**   (2.70)**   (2.19)**
    r2(adj) = 0.994; SE = 0.28; DW = 2.82; Durbins H = -3.33; F = 907.8***

(3)   Defense Expenditures (MILX)
MILX = - 4.77 + 0.13GDP-1 - 0.24 IGTP-1 - 0.23 BORFP-1 - 0.14 PDII
        (-1.32)   (6.49)***   (-3.08)***   (-2.44)**   (-2.08)**
    r2(adj) = 0.990; SE = 1.11; DW = 1.66; F = 403.2***

(4)   Nondefense Public Expenditures (NILX)
NILX = -29.71 + 0.23 GDP-1 - 2.81 Δ MILX-1
        (-7.01)*** (19.74)***   (-2.50)**
    r2(adj) = 0.964; SE = 5.38; DW = 1.74; F = 229.61***

(5)   Gross National Savings (GNS)
GNS = -30.12 + 0.18 GDP-1 - 0.73 GDEF - 0.71 GDEF-1
        (-5.08)*** (10.88)***   (-2.35)**   (-2.41)**
    r2(adj) = 0.944; SE = 5.96; DW = 2.21; F = 96.15***

(6)   Total Public Investment (IGT)
IGT = 6.81 + 0.47 IGT-1 + 1.04 IGGT
        (3.31)*** (3.68)***   (3.39)***
    r2(adj) = 0.951; SE = 2.37; DW = 2.61; Durbins H = -1.76; F = 144.30

(7)   General Government Investment (IGGT)
IGGT = 3.08 + 0.71 IGGT-1 + 0.23 IPMT
        (2.77)** (5.47)***   (2.11)**
    r2(adj) = 0.951; SE = 1.02; DW = 1.81; Durbins H = 0.46; F = 167.05

Table 9.1 continued
Pakistan: Defense and the Macroeconomy, Simulation Model, 1973–91

(constant 1985 prices)

Structural Equations

(8)   Total Public Revenue (GRT)
$$GRT = -20.77 + 0.21 \, GDP\text{-}1 + 0.26 \, \Delta GDP\text{-}1$$
    (-9.27)*** (25.25)***   (2.35)**
    r2(adj) = 0.941; SE = 2.87; DW = 1.85; F = 906.67***

(9)   Public Domestic Borrowing (BORD)
$$BORD = 12.99 + 0.73 \, GDEF\text{-}1 - 0.91 \, BORF$$
    (4.00)*** (5.10)***   (-2.91)**
    r2(adj) = 0.610; SE = 5.27; DW = 2.37; F = 14.30***

(10) Public Foreign Borrowing (BORF)
$$BORF = 14.74 + 0.48 \, GDEF + 0.27 \, GDEF\text{-}1 - 0.59 \, MILX$$
    (8.40)*** (4.13)***   (2.48)**   (-6.02)***
    r2(adj) = 0.715; SE = 2.30; DW = 1.91; F = 15.19***

(11) Private Investment in Large-Scale Manufacturing (IPML)
$$IPML = -4.37 + 0.78 \, IPML\text{-}1 - 0.07 \, BORD\text{-}1 + 0.24 \, MILX\text{-}1 + 0.13 \, BORF$$
    (-3.36)*** (5.96)***   (-2.63)**   (3.75)***   (2.66)**
    r2(adj) = 0.990; SE = 0.59; DW = 1.99; Durbins H = -0.54; F = 413.6***

(12) Private Investment in Small-Scale Manufacturing (IPMS)
$$IPMS = 0.02 + 0.85 \, IPMS\text{-}1 - 0.006 \, BORD + 0.007 \, NILX$$
    (0.43)   (8.87)***   (-2.82)**   (-4.26)***
    r2(adj) = 0.994; SE = 0.05; DW = 2.12; Durbins H = -0.93; F = 934.7***

(13) Private Investment in Non-Manufacturing (IPNMT)
$$IPNMT = 2.39 + 0.07 \, GDP - 0.36 \, MILX + 0.08 \, GNS$$
    (3.06)*** (7.54)*** (-3.31)***   (3.24)***
    r2(adj) = 0.987; SE = 0.81; DW = 1.75; F = 415.55***

(14) Total Public External Debt (PDF)
$$PDF = 14.27 + 0.43 \, PDF\text{-}1 + 1.05 \, IGT + 9.96 \, \Delta BORF\text{-}1$$
    (1.52)   (2.84)**   (4.13)***   (2.37)**
    r2(adj) = 0.874; DW = 2.14; Durbins H = -0.78; F = 40.20***

Table 9.1 continued
Pakistan: Defense and the Macroeconomy, Simulation Model, 1973–91

(constant 1985 prices)

Structural Equations

(15) Public External Debt to International Institutions (PDII)
PDII = - 10.78 + 0.97 PDII-1 + 1.05 IGGT
      (-3.47)*** (13.57)***   (3.13)***
    r2(adj) = 0.990; SE = 2.51; DW = 2.28; F = 869.97***

(16) Imports (ZN)
ZN = -24.78 + 0.35 GDP-1 -2.37 REALEX + 0.96 Δ IGTP
    (-1.99)*   (21.55)***   (-2.37)**   (2.15)**
    r2(adj) = 0.983; SE = 5.98; DW = 1.60; F = 271.41***

(17) GDP Deflator (GDPDF)
GDPDF = 0.081 + 0.73 GDPDF-1 + 0.0016 MSGC-1 + 0.076 UVZ
      (3.25)*** (13.24)***   (5.50)***   (2.50)**
r2(adj) = 0.998; SE = 0.02; DW = 2.07; Durbins H = -0.69; F = 2753***

(18) Government Credit from the Monetary System (MSGCP)
MSGCP = 28.20 + 1.70 GDEF-1 + 1.73 GDEF-2 + 11.49 Δ MILXP-1
      (3.26)*** (2.50)**   (2.39)**   (3.81)***
    r2(adj) = 0.842; SE = 16.44; DW = 1.96; F = 24.96***

Identities
(19) Government Expenditures (GD)
GE = MILX + NILX

(20) Government Deficit (GDEF)
GDEF = GE - GR

(21) Change in GDP (Δ GDP)
Δ GDP = GDP - GDP-1

(22) Lagged Change in Defense Expenditures (Δ MILX-1)
Δ MILX-1 = MILX-1 - MILX-2

Table 9.1 continued
Pakistan: Defense and the Macroeconomy, Simulation Model, 1973–91

(constant 1985 prices)

---

(23) Nominal Public-Sector Credit from the Financial System (MSGC)
MSGC = MSGCP*GDPDF

(24) Real Exchange Rate (REALEX)
REALEX = EXR*UVZ/GDPDF

(25) Private Investment in Manufacturing (IPMT)
IPMT = IPML + IPMS

(26) Total Private Investment (IPT)
IPT = IPMT + IPNMT

(27) Private Capital Stock (PK)
PK = IPT + IPT-1 + IPT-2

(28) Public Capital Stock (GK)
GK = IGGT + IGGT-1 + IGGT-1

(29) External Gap (EGAP)
EGAP = EP + NFP - ZN

Exogenous Variables
(30) Population (POP)
(31) Exchange Rate (EXR)
(32) Import Price Index (UVZ)
(33) Exports (EP)
(34) Net Factor Payments (NFP)

Notes: Two Stage least squares estimations. See: *SORITEC Integrated Econometric and Statistical Analysis Language, Version 6.6 Reference Manual* (Springfield, Virginia: Sorites Group, Inc., 1993) for a description of the procedure. r^2(adj) = adjusted coefficient of determination; SE = Standard Error of Regression; DW = Durbin Watson Statistic; Durbins H = Durbin's H Statistic; F = F Statistic; ( ) t-statistic; * = significant at the 90 percent level; ** = significant at the 95 percent level; *** = significant at the 99 percent level.

Δ = year-to-year difference.

2. *Employment* increases with an expanded population together with increments to the stock of public infrastructure.

3. *Defense Expenditures* expand in line with the general size of the economy. However, allocations to the military compete with infrastructure for funding. In addition, expanded levels of foreign borrowing in the previous year constrain allocations to the military. The same is also true for increased levels of indebtedness to the international institutions.

4. *Nondefense* public expenditures also expanded in line with GDP. However, allocations to this category were reduced by short-run increases in the defense budget.

5. *Gross National Savings* expand with the general growth of the economy. However, these funds are preempted (or crowded out) by the current fiscal deficit, as well as the deficit in the previous year.

6. *Private Investment in Large-Scale Manufacturing* followed a lag adjustment pattern whereby investment in any one year was undertaken to bridge the gap between investor's optimal and actual capital stocks. The optimal level of private investment was in turn influenced by defense expenditures and ability to attract foreign funding. Again, however, this category of private investment was crowded out by the fiscal deficit.

7. *Private Investment in Nonmanufacturing* activities expanded with the total size of the economy and availability of savings. In contrast to investment in manufacturing, however, this type of investment was discouraged by expanded defense expenditures.

8. *Government Credit* from the monetary system was also related to past deficits and short-run movements in defense expenditures.

9. *Inflation.* is largely a function of expanded credit to the public sector, together with movements in the international price level.

10. *Public Borrowing in the Domestic Markets* was largely a function of the fiscal deficit. However, the authorities' ability to borrow internationally reduced some of the pressures on the domestic capital markets.

11. *Public Borrowing in the Foreign Capital Markets* was also largely a function of the fiscal deficit. Again, however, increases in defense expenditures ceteris paribus reduced the amount of funding from this source.

In summary the model captures the fundamental dilemma facing Pakistani policymakers. Looked at in isolation, defense expenditures have tended to positively influence the economy. However, if these expenditures are funded with increased levels of deficit financing, the subsequent crowding out of private investment may actually result not only in increased inflation, but, more importantly, in a net negative impact on the economy. The inability of nondefense expenditures other than infrastructure to impact positively on the economy has only compounded this dilemma. In any case, the concern of external creditors over the country's high defense burden will in all likelihood increasingly constrain allocations to the military.

FISCAL OPTIONS

Realistically Pakistan's fiscal options are likely to be narrowly constrained by the International Monetary Fund (IMF). In November 1993 the government negotiated an agreement with the IMF to borrow a total of Special Drawing Rights (SDR) 1.2 billion ($1.67 billion) in a combination of concessionary and market rate loans if it implements reforms and reaches certain economic targets (MEED 1993).

Policy Constraints and Objectives

The loans will be a combination of an enhanced structural adjustment facility that carries an interest rate of 0.5 percent, an extended fund facility at market rates and a public-sector adjustment loan (the $350 million standby credit approved by the IMF in September 1993 is not included in the new agreement). As part of the agreement, the government pledges to take measures to meet the following economic targets (MEED 1993):

1. Reach an average GDP growth rate of 6.5 percent over the next three years. The GDP was expected to grow by 7.5 percent in 1994 depending on the size of the crucial cotton crop, compared with a record low of 3 percent GDP growth in 1993.
2. Bring inflation down to 5 percent. The government has forecast an inflation rate of 8 percent for 1994 compared with more than 10 percent in 1993.
3. Boost foreign exchange reserves. Reserves fell steadily in 1993 to reach $222 late that year (compared with $1,000 in January 1993).
4. Reduce the burden of foreign and local debt. In late 1993 the state owed $23 billion to foreign lenders, of which $4.5 billion was short-term debt.
5. Continue the tariff, tax, and financial reforms, privatization and deregulation policies launched in the late 1980s.

By late 1994 the government had complied with IMF pressure by increasing energy prices and introducing a controversial agricultural tax as a means of reducing the fiscal deficit (MEED 1993). Petroleum and utility prices have been adjusted substantially, together with the introduction of a mechanism to make domestic petroleum prices more responsive to changes in international prices. In addition, the authorities' fiscal program for 1993/94 envisages a reduction in defense expenditures by about 1 percent of GDP, along with a containment of nonessential expenditures (IMF 1994).

The authorities have tightened monetary policy through upward adjustments in the rates of return and reductions in the scope of concessional and mandatory credit schemes. The framework for concluding effective monetary policy has been strengthened through the provision of increased autonomy to the central bank.

Finally the Pakistan rupee was devalued by 10 percent at the outset of the 1993/94 fiscal year. This has been followed by a series of small exchange rate adjustments implying a total devaluation of 12 percent relative to the U.S. dollar and a real effective depreciation.

Against these positive initiatives, the government began in late-1994 to experience experienced a number of setbacks (Rashid 1995; Rogers 1994; Bokhari 1995a):

1. During December 1994, inflation rose to 14.3 percent from 11 percent a year earlier. This figure is considerably higher than the agreed-to 5 percent target to be reached by 1997.
2. For the July–December 1994 period, net tax receipts are estimated to have fallen 37 percent short of target. The shortfall in the collection of indirect taxes during the period was around 36 percent while income tax collection is off its mark by 39 percent.
3. Government spending, which was supposed to be curtailed under the IMF guidelines, was around 18 percent higher than over the previous July–December period. The situation is so critical that the government has stopped all ministries from issuing checks of more than 100,000 rupees and canceled all development funds for December.
4. Finally, the agricultural sector has experienced a series of setbacks. A series of natural disasters and poorly thought-out policies has led to a drastic slowdown in production. After growing by 9.5 percent in 1991–92 farm output dropped 5.3 percent in the falling year. For 1994 is expended by just 2.6 percent. During the current twelve months, the cotton harvest may be up to 7.5 million bales or up to 20 percent short of target. Estimates are that for every one million cotton bales lost GDP growth is reduced by one percentage point. If this relationship is accurate, the projected GDP growth of 6.9 percent for 1994–95 could be as low as 3.5 percent.

If we can assume that the government's current fiscal problems reflect primarily the transitional difficulties of shifting from tariffs to a general sales tax and that the agricultural crisis is largely a result of natural disasters, then the country should be able to realistically pursue its major objectives throughout the remainder of the 1990s. These include

1. A stable rate of GDP growth of between 6.0 percent and 7.0 percent per annum—this is in line with the average rate of growth since 1976
2. Employment growth of 2.8 percent to 3.1 percent—around the rate of growth of population and consistent with past rates of job creation
3. Inflation 5 percent or lower—somewhat below the historical range of 7–8 percent
4. Foreign borrowing to expand at a rate slower than the general expansion in economic activity; that is, around 5 percent or less
5. Defense expenditure to decline to around 4–5 percent of GDP—down from the 6–7 percent range in the late 1980s early 1990s.
6. Government deficits to fall to 3–4 percent of GDP—down from the 6 percent figure reached in the early 1990s
7. A general expansion in the share of savings in GDP up toward the range of 18–20 percent—typical values for countries at Pakistan's stage of development
8. An expanded share of private investment in GDP

Alternative Policy Mixes

The critical question is whether and to what extent these objectives are consistent and attainable. Of particular importance for the current study are the defense expenditure levels that would aid in the attainment of these goals. Again, using the model developed in Table 9.1, several policy packages were examined in terms of their ability to improve the country's economic fortunes.

Simulation I—No Major Policy Initiatives. As a benchmark, the policy simulation model outlined in Table 9.1 was solved with the world rate of inflation set at 3 percent per annum, population growth at 3 percent per annum and exports at constant prices assumed to growth at an annual rate of 7.5 percent per annum. Here we are assuming no major shifts in past public expenditure or revenue decisions. Under these assumptions:

1. The economy (GDP) would continue to expand in the 6.5–7.5 range, with defense expenditures gradually slowing to less than 5 percent per annum by the end of the century.
2. Despite this slowing in defense expenditures the military burden (defense as a share of GDP) would remain well above 6 percent throughout this period.
3. There would be a gradual increase in nondefense expenditures as a share of GDP— increasing from around 16 percent in 1992 to 18.4 percent by 2000. This pattern reflects the rapid expansion in government consumption during the 1980s.
4. Employment targets would be met with rates of growth averaging around 3 percent.
5. The savings rate would increase, but only very gradually, reaching around 16 percent by the end of the century. This is well below the 18–20 percent assumed to be a precondition for self-sustained growth.

In summary:

1. The fiscal deficit would expand throughout this period with its share in GDP also reaching unacceptable rates.
2. Most unsatisfactory of the major indicators is the rate of inflation. With expenditure, savings, and deficits in the ranges noted, inflation would increase during this period, reaching slightly over 20 percent by the end of the century.
3. Reflecting these patterns, the external gap would reach nearly 8 percent of the GDP, a figure probably unattainable given the likely reluctance of foreign creditors to finance deficits of this magnitude.

Simulation II—Alternative Defense Expenditure Strategies. For most developing countries, a logical alternative at this point would be to determine the extent to which economic performance might be improved through cutting defense expenditures. As noted above, however, the consequences of this approach are not clear. On the one hand, defense expenditures appear to provide a positive stimulus to the economy, and on the other, the deficits associated with increased allocations to the military may be financed in a way that preempts funds that might flow into private investment. To assess the net magnitude of these effects, several alternative defense budgets were examined. In these simulations defense expenditures were assumed to expand at a constant rate (2.5 percent, 5.0 percent and 7.5 percent) over the period to 2000. As a frame of reference, defense expenditures averaged 7.2 percent over the 1981–91 and 1986–91 periods. Under these assumptions:

1. The growth in GDP begins to decline after 1994, with the rate of decline largely a function of the expansion in defense.
2. With defense expenditures endogenous (determined by the model's equations—Simulation I) the deceleration in the GDP growth is gradual, leveling off at around 6.5 percent per annum by the end of the century.
3. With defense expanded at a rate of 7.5 percent per annum (providing there were no fiscal or inflationary constrains) it would be possible to stabilize the growth of the GDP at slightly over 7 percent per annum.
4. Increases in defense expenditures at a constant 5.5 percent or 2.5 percent would (in the absence of any other policy changes) causes the economy to decelerate fairly rapidly, reaching a growth of about 5.8 percent and 4.6 percent respectively by the end of the century.
5. The impact of defense expenditures on private investment reflected the anticipated pattern. The share of national resources devoted to private investment, increases with lower rates of expansion in military expenditures.
6. Concerning the fiscal imbalance, only the deficit associated with a 2.5 percent expansion in defense expenditures is likely to fall within an acceptable range (around 4.8 percent of the GDP). Without simultaneous reforms in tax structure or collection, significant reductions in the deficit as a share of GDP are unlikely under any of the proposed scenarios.
7. Simply just constraining defense expenditures, even at low rates of growth (with no other complementary stabilization measures), would most likely not stave off increases in inflation. As noted above, inflationary pressures have been building for some time. Even at an average annual growth of only 2.5 percent defense expenditures, it would be difficult for the country to reduce inflation below 10 percent per annum during the remainder of this century.

FISCAL OPTIONS WITH CONSTRAINED DEFENSE

These simulations suggest that although the general rate of growth of GDP may increase with defense expenditures, the adverse effects associated with this expansion negate any resort to a defense-led growth model. The real question for policy makers must center on ways of improving economic performance while constraining defense expenditures to lower than historic rates of expansion.

Several policy packages are examined under the assumption that the government will gradually be forced move to more austere programs if more moderate fiscal restraints fail to achieve the country's major macroeconomic objectives. Specifically Fiscal Program I outlined below would be one of the mildest attempts at reform. Macroeconomic objectives not achieved by that program suggest the modifications introduced into Fiscal Program II and so on. Analysis is confined to the use of policy tools directly under the control of the authorities—external borrowing, expenditures and taxes.

Fiscal Program I. First while holding defense expenditures at a 2.5 percent rate of growth, the authorities might also constrain foreign borrowing. Given the country's current debt situation and the high proportion of the budget allocated to debt servicing, reduced rates of external borrowing are probably a good objective in and of themselves. Credit from this source is set to grow at 5.0 percent per annum. This rate is considerably lower than the average of 22 percent over the 1986–91 period, but in line with the average of 4.6 percent for the 1981–91 period as a whole.

Fiscal Program II. To strengthen the country's acute infrastructural bottlenecks, this policy package would shift more resources toward public investment in transport, energy, communications, and the like. Expanded expenditures in these areas would also help to offset the deflationary effects associated with the planned reductions in defense expenditures. As a starting point, infrastructure investment was set at an expansion of 7.5 percent per annum, up somewhat from the 6.1 percent average over the 1981–91 and 5.1 percent expansion during the 1986–91 period.

Fiscal Program III. This set of policies would add increased revenue collection to Program II. Here, implementation of the agriculture tax and better tax collection should be enough to sustain an increase in revenues of around 7.5 percent per annum. This rate is up some from the 6.8 percent growth during 1981-91 and 5.5 percent for the 1986-91 period.

Fiscal Program IV. Finally the last package of reforms would modify Program III by constraining nondefense (and noninfrastructure) expenditures to a maximum rate of expansion of 7.5 percent per annum. As noted above, one of the main causes of the country's current fiscal crisis has been an acceleration in nondefense expenditures. These averaged 8.4 percent during 1981–91, accelerating to 9.4 percent from 1986–1991.

Of the expenditure and revenue programs noted above, those associated with increased taxation are likely to be the most difficult to attain. In part, this will be due to the likely slowdown in economic growth, but also to a fall in import tariff revenue, widespread tax evasion (only 1 million of Pakistan's 120 million population pay an income tax (Rashid 1994), and the difficulties of taxing the country's large black-market economy (Bokhari and Bowley 1995). In addition in early 1995, businesses in Karachi began threatening a tax strike (IHT 1995) unless the government restored law and order to that city. Given the current problems faced by cotton and sugar producers, there is also sufficient reason to believe that it may be some time before the recently enacted agricultural tax will yield significant increases in revenues.

Main Findings

Of particular interest is the manner in which these packages might improve economic performance over that likely to occur simply through constraining the growth in defense expenditures at 2.5 percent per annum.

Growth. The GDP growth gradually improves as the fiscal programs are made more comprehensive. That is, simply restraining foreign borrowing does not significantly improve the general rate of expansion of the economy. Nor is there little difference between the growth path obtained through carrying out Program I and that of simply expanding defense expenditures with foreign borrowing being determined though the models' relationships. There are several other patterns of interest:

1. While Program IV yields the highest rate of growth throughout the 1990s, it converges with Program III by the end of the century.
2. Program II starts out the 1990s with relatively low rates of growth. However, after 1994/95 this programs' performance improves significantly over that associated with Program I.

Inflation. Inflationary pressures proved relatively hard to dampen. Constraining defense expenditures to a 2.5 percent growth path, together with restricting foreign borrowing (Program I) and increasing infrastructure investment (Program II) while keeping the rate of inflation considerably below that of the purely endogenous forecast were unable to put the economy on a declining inflation path. This leads to several important policy implications:

1. A clear ingredient of any anti-inflationary program must be tax reform. Even expanding government revenues at 7.5 percent per annum (Program III) were not sufficient to reduce inflation below 6 percent per annum.
2. However supplementing tax reform with constraints on nondefense expenditure (Program IV) quickly suppressed inflation. This policy package lowered inflation below 5 percent through much of the period under consideration.

Budget Deficit. The pattern of budget deficits was similar to those characterizing inflation. Without tax reform, the programs were not capable of significantly reducing their share of the fiscal deficit in GDP. Specifically constrained defense expenditures at 2.5 percent, Program I and Program II all stabilized the deficit at around 5.0 percent (with program II eventually reducing this ration to 4.5 at the end of the century).

On the other hand, fiscal performance improved dramatically with expanded revenues (Program III) and constrained nondefense expenditures (Program IV). Specifically by 2000, Program III will bring the deficit down to around 2.6 percent of GDP and Program IV will bring the deficit down further toward 2.0 percent.

Savings. As noted increasing the rate of national savings must be an essential objective in any fiscal program. In this regard, all four programs produced some improvement in this aggregate. Again the results from the defense expenditure expansion of 2.5 percent, Program I and Program II were fairly similar, with savings increasing from about 14.5 percent in 1992 to slightly over 17 percent by 2000.

Tax reforms however contributed greatly to this objective, raising the savings rate to nearly 19 percent at the end of the period. Finally, constraints on nondefense expenditure will expand this rate a further 2 percent to slightly under 21 percent by 2000.

Private Investment. Finally increasing the share of national resources invested by the private sector is possible under all of the programs examined. Here improvements up to around 10.2 percent (from around 9.2 in 1992) are easily obtained. As with the other macroeconomic aggregates, however, a significant improvement in private investment depends critically on the willingness of the government to reduce its deficit.

SUMMARY

In summing up, the fiscal pattern that developed in Pakistan during the 1980s and extending into the 1990s is not sustainable. Overexpansion in expenditures, both for defense and nondefense purposes, together with sluggish revenues and excessive foreign borrowing have created a situation in which further growth will be increasingly constrained by debt servicing, inflation, and shortages of domestic savings for private investors.

However, given the complex nature of defense expenditures in both stimulating and suppressing growth, budgetary reductions in this area in and of themselves are unlikely to improve the country's economic performance. In fact, rapid reductions in defense are likely to impair the situation even further. On the other hand, modest efforts in tax reform are by far the most effective means at restoring fiscal stability (Khan 1989). The optimal policy mix is one of tax reform together with defense expenditures expansion that is constrained in the 2.5 percent range. Unforeseen events aside, this package would enable the country to meet the goals established by itself and its major creditors in restoring a rapid, self-sustaining growth in an environment characterized by a declining defense burden.

PROSPECTS

The results summarized above are suggestive of the country's future macroeconomic environment. They show that the country has, through fiscal reforms, the potential of sustaining a relatively high rate of economic expansion throughout the 1990s. Combining the fiscal simulations summarized above with an (admittedly subjective) estimate of their likely occurrence, the country has, in most likelihood, a probability of around 40 percent of sustaining a strong economic expansion through the remainder of the 1990s.

A broader issue is whether this expansion is broadbased enough and sustainable to the point that the country might evolve into a dynamic South Asian Tiger. In this regard, the present Southeast Asian Tigers have a number of characteristics that set them apart from Pakistan and most other developing countries. These include (IBRD 1993b) the following:

1. More rapid output and productivity growth in agriculture
2. Higher rates of growth of manufactured exports
3. Earlier and steeper declines in fertility
4. Higher growth rates of physical capital supported by higher rates of domestic savings
5. Higher initial levels of growth rates of human capital
6. Generally higher rates of productivity growth
7. Declining income inequality and reduced poverty

Although Pakistan's overall economic growth rates have been roughly comparable to those of the Southeast Asian (Singapore, Malaysia, South Korea, and Thailand) countries (Table 9.2), it is apparent that the country has not been able to lay the foundation necessary for high and sustained growth. In particular

1. The country's savings rate is one of the lowest in the world
2. Export performance has been erratic
3. Manufacturing has not shown an ability to grow at a faster rate then the overall economy
4. Government consumption accounts for a relatively high share of the GDP
5. The country's population growth rate remains relatively high
6. As opposed to the Southeast Asian countries, Pakistan would be beginning its phase of high growth with an extremely high debt ratio
7. By most measures, Pakistan's military expenditures are considerably above those in Southeast Asia

Most important, the country has seriously neglected the development of human capital. Despite rapid economic growth, there has been little improvement in literacy, the proportion of children in school, or the number of available teachers. The unequal distribution of human capital in turn has created an income distribution much more unequal that found in Southeast Asia. Most analysts feel that the success of the Southeast Asian economies is liked to their initial, equitable distribution of income and assets.

Given the budgetary constraints that the government is likely to be faced with during the remainder of the decade, it is difficult to see how the country could significantly improve its social infrastructure. Without these human assets and capabilities, the country will be unable to achieve the productivity increases necessary to transform itself along the lines of the Southeast Asian model.

Table 9.2
International Comparisons of Economic and Social Performance

Measure	Region			
	Total	SE. Asia	S. Asia	Pakis
Economic Performance (% Growth)				
Gross Domestic Product, 1970–80	4.9	8.2	4.1	4.9
Gross Domestic Product, 1980–91	2.8	7.5	5.2	6.1
Investment, 1970–80	6.5	10.0	7.3	3.7
Investment, 1980–91	0.3	7.8	4.0	5.6
Exports, 1970–1980	4.0	7.9	2.3	0.7
Exports, 1980–91	4.7	10.7	7.9	9.9
Government Expenditures, 1970–79	8.1	9.4	5.9	7.4
Government Expenditures, 1981–91	0.8	4.9	5.0	7.0
Population, 1970–80	2.6	2.2	2.4	3.1
Population, 1980–91	2.5	1.8	2.2	3.1
Economic Structure (% GDP)				
Investment, 1970	21.7	28.0	17.3	16.0
Investment, 1991	20.5	37.8	20.7	19.0
Savings, 1970	18.6	20.3	13.7	9.0
Savings, 1991	14.0	36.3	14.7	12.0
Private Consumption, 1970	69.1	67.8	76.0	81.0
Private Consumption, 1991	72.2	52.5	73.7	75.0
Exports, 1970	22.7	43.3	12.3	8.0
Exports, 1991	28.5	83.3	17.7	16.0
Resource Balance, 1970	-2.7	-7.5	-3.7	-7.0
Resource Balance, 1991	-6.8	-1.5	-6.0	-7.0
Government Consumption, 1970	13.8	12.3	10.3	10.0
Government Consumption, 1991	13.9	11.5	11.7	13.0
Manufacturing, 1970	14.2	17.3	16.0	16.0
Manufacturing, 1991	15.2	28.0	16.3	17.0
Infrastructure Investment (% Growth)				
Paved Roads, 1970–80	8.6	8.5	5.6	4.4
Paved Roads, 1980–90	3.0	4.8	5.3	8.6
Irrigated Land, 1970–80	4.5	2.5	1.6	1.3
Irrigated Land, 1980–90	2.4	1.5	1.0	1.5
Electric Generating Capacity, 1970–80	8.9	11.8	6.6	8.3
Electric Generating Capacity, 1980–90	6.2	7.9	10.1	10.0

Table 9.2 continued
International Comparisons of Economic and Social Performance

Measure	Region			
	Total	SE. Asia	S. Asia	Pakis
Debt (%)				
External Debt/Exports 1980	152.4	90.7	156.1	208.8
External Debt/Exports 1991	392.3	65.4	250.4	244.9
External Debt/GDP 1980	40.9	34.2	33.5	42.4
External Debt/GDP 1991	82.5	33.7	50.7	50.1
Debt Service/Exports, 1980	17.3	15.0	13.1	17.9
Debt Service/Exports, 1991	21.0	9.5	21.9	21.1
Military (Average % Share)				
Defense Expend./Budget, 1970–80	15.2	22.0	17.7	29.5
Defense Expend./Budget, 1980–91	16.1	18.9	17.0	26.2
Arms Imports/Total Imp., 1970–80	8.5	2.4	5.3	8.5
Arms Imports/Total Imp., 1980–91	17.7	1.3	6.9	6.9
Defense Expend./GDP, 1970–80,	5.6	9.1	7.0	6.1
Defense Expend./GDP, 1980–91	5.3	4.5	4.1	6.2
Armed Forces/1000 Pop., 1970–80	7.1	10.8	3.3	6.5
Armed Forces/1000 Pop., 1980–91	8.0	12.2	3.4	6.3
Social				
Population per Physician, 1970	15470.4	4047.5	5033.3	4310.0
Population per Physician, 1990	10570.2	2472.5	2700.0	2940.0
Life Expectancy (years) 1991	60.4	71.0	63.3	59.0
Illiteracy (%) 1991	37.4	11.0	43.0	65.0
Malnourishment (%), 1991	25.4	25.0	51.0	57.0
Education (% Relevant Age Group in School)				
Primary School, 1970	71.9	94.5	70.7	40.0
Primary School, 1990	87.5	99.0	80.3	37.0
Secondary School, 1970	20.8	34.8	28.7	13.0
Secondary School, 1990	39.8	61.0	46.7	22.0
Tertiary School, 1970	8.1	11.0	4.5	4.0
Tertiary School, 1990	10.8	17.5	3.5	3.0
Primary Pupil/Teacher Ratio, 1970	38.5	38.3	41.0	41.0
Primary Pupil/Teacher Ratio, 1990	35.4	25.0	51.0	41.0

Sources: Economic/Social, World Bank. Military, United States Arms Control and Disarmament Agency.

Appendix: Tests for Causality

GRANGER TEST

Granger (Granger 1969) defines causality such that X Granger causes (G-C) Y if Y can be predicted more accurately in the sense of mean square error, with the use of past values of X than without using past values of X. Based upon the definition of Granger causality, a simple bivariate autoregressive (AR) model for public-sector deficits (DEF) and PIM can be specified as follows:

$$(1) \quad PIM(t) = c + \sum_{i=1}^{p} a(i)DEF(t-i) + \sum_{j=1}^{q} b(j)DEF(t-j) + u(t)$$

$$(2) \quad DEF(t) = c + \sum_{i=1}^{r} d(i)DEF(t-1) + \sum_{j=1}^{s} e(j)PIM(t-j) + v(t)$$

where PIM is the growth in private-sector investment in manufacturing and DEF = the growth in public-sector deficits; p, q, r, and s are lag lengths for each variable in the equation; and u and v are serially uncorrelated white noise residuals. By assuming that error terms (u, v) are "nice", ordinary least squares (OLS) becomes the appropriate estimation method (Hsiao 1981).

Within the framework of unrestricted and restricted models, a joint F-test is appropriate for causal detection. Where

$$(3) \quad F = \frac{RSS(x) - RSS(u)/ \ df(x) - df(u)}{RSS(u)/df(u)}$$

RSS(r) and RSS(u) are the residual sum of squares of restricted and unrestricted models, respectively; and df(r) and df(u) are, respectively, the degrees of freedom in restricted and unrestricted models.

The Granger test detects causal directions in the following manner: first, unidirectional causality from DEF to PIM if the F-test rejects the null hypothesis that past values of DEF in equation (1) are insignificantly different from zero and if the F-test cannot reject the null hypothesis that past values of PIM in equation (2) are insignificantly different from zero. That is, PIM causes DEF but PIM does not cause DEF. Unidirectional causality runs from PIM to DEF if the reverse is true.   Second, bidirectional causality runs between DEF and PIM if both F-test statistics reject the null hypotheses in equations (1) and (2). Finally, no causality exists between DEF and PIM if we can not reject both null hypotheses at the conventional significance level.

HSIAO'S PROCEDURE

The first step in Hsiao's procedure is to perform a series of autoregressive regressions on the dependent variable. In the first regression, the dependent variable has a lag of one. This increases by one in each succeeding regression. Here, we estimate m regressions of the form

$$(4) \quad G(t) = a + \sum_{i=1}^{m} b(t\text{-}1)G(t\text{-}1) + e(i)$$

where the values of m range from 1 to m. For each regression, we compute the FPE in the following manner:

$$(5) \quad FPE(m) = \frac{T + m + 1}{T - m - 1} \; ESS(m)/T$$

Where: T is the sample size, and FPE(m) and ESS(m) are the final prediction error and the sum of squared errors, respectively. The optimal lag length, m*, is the lag length which produces the lowest FPE. Having determined m* additional regressions expand the equation with the lags on the other variables added sequentially in the same manner used to determine m*. Thus, we estimate four regressions of the form:

$$(6) \quad G(t) = a + \sum_{i=1}^{m*} b(t\text{-}1)G(t\text{-}1) + \sum_{I=1}^{n} c(t\text{-}1)D(t\text{-}1) + e(i)$$

with n ranging from one to four. Computing the final prediction error for each regression as

$$FPE(m^*,n) = \frac{T + m^* + n + 1}{T - m^* - n - 1} \; ESS(m^*,n)/T$$

we choose the optimal lag length for D, n^* as the lag length which produces the lowest FPE. Using the final prediction error to determine lag length is equivalent to using a series of F tests with variable levels of significance.

The first term measures the estimation error and the second term measures the modeling error. The FPE criterion has a certain optimality property that "balances the risk due to bias when a lower order is selected and the risk due to increases in the variance when a higher order is selected" (Hsiao 1979). An intuitive reason for using the FPE criterion is that longer lags increase the first term but decrease the RSS of the second term, and thus the two opposing forces are optimally balanced when their product reaches its minimum (Judge, Griffiths et al. 1982).

Bibliography

Abe, S. et al. "Financial Liberalization and Domestic Saving in Economic Development: An Empirical Test for Six Countries." *The Pakistan Development Review* 16, no. 3 (1977): 298–308.

Aghevli, B., S. Kim, and H. Neiss. "Growth and Adjustment in South Asia." *Finance and Development* (1987): 12–15.

Ahmad, M. "The Effects of Government Budget Deficits on Interest Rates: A Case Study of a Small Open Economy." *Economia Internazionale* 47, no. 1 (1994): 1–6.

Ahmed, I. "State Military and Modernity: The Experience of South Asia." *Contemporary South Asia* 3, no. 1 (1994): 53–66.

Ali, G. "Development in Transport of Goods by Road." *Economic Review* 25, no. 8 (1994): 115.

Ali, S.A. "Pak-Iran Textile Project." *Pakistan & Gulf Economist* 11, no. 21 (1992): 38–39.

Amin, K.M. "Outline of a Transport Policy: Transportation System in Pakistan." *Economic Review* 22, no. 6 (1991): 6.

Anwar, M. "Islamic Banking in Iran and Pakistan: A Comparative Study." *The Pakistan Development Review* 31, no. 4 (1992): 1089–1100.

Arms Control and Disarmament Agency (ACDA). *World Military Expenditures and Arms Transfers, 1995*. Washington, DC: U.S. Arms Control and Disarmament Agency, 1996.

Arshad, Mohammad F. "Regional Patterns of Industrialization in Pakistan." *Pakistan Economic & Social Review* 27, no. 1 (1989): 17–32.

Asian Development Bank (ADB). *Appraisal of the Third Telecommunications Project in the Islamic Republic of Pakistan*. Manila: Asian Development Bank, 1990.

Awan, A. and A.U. Rahman. "The $5 Billion Company." *Pakistan & Gulf Economist* 13, no. 32 (1994): 6–13.

Bamford, D.J. "Paktel Communication on the Move." *Economic Review* 23, no. 11 (1992): 43.

Banker. "Making All the Right Noises." *The Banker* (1991): 51.

Barro, R.J. "Democracy: A Recipe for Growth?" *The Wall Street Journal,* December 1 (1994): A-24.

———. "Democracy and Growth: Do They Go Together?" *Straits Times,* December 11 (1994a): 13.

———. "Government Spending in a Sample Model of Endogenous Growth." *Journal of Political Economy* 98, October, Part 2 (1990): S103–125.

Bayoumi, T., D. Hewitt, and J. Schiff. *Economic Consequences of Lower Military Spending: Some Simulation Results.* Washington, DC: International Monetary Fund, 1993.

Beg, A.A.A. "Transportation Scenario." *Pakistan & Gulf Economist* 14, no. 3 (1995): 35–36.

———. "Highways and Reorientation for Trade: Making Amends for Low Priority in the Past." *Pakistan & Gulf Economist* 13, no. 43 (1995a): 11.

———. "Infrastructure Facilities: A Vital Component to Economic Growth." *Pakistan & Gulf Economist* 13, September 23 (1995b): 7–14.

———. "Development in Transportation of Goods by Road." *Economic Review* 25, no. 8 (1994): 115.

———. "Pakistan-ECO Rail and Road Links." *Pakistan & Gulf Economist* 13, no. 26 (1994a): 35–37.

Benoit, E. *Defense and Growth in Developing Countries.* Lexington, MA: Lexington Books, 1973.

Bergsman, J. "Commercial Policy, Allocative and X-Efficiency." *Quarterly Journal of Economics* 88, no. 3 (1974): 409–433.

Bilquees, F. "Monetary Approach to Balance of Payments: The Evidence on Reserve Flow From Pakistan." *The Pakistan Development Review* 28, no. 3 (1989): 195–206.

Blejer, M.I., and M.S. Khan. "Government Policy and Private Investment in Developing Countries." *IMF Staff Papers* 31 (1984): 379–413.

———. "Public Investment and Crowding Out in the Caribbean Basin Countries." In *The Economics of the Caribbean Basin Countries,* edited by M. Connolly and J. McDermott, 219–236. New York: Praeger, 1985.

Blum, C. "Can Bhutto Keep Her Promises?" *Middle East Economic Digest,* July 1 (1994): 2.

Bio-Medical Data Processor. *BMDP Statistical Software Manual: 1990 Version, Volume 1.* Berkeley: University of California Press, 1992.

Bokhari, F. "Pakistani Cotton Farmers Play for High Stakes: The Success of the Crop is Vital for the Country's Economy." *Financial Times,* July 26 (1996): 26.

———. "Pakistan Set to Grasp Farm Tax Nettle." *Financial Times,* June 13 (1996a): 19.

———. "Taxpayers Sought to Fill Pakistan's Budget Hole." *Financial Times,* no. June 13 (1996b): 6.

———. "Pakistan Faces Dilemma Over Farm Taxation." *Financial Times,* January 12 (1996c): 25.

———. "Shutdown for Mobile Phones to Cut Karachi Violence." *Financial Times,* July 3 (1995): 16.

———. "Pakistani Team to Meet IMF Over Three-Year Programme." *Financial Times,* January 25 (1995a): 6.

———. "Pakistan Falls Short of Growth Target." *Financial Times,* May 20 (1994): 5.

————. "Testing Time for Privatization." *Financial Times*, August 5 (1991): 3.
————. "Pakistan Resists Pressure to Tax Farmers." *Financial Times*, June 5 (1991a): 8.
Bokhari, F. and G. Bowley. "Shadow of Unrest Shakes Confidence." *Financial Times*, April 7 (1995): 23.
Brauchli, M.W. "Few Options: A Rising Middle Class Clamors for Changes in Troubled Pakistan." *The Wall Street Journal*, December 14 (1995).
Burney, N.A. "Sources of Pakistan's Economic Growth." *The Pakistan Development Review* 25, no. 4 (1986): 573–587.
Burney, N., and A. Yasmeen. "Government Budget Deficits and Interest Rates: An Empirical Analysis for Pakistan." *The Pakistan Development Review* 28, no. 4, Part II (1989): 971–980.
Butler, Stuart. *Privatization Federal Spending: A Strategy to Eliminate the Budget Deficit*. New York: Universe Books, 1985.
Byerlee, D. *Agricultural Productivity in Pakistan: Problems and Potential*. Washington, DC: The World Bank, 1994.
Cahill, J. "SPRINT's International Presence." *Latin Finance*, no. 54 (1994): 45.
Cane, A. "Demand on a Grand Scale." *Financial Times*, May 9 (1995): 23.
Cebula, J.R. "Federal Budget Deficit and Interest Rates: An Empirical Analysis for the United States." *Public Finance* 43, no. 3 (1988): 337–347.
Chan, S. "Military Expenditures and Economic Performance." In *World Military Expenditures and Arms Transfers. 1986*, 29–38. Washington, DC: United States Arms Control and Disarmament Agency, 1986.
Chapra, M.U. *Islam and Economic Development*. Islamabad: International Institute of Islamic Thought, 1993.
Chaudhary, Aslam. "Economic Growth and Regional Disparity in Production Activities in Pakistan." *Pakistan Economic and Social Review* 27, no. 2 (1990): 105–120.
Chaudhry, M.H. "Economic Liberalization of Pakistan's Economy: Trends and Repercussions." *Contemporary South Asia* 4, no. 2 (1995): 187–192.
Child, F.C., and H. Kaneda. "Links to the Green Revolution: A Study of Small Scale Agriculturally Related Industry in the Pakistan Punjab." *Economic Development and Cultural Change* 23, no. 2 (1975): 249–275.
Communications International. "Asian States Take Different Routes to Similar Goals, Telecommunications Infrastructure." *Communications International* 19, no. 5 (1992): 76.
Clifford, M. "Pressure for Change: Technology Brings a Wide Array of Growth Options." *Far Eastern Economic Review* 157, no. 14 (1994): 36–38.
Concrete Products. "Riding the Waves of Pakistan's Road Building Program." *Concrete Products* 98, no. 3 (1995): S64.
Crossette, B. "Premier Takes a Chance on Reform in Pakistan." *The New York Times*, June 30 (1991): 7.
Currie, L. "The 'Leading Sector' Model of Growth in Developing Countries." *Journal of Economic Studies* 1, no. 1 (1974): 1–16.
Dahlburg, J.T. "Pakistan's Leaders Still Need to Take Tough Economic Steps." *Los Angeles Times*, April 21 (1994): D-6.
Dawn. "Highly Ill-Advised." *Dawn* February 23 (1981).

Deleuw, F., and T. Holloway. "The Measurement and Significance of Cyclically Adjusted Federal Budget and Deficits." *Journal of Money, Credit and Banking* 17, no. 2 (1985): 20–29.

Dewald, H.G. "Federal Deficits and Real Interest Rates: Theory and Evidence." *Federal Reserve Bank of Atlanta Economic Review* 68 (1983): 20–29.

Dickey, D.A.   and W.A. Fuller. "Likelihood Ratio Statistics for Autoregressive Time Series With a Unit Root." *Econometrica* 49 (1981): 1057–72.

Doan, T.A. *RATS User's Manual Version 4.* Evanston, IL: Estima, 1992.

Donyal, O. "Cellular War." *Politics and Business,* November 2 (1994): 37–42.

Doornik, J.A., and D.F. Hendry. *PcGive Version 8.0.* London: Thompson Publishing (1994), London.

Dwyer, G. "Inflation and Government Deficits." *Economic Inquiry* 20 (1982): 315–329.

Economist. "Economic Freedom: Of Liberty, and Prosperity." *The Economist,* January 13 (1996): 21–24.

Economic Review. "Modarabas: Excessive Control Stunts Development." *Economic Review* 27, no. 3 (1995): 21.

———. "Asian Leasing Corporation Limited: Company Profile." *Economic Review* 25, no. 2 (1994): 25.

———. "The Role of Modarabas in the Financial Sector." *Economic Review* 25, no. 8 (1994a): 28.

———. "First Al-Noor Modaraba: Pakistan." *Economic Review* 24, no. 6 (1993): 156.

Economic and Social Commission for Asia and the Pacific (ESCAP). *Economic and Social Survey of Asia and the Pacific, 1990.* New York: United Nations, 1991.

Evans, P. "Do Large Deficits Produce High Interest Rates." *American Economic Review* 75, no. 1 (1982): 55–72.

Faiz, A. "Financing Infrastructure Investment." In *Financing Pakistan's Development in the 1990s,* edited by A. Nasim, 191–224. Karachi: Oxford University Press, 1992.

Feng, Y. "Regime, Polity, and Economic Growth: The Latin American Experience." *Growth and Change* 26, no. Winter (1995): 77–104.

FinTech Mobile Communications (FMC). "Fast Growing Asia Presents Problems for Would-be Operators." *FinTech Mobile Communications,* no. July 28 (1994).

FitzGerald, E.V.K. "A Note of Capital Accumulation in Mexico: The Budget Deficit and Investment Finance." *Development and Change* 11, no. 3 (1980): 391–417.

———. *The Fiscal Deficit and Development Finance: A Note on the Accumulation Balance in Mexico.* Cambridge: Cambridge University Centre of Latin American Studies, 1979.

Frane, James W., and M. A. Hill. *Annotated Computer Output for Factor Analysis: A Supplement to the Write-up for Computer Program BMDP 4M.* Los Angeles: BMDP Statistical Software, 1987.

Frederiksen, P.C., and R. E. Looney. "Budgetary Consequences of Defense Expenditures in Pakistan: Short-Run Impacts and Long-Run Adjustments." *Journal of Peace Research* 31, no. 1 (1994): 11–18.

———. "Another Look at the Defense Spending and Development Hypothesis." *Defense Analysis* 1, no. 3 (1985): 205–210.

Galbis, V. "Money, Investment and Growth in Latin America, 1961–1973." *Economic Development and Cultural Change* 27 (1979): 423–443.

Gauhar, H. "Mobilink Woes or How to Chase Investors Away." *Politics and Business*, January 30 (1995): 22.

Gauhr, H. "Where is Your Paktel?: A Talk With David Bamford, The Paktel Chief." *Politics & Business*, February 27 (1995): 32–34.

Gold, D.M., and R.J. Ruffin. "What Determines Economic Growth?" *Federal Reserve Bank of Dallas Economic Review*, Second Quarter (1993): 25–40.

Goldsmith, R. *Financial Structure and Development*. New Haven: Yale University Press, 1969.

Government of Pakistan. *Seventh Five Year Plan 1988–93 & Perspective Plan 1988–2003*. Islamabad: Government of Pakistan, 1988.

———. *Economic Survey 1994–95*. Islamabad: Finance Division, Economic Advisor's Wing (1995).

Granger, C.W.J. "Some Recent Developments in a Concept of Causality." *Journal of Econometrics* 39 (1988): 199–211.

———. "Developments in the Study of Cointegrated Economic Variables." *Oxford Bulletin of Economics and Statistics* 48 (1986): 213–228.

———. "Testing for Causality." *Journal of Economic Dynamics and Control* 2 (1980): 329–352.

———. "Investigating Causal Relations by Econometric Models and Cross-Spectral Methods." *Econometrica* 37 (1969): 424–438.

Gray, F. "Pakistan's $1.3 Billion Power Deal." *Financial Times*, June 7 (1991): 4.

Greenwood, J.G., and S.L. Ogus. "A Survey of Economic Freedom in Asia—1991." *Hong Kong Economic Papers*, no. 23 (1994): 31–43.

Guisinger, S., and C.W. Scully. *The Timing and Sequencing of a Trade Liberalization Policy: The Case of Pakistan*. London: Basil Blackwell, 1989.

Gupta, K.L. "Ricardian Equivalence and Crowding Out in Asia." *Applied Economics* 24 (1992): 19–25.

Gwartney, J., R. Lawson, and W. Block. *Economic Freedom of the World: 1975–1995*. Washington, DC: Cato Institute, 1996.

Hamid, I.N. and A. Nasim. *Trade, Exchange Rate, and Agricultural Pricing Policies in Pakistan*. Washington: The World Bank, 1990.

Hamid, N. "Growth of Small Scale Industry in Pakistan." *Pakistan Economic and Social Review* 21, no. 1&2 (1983): 37–76.

Hanke, Steve H., ed. *Privatization and Development*. San Francisco: International Center for International Growth, 1987.

Hansen, H., and K. Juselius. *CATS in RATS: Cointegration Analysis of Time Series*. Evanston, Il: Estima, 1995.

Haq, I. "The Role of Non-Bank Financial Institutions." In *Financing Pakistan's Development in the 1990s*, edited by A. Nasim, 419–430. Karachi: Oxford University Press, 1992.

Haque, I. "Profile, Growth and Trends of Pakistan's Textile Exports in the Past Decade." *Pakistan & Gulf Economist* 11, no. 9 (1992): 9–17.

Haque, N.U., and P. Montiel. "Fiscal Adjustment in Pakistan: Some Simulation Results." *IMF Staff Papers* 40, no. 2 (1993): 471–482.

———. "Fiscal Policy Choices and Macroeconomic Performance in the Nineties." In *Financing Pakistan's Development in the 1990s*, edited by A.Nasim, 101–162. Karachi: Oxford University Press, 1992.

———. *The Macroeconomics of Public Sector Deficits: The Case of Pakistan.* Washington, DC: International Monetary Fund, 1991.

Harris, G.T. "Economic Aspects of Military Expenditures in Developing Countries: A Survey Article." *Contemporary Southeast Asia* 8, June (1988): 82–102.

Henderson, D.R. "Why Some Latinos Prosper, and Others Don't." *Wall Street Journal,* March 29 (1996).

Hirschman, A.O. *The Strategy of Economic Development.* New Haven, CT: Yale University Press, 1958.

Hoelscher, G. "New Evidence on Deficits and Interest Rates." *Journal of Money, Credit and Banking* 18, no. 1 (1986): 1-17.

———. "Federal Borrowing and Short Term Interest Rates." *Southern Economic Journal* 50, no. 2 (1983): 319–333.

Hsiao, C. "Autoregressive Modeling and Money-Income Causality Detection." *Journal of Monetary Economics* (1981): 85–106.

———. "Causality Tests in Econometrics." *Journal of Economic Dynamics and Control* 7 (1979): 326–335.

Hunter, T.C. "Pakistan Telecommunications." *Global Communications* 16, no. 4 (1994): 16.

Huntington, S. "Democracy for the Long Haul." *Straits Times,* September 19 (1995): 1, SR4.

Husain, S.I. "Modaraba Operations, Challenges and Future Prospects." *Economic Review* 26, no. 3 (1994): 39.

Hyman, A. "Pakistan." In *The Middle East Review 1991/92.* Walden, Essex: The World of Information, 1991.

Ijaz, M. "The IMF's Recipe for Disaster." *The Wall Street Journal,* June 10 (1996).

International Bank for Reconstruction and Development (IBRD). *World Development Report 1995.* New York: Oxford University Press, 1995.

———. *Pakistan: A Strategy for Sustainable Agricultural Growth.* Washington, DC: World Bank, 1994.

———. *Pakistan Irrigation and Drainage: Issues and Options.* Washington, DC: World Bank, 1994a.

———. *Pakistan: Country Memorandum FY93, Progress Under the Adjustment Program.* Washington, DC: The World Bank, 1993.

———. *The East Asian Miracle: Economic Growth and Public Policy.* New York: Oxford University Press, 1993b.

———. *Pakistan: Current Economic Situation and Prospects.* Washington, DC: The World Bank, 1992.

———. *Pakistan: Current Economic Situation and Prospects.* Washington, DC: The World Bank, 1991.

———. *World Development Report, 1991.* New York: Oxford University Press, 1991a.

———. *Pakistan: Review of the Sixth Five-Year Plan.* Washington, DC: The World Bank, 1983.

International Herald Tribune (IHT). "Karachi Strife Prompts Businesses to Threaten Tax Strike." *International Herald Tribune,* March 17 (1995): 5.

International Monetary Fund. *Pakistan Recent Economic Developments.* Washington, DC: International Monetary Fund, 1996.

———. *International Financial Statistics Yearbook.* Washington: International Monetary Fund, 1995.

————. "Pakistan." IMF Survey (1994): 76–77.

Islam, S.   and A. Rashid. "Talking Tough: Donors Tell Pakistan to Clean Up Its Fiscal Act." *Far Eastern Economic Review* 159, May 3 (1996): 77.

Ismail, I. "Cover Story: Who Killed Cock Robin." *Politics & Business*, February 6 (1995): 9–14.

Jabir, R. "Leasing Companies' Role in Pakistan's Economic Growth." *Economic Review* 21, no. 3 (1990): 15.

Jaffery, S.A. "The Feasibility of Plastic Money in Pakistan." *Economic Review* 26, no. 3 (1995): 13–15.

James, W.E., and S. Naya. "Trade and Industrialization Policies for an Accelerated Development in Pakistan." *The Pakistan Development Review* 29, no. 3 & 4 (1990): 201–222.

Johnston, B.F. "Agriculture and Structural Transformation in Developing Countries: ASurvey of Research." *Journal of Economic Literature* 8, no. 2 (1970): 369–404.

Judge, G.G., H. Griffiths, H. Lutkephol, and T.C. Lee. *Introduction to the Theory and Practice of Econometrics*. New York: John Wiley and Sons, 1982.

Jussawalla, M.   and D.M. Lamberton. *Communication in Economics and Development*. New York: Pergamon, 1982.

Kalam, B.A. "Technology Planning for Industrial Development." *Economic Review* 22, no. 6 (1991): 36.

Kaneda, H. "Economic Implications of the Green Revolution and the Strategy of Agricultural Development in West Pakistan." In *Growth and Inequality in Pakistan*, edited by K & Griffin and A.H. Khan, 94–112. New York: St. Martin's Press, 1971.

Kay, J.A., and D.J. Thompson. "Privatization: A Policy in Search of a Rationale." *The Economic Journal* 96 (1986): 18–32.

Kazmi, S.H. "Modaraba: A Viable Alternative." *Pakistan & Gulf Economist* 13, March 26-April 1, 1994 (1994): 16–17.

————. "Modarabas: Thriving Now." *Pakistan & Gulf Economist* 13, September 24-30 (1994a).

————. "Expressways: Pressing Need of Changing Times." *Pakistan & Gulf Economist* 13, October 22 (1994b): 15–17.

Kemal, A.R. "Options for Financing the Budgetary Deficit, Money Supply, and Growth of the Banking Sector." *The Pakistan Development Review* 30, no. 4, Part II (1991): 769–784.

————. "Fiscal Imbalances as an Obstacle to Privatization Effort." *Pakistan Development Review* 28, no. 4, Part II (1989): 1009–1019.

Khan, A.H., and Z. Iqbal. "Fiscal Deficit and Private Sector Activities in Pakistan." *Economia Internazionale* 44, no. 2 and 3 (1991): 182–90.

Khan, A.H. "Budgetary Deficit: Options and Limitations." *PIDE Tidings* 1, no. 3 (1989): 19–22.

————. "Macroeconomic Policy and Private Investment in Pakistan." *The Pakistan Development Review* 27, no. 3 (1988): 277–294.

————. "Financial Repression, Financial Development and Structure of Savings in Pakistan." *The Pakistan Development Review* 27, no. 4 (1988a): 701–711.

Khan, A.H. and L. Hasah, and A. Malik. "Dependency Ratio, Foreign Capital Inflows and the Rate of Savings in Pakistan." *The Pakistan Development Review* 31, no. 4, Part II (1992): 843–856.

Khan, M.   and A. Mirakhor, eds. *Theoretical Studies in Islamic Banking and Finance.* Houston: Institute for Research and Islamic Studies, 1987.

Khan, M.H. "Public Policy and Agricultural Transformation in Pakistan." *The Pakistan Development Review* 24, no. 3 and 4 (1985): 305–329.

Khan, M.S. and A. Mirakhor. "Islamic Banking: Experiences in the Islamic Republic of Iran and Pakistan." *Economic Development and Cultural Change* 38, no. 2 (1990): 353–376.

Khan, Z.H. "Government Budget Deficits and Interest Rates: The Evidence Since 1971 Using Alternative Deficit Measures." *Southern Economic Journal* 50, no. 2 (1986): 1–17.

Khawaja, K.N. "Islamic Concept of Banking." *Economic Review* 25, no. 3 (1994): 30–31.

Komiya, M. "Fixed Wireless Local-loop System: A New Recipe for Success?" *Microwave* Journal 37, no. 6 (1994): 24.

Lawai, H. "Essentials of Successful Islamic Banking." *Economic Review* 25, no. 10 (1994): 79.

Lee, J., and Y. Iwasaki. *Promotion of Manufactured Exports in Pakistan.* Manila: Asian Development Bank, 1991.

Leff, N.H.   and K. Sato. "Macroeconomic Adjustment in Developing Countries: Instability, Short-run Growth and External Dependency." *The Review of Economics and Statistics* 62, no. 2 (1980): 170–179.

Leibenstein, H. "Allocative Efficiency vs. X-Efficiency." *American Economic Review* 61, June (1966): 392–415.

Lewis, S.R. Pakistan: *Industrialization and Trade Policies.* London: Oxford University Press, 1970.

Looney, R.E. "Public Sector Deficits and Private Investment: A Test of the Crowding-out Hypothesis in Pakistan's Manufacturing Industry." *The Pakistan Development Review* 34, no. 3 (1995): 277–299.

———. "Macroeconomic Constraints on Private Sector Investment in Pakistan." *METU Studies Development* 22, no. 4 (1995a): 397–424.

———. "Budgetary Dilemmas in Pakistan: Costs and Benefits of Sustained Defense Expenditures." *Asian Survey* 34, no. 5 (1994): 417–429.

———. "The Impact of Infrastructure on Pakistan's Agricultural Sector." *Journal of Developing Areas* 28, July (1994a): 469–486.

———. "Manufacturing's Contribution to Pakistan's Economic Expansion." *Development Policy Review* 12, no. 4 (1994b): 369–386.

———. "Defense Expenditures, Investment and Crowding Out: Problems of Capital Formation in Pakistani Manufacturing." *Journal of Third World Studies* XI, no. 2 (1994c): 292–316.

———. *The Economics of Third World Defense Expenditures.* Greenwich, Conn.: JAI Press, 1994d.

———. "The Budgetary Impact of Defense Expenditures in the Middle East." *Middle East Business and Economic Review* 5 (1993): 38–49.

————. "Real or Illusory Growth in an Oil-Based Economy: Government Expenditures and Private Sector Investment in Saudi Arabia." *World Development* 20 (1992): 1367–1376.

————. "Infrastructure and Private Sector Investment: The Case of Pakistan's Transportation and Communications Sector." *Rivista Internazionale di Scienze Economiche e Commerciali* 39, no. 9 (1992a): 771–792.

————. "Budgetary Balance and Private Sector Activity in Pakistan: The Net Impact of Defense Expenditures on Investment in Manufacturing." *Journal of Economics and Administrative Sciences* 6 (1992b): 83–111.

————. "Infrastructural Constraints on Transport and Communications: The Case of Pakistan." *International Journal of Transport Economics* 19, no. 3 (1992c): 287–306.

————. "Defense Expenditures and Economic Performance in South Asia: Tests of Causality and Interdependence." *Conflict Management and Peace Science* 11, no. 2 (1991): 37–68.

————. "A Post-Keynesian Analysis of Third World Military Expenditures." *Rivista Internazionale di Scienze economiche e Commerciali* 38 (1991a): 779–98.

Looney, R.E., and P.C. Frederiksen. "Fiscal Policy in Mexico: The Fitzgerald Thesis Reexamined." *World Development* 15 (1987): 399–404.

————. "Regional Impact of Infrastructure Investment in Mexico." *Regional Studies* 14, no. 4 (1981): 285–296.

Looney, R.E., and D. Winterford. "The Role of Infrastructure in Pakistan's Economic Development: 1972–1991." *Pakistan Economic and Social Review* 30, no. 1 (1992): 69–94.

Makin, J.H. "Real Interest Money Surprises, Anticipated Inflation and Fiscal Deficits." *Review of Economics and Statistics* 65, no. 3 (1983): 374–384.

Mascaro, A.   and A.H. Meltzer. "Long and Short Term Interest Rates in a Risky World." *Journal of Monetary Economics* 10 (1983): 151–200.

McKinnon, R.I. *Financial Liberalization in Retrospect: Interest Rate Policies in LDCs.* Stanford, California: Stanford University, 1986.

————. *Money and Capital in Economic Development.* Washington, DC: The Brookings Institution, 1973.

McMillin, W.D. "Federal Deficits and Short Term Interest Rates." *Journal of Macroeconomics* 8 (1986): 403–22.

Mehdi, Istaqbal. "Privatization—A Device for Reforming Public Enterprise Sector in Pakistan." *The Pakistan Development Review* 30, no. 4 Part II (1991): 895–905.

Memon, N.A. "A Whisker of Pride: Forty-Five Years of Textile Industry Experience Have Given Us a Competitive Edge." *Pakistan & Gulf Economist* 12, no. 15 (1993): 11–12.

Messick, R. E. "Economic Freedom Around the World." *The Wall Street Journal,* May 6 (1996).

Middle East Economic Digest (MEED). "IMF Agrees to Lend $1.7 Billion." *Middle East Economic Digest,* November 26 (1993): 34.

Mobile Phone News (MPN). "Mobilink Awaits Monitoring Equipment in Hopes Karachi Service Will be Restored." *Mobile Phone News* 3, no. 11 (1995).

Motley, B. "Real Interest Rates, Money and Government Deficits." *Federal Reserve Bank of San Francisco Economic Review* 9, no. 3 (1983): 31–45.

Nabi, I. *Entrepreneurs & Markets in Early Industrialization: A Case Study from Pakistan.* San Francisco: International Center for Economic Growth, 1988.

Naqvi, S.N.H. *Islam, Economics and Society.* London: Kegan Paul International, 1994.

Naqvi, S.N.H., and A.R. Kemal. *Protectionism and Efficiency in Manufacturing: A Case Study of Pakistan.* San Francisco: International Center for Economic Growth, 1991.

Noman, A. "Comments to A.R. Kemal, 'Options for Financing The Budgetary Deficit, Money Supply and Growth of Banking Sector.' " *The Pakistan Development Review* 30, no. 4 (1991a): 782–784.

———. "Industrial Development and Efficiency in Pakistan: A Revisionist Overview." *The Pakistan Development Review* 30, no. 4, Part II (1991): 849–861.

Pakistan & Gulf Economist. "First Interfund Modaraba: Positive Contribution to the Economy." *Pakistan & Gulf Economist* 8, no. May 14–20, 1994 (1994): 45.

———. "Textile Industry: Special Report." *Pakistan & Gulf Economist* 8, no. April 15 (1989): 26–42.

Panni, J.M. "Leasing in Pakistan: Past, Present and Future, Industry Overview." *Economic Review* 24, no. 3 (1993): 15–16.

Patrick, H.T. "Financial Development and Economic Growth in Underdeveloped Countries." In *Leading Issues in Economic Development*, edited by G. Meier, 203–205. New York: Oxford University Press, 1989.

Plosser, C.Z. "Government Financing Decisions and Asset Returns." *Journal of Monetary Economics* 9, no. 3 (1982): 325–352.

Pourgerami, A. "Authoritarian versus Nonauthoritarian Approaches to Economic Development: Update and Additional Evidence." *Public Choice* 74, no. 3 (1992): 365–377.

Pourgerami, A., and J. Assane. "Macroeconomic Determinants of Growth: New Measurement and Evidence on the Effect of Political Freedom." *Applied Economics* 24, no. 1 (1992a): 129–136.

Prowse, M. "Investment in People Seen as Key to Third World Growth." Financial Times, July 8 (1991): 4.

Quigley, P. "Watchword for the Future: Global Mobile Communications." Financial Times, March 16 (1994): 8.

Rashid, A. "Bad Math: Pakistan's Budget Shortfall Brings on Fiscal Crisis." Far Eastern Economic Review, January 26 (1995): 49.

———. "Getting Tough: Pakistan's Bhutto Tries for Fiscal Austerity." *Far Eastern Economic Review*, June 23 (1994): 61.

Rasmussen, J., H. Schmitz, and M. van Dijk. "Introduction: Exploring a New Approach to Small-Scale Industry." *IDS Bulletin* 23, no. 3 (1992).

Rees, Ray. "Is There a Case for Privatization?" *Public Money* 5, March (1986): 19–26.

Robinson, J. *The Rate of Interest and Other Essays.* London: Macmillan, 1952.

Rogers, E. "Bhutto Chases the Asian Tigers." *Middle East Economic Digest* 38, December 16 (1994): 2–3.

Rosett, C. "Pakistan's Free Marketeer." *The Wall Street Journal*, (July 11) (1991): A-10.

Rostow, W.W. *Theorists of Economic Growth from David Hume to the Present.* New York: Oxford University Press, 1990.

Sakr, K. *Determinants of Private Investment in Pakistan.* Washington: International Monetary Fund, 1993.

Sarmad, Khwaja. "The Profitability of Public Enterprises in Pakistan." *The Pakistan Development Review* 22, nos. 2, 3 (1984): 147–153.

――――. *A Review of Pakistan's Development Experience: 1949 to 1979/80*. Islamabad: Pakistan Institute of Development Economics, 1984a.

Sattar, Z. "Interest Free Economics and the Islamic Macroeconomic System." *Pakistan Economic and Social Review* 27, no. 2 (1989): 109–138.

Saunders, R.J., J.J. Warford, and B. Wellenius. *Telecommunications & Economic Development*. Second ed. Baltimore: Johns Hopkins University Press, 1994.

Schiantarelli, F. "Financial Constraints and Investment: Methodological Issues and International Evidence." *Oxford Review of Economic Policy* 12, no. 2 (1996): 70–9.

Siddiqi, S.H. *Islamic Banking*. Karachi: Royal Book Company, 1994.

Smith, P.L., and G. Staple. *Telecommunications Sector Reform in Asia: Toward a New Pragmatism*. Washington, DC: The World Bank, 1994.

Statistical Package for the Social Sciences (SPSS). "Logistic Regression Analysis." In *SPSS/PC+ Advanced Statistics*. Chicago: SPSS International, 1992.

Sundararajan, V., and S. Thakur. "Public Investment, Crowding Out and Growth: A Dynamic Model Applied to India and Korea." *IMF Staff Papers* 27, no. 4 (1980): 814–855.

Taylor, L. *Varieties of Stabilization Experiences*. Oxford: Clarendon Press, 1988.

Thomas, V. "Development Means Hard Decisions." *International Herald Tribune*, August 15 (1991): 6.

Thornton, D.L.   and D.S. Batten. "Lag-Length Selection and Tests of Granger Causality Between Money and Income." *Journal of Money, Credit and Banking* (1985): 164–178.

Time Series Processor (TSP) Reference Manual: Version 4.3. Palo Alto, California: TSP International, 1995.

Treddenick, J. "The Arms Race and Military Keynesianism." *Canadian Journal of Public Policy* 5 (1985): 64–80.

United Nations Industrial Development Organization (UNIDO). *Pakistan: Toward Industrial Liberalization and Revitalization*. Oxford: Basil Blackwell, 1990.

Wai, U.T. and C. Wong. "Determinants of Private Investment in Developing Countries." *Journal of Development Studies* 19, no. 1 (1982): 19–36.

Walle, van de. "Privatization in Developing Countries: A Review of the Issues." *World Development* 17, no. 5 (1989): 601–615.

Wellenius, B. *Telecommunications: World Bank Experience and Strategy*. Washington, DC: The World Bank, 1993.

World Bank. *Islamic Republic of Pakistan: Financial Sector Deepening and Intermediation Project. Report No. 12733-PAK*. Washington, DC: The World Bank, 1994.

Zafarunnin, M. "Modarabas: Progress and Future Prospects." *Pakistan & Gulf Economist* 13, no. 39 (1995): 7.

Zaidi, N.A. *Eliminating Interest from Banks in Pakistan*. Karachi: Royal Book Company, 1987.

Zanganeh, Hamid. "Islamic Banking: Theory and Practice in Iran." *Comparative Economic Studies* 31 (1989): 67–81.

Zuberi, H.A. "Interest Free Banking and Economic Stability." *The Pakistan Development Review* 31, no. 4 (1992): 1077–1088.

Index

About the Author

ROBERT E. LOONEY is Professor of National Security Affairs at the Naval Post-graduate School, Monterey, California. An advisor to the governments of Iran, Saudi Arabia, Panama, Jamaica, and Mexico, he has written twenty books on various aspects of economic development including *Manpower Policies and Development in the Persian Gulf Region* (Praeger, 1994).

ISBN 0-275-94737-8

90000>

EAN

9 780275 947378

HARDCOVER BAR CODE